LEGENDARY LOCALS

OF

EAST AURORA

NEW YORK

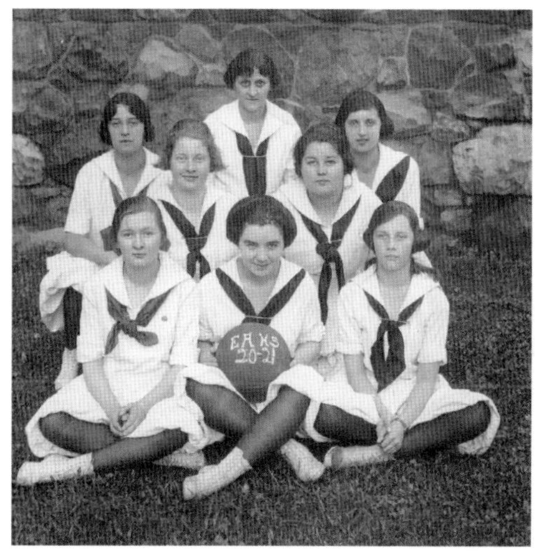

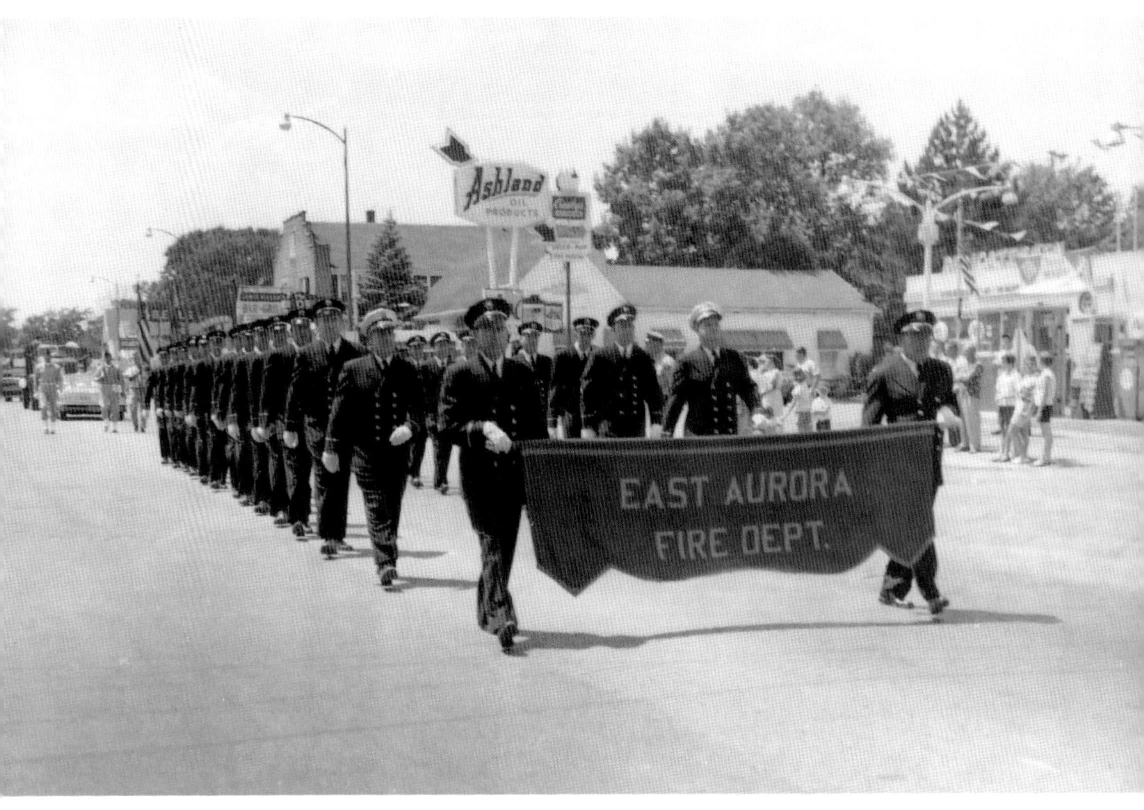

The East Aurora Fire Department

Members of the East Aurora Fire Department, pictured during a parade around 1959, have been protecting historic East Aurora since the early 1870s. Four fire companies, which operated out of separate fire halls around the village, consolidated into one fire hall for the first time in 1954. (Courtesy of the Aurora Town Historian's Office.)

Page 1: Sports Pioneers

Long before Title IX guaranteed equal athletic opportunities for female athletes, East Aurora High School had a competitive girls' basketball team. See page 56. (Courtesy of the Aurora Town Historian's Office.)

LEGENDARY LOCALS

OF

EAST AURORA

NEW YORK

ROBERT LOWELL GOLLER

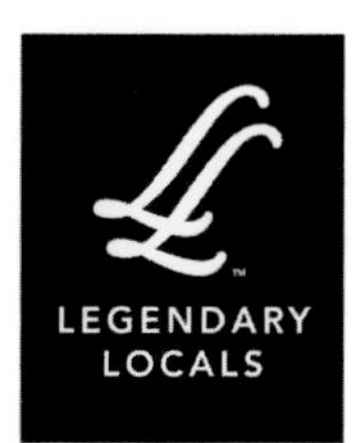

ISBN 978-1-4671-0170-7

Legendary Locals is an imprint of Arcadia Publishing
Charleston, South Carolina

Printed in the United States of America

Library of Congress Control Number: 2014934389

For all general information, please contact Arcadia Publishing:
Telephone 843-853-2070
Fax 843-853-0044
E-mail sales@arcadiapublishing.com
For customer service and orders:
Toll-Free 1-888-313-2665

Visit us on the Internet at www.arcadiapublishing.com

Dedication
To my best friend, Jason Gonser.

On the Front Cover: Clockwise from top left:
Roycroft founder Elbert G. Hubbard (courtesy of the Aurora Town Historian's Office; see page 66), Edward Godfrey with Barbara "Bobbie" Kelly and East Aurora mayor Robert Kelly (courtesy of the Aurora Town Historian's Office; see page 47), Martha Richardson Adams, (courtesy of the Aurora Town Historian's Office; see page 82), Edward Vidler with "Vidler on the Roof" (courtesy of the Vidler family; see page 25), champion horse Mambrino King (courtesy of the Aurora Town Historian's Office; see page 108), Gen. Aaron Riley (courtesy of the Aurora Town Historian's Office; see page 10), Fisher-Price founder Helen Schelle (courtesy of the Aurora Town Historian's Office; see page 90), pianist Eleanor Fattey (courtesy of the Aurora Town Historian's Office; see page 76), art gallery owner Grace Meibohm (photograph by the author; see page 35).

On the Back Cover: From left to right:
Musician Charles Nyhart (courtesy of the Nyhart family, see page 21), sidewalk sweeper Arthur Dorshide (courtesy of the Aurora Town Historian's Office, see page 119).

CONTENTS

ACKNOWLEDGMENTS

Legendary Locals of East Aurora would not have been possible without the assistance and guidance of many friends. I am grateful to the previous town historians and Aurora Historical Society volunteers, whose hard work and dedication have preserved our community's history for the citizens of today and tomorrow. Thanks go to all those who helped me track down information and photographs for this book, especially the Aurora Historical Society, Grant M. Hamilton and the team at the *East Aurora Advertiser*, fellow history enthusiast Mike Kelly, and Grace Meibohm and Mark Strong at Meibohm Fine Arts. It was an absolute pleasure to meet the East Aurorans—both past and present—who have helped make our community such a special place.

Regrettably, errors in the available historical records are inevitable, but a thank-you is owed to all who helped verify information to avoid mistakes in this book as much as possible.

I am especially grateful to my best friend and husband, Jason Gonser, for his patience and support of all my projects.

Finally, I thank the citizens of the town of Aurora and village of East Aurora for entrusting the Aurora Town Historian's Office to me since 2007.

Unless otherwise noted, all photographs in this book are from the archives of the Aurora Town Historian's Office.

—Robert Lowell Goller

INTRODUCTION

East Aurora has always been a popular place to live. Native Americans called it home for thousands of years before Vermont native and Revolutionary War veteran Jabez Warren discovered the beauty of the area while surveying the 43-mile Middle Road for the Holland Land Company in 1803. He came back a year later and spent the rest of his life here. Other settlers, including Warren's son, quickly followed. They endured many challenges as they built their new community on the banks of Cazenovia Creek.

East Aurora grew rapidly after the War of 1812, evolving into a business and cultural center south of Buffalo. The community found a place on the national map in 1850, when Millard Fillmore, who served as the town's only lawyer two decades earlier, ascended to the US presidency. His home, the only house built with a president's own hands, is now a museum operated by the Aurora Historical Society.

East Aurora shared the success of the city of Buffalo 17 miles to the north thanks to the plank road that connected the two communities. However, when the longtime goal to bring the railroad through town was finally realized after the Civil War, East Aurora prospered beyond anyone's expectations.

By the 1880s, the village had become a horse-racing capital, where thousands came to get a glimpse of Cicero Hamlin's legendary horse, Mambrino King, or to see the world's only covered mile-long racetrack at the Jewett Farm off Grover Road.

Thousands more came to East Aurora at the turn of the 20th century to be part of the Roycroft Arts and Crafts community on South Grove Street. The creative energy was contagious, resulting in the launch of several other successful business ventures in the next few decades, including Fisher-Price Toys, Moog, and Vidler's 5 & 10.

With the construction of Route 400 in the late 1960s, East Aurora faced modernization. Some of the older homes and hotels along the west end of Main Street were taken down to make way for more suburban-like buildings. However, through zoning regulations, East Aurora in the early 1990s was one of the first communities in the nation to successfully keep out big-box chain retail stores. East Aurora remains a small village at heart, where most businesses can still be considered "mom-and-pop" operations.

Though many East Aurora High School graduates have left the community, most cannot wait for Reunion Weekend each July to experience their legendary hometown once again. As the *East Aurora Advertiser* has indicated more than once, East Aurora is "the hometown you've always imagined."

More than 100 years ago, Elbert G. Hubbard, founder of the Roycroft, called East Aurora a "condition of mind." To him, and to the residents who still make the same observation today, the village is more than just a dot on the map.

Communities often define their history through their structures, old buildings, and houses. Historic buildings are certainly important. In fact, the village of East Aurora has the unique distinction of two National Historic Landmarks: Pres. Millard Fillmore's house and the Roycroft campus. East Aurora's streets are lined with well-maintained 19th-century homes, and many of the businesses are still located in buildings that were constructed more than a century ago.

However, East Aurora evolved into—and has remained—a "condition of mind" not because of its historic buildings, but because of its people.

Legendary Locals of East Aurora offers a glimpse into the lives of some of the people throughout the community's history who have made the village such a unique place. Of course, it is impossible to include every legendary person from East Aurora in just one book, and this book is certainly not meant to be an all-inclusive list or a ranking of everyone who has made—or is still making—a mark on the village.

Some of East Aurora's legendary locals from years past are not included because they already have been featured in previous books about the history of the community. They include Lawrence

Ernst, the first young man from East Aurora to sacrifice his life in war oversees; Raymond and Irene Hubbs, who were locally famous for the small grocery store they operated for many years across from Hamlin Park; William Moog, founder of the international company that bears his name; and First Lady Abigail Fillmore.

Although there are a few famous names in this book, including those of Millard Fillmore, Elbert Hubbard, and Margaret Evans Price, this book is not meant to focus just on those who are already famous. It is about the everyday people who keep the gears of the community turning. There is the woman who helped launch one of the most successful toy companies in the world but who does not get the credit, because her name is not part of the company name. There is the man who has kept the sidewalks of the business district clear of snow each winter for more than a decade.

Local legends come from a variety of backgrounds, but all their stories are equally important. The man who has changed the letters on the theater marquee for three decades is just as vital to the community's story as the world-famous founder of the Roycroft, and the young artist who painstakingly documented the architecture of the village is just as interesting as the country lawyer who went on to become president of the United States.

CHAPTER ONE

Business Leaders

Some of the most legendary East Aurorans have been the business owners. The wide variety of stores, hotels, taverns, and shops has been a reflection of the many personalities who have owned and operated them.

Main Street has been the center of East Aurora's business community since the beginning. A few years after the first settlement, William Warren established a tavern on the east end of Main Street. (It also served as the first school.) On the west end, travelers to and from Buffalo spent nights at the Eagle Tavern, a log cabin built on the current site of McDonald's. Shortly after the War of 1812, Robert Persons started the first permanent general store in East Aurora at the corner of Main Street and Olean Road. It did not take long for business to begin booming along both ends of Main Street. The end of the war brought more settlers to East Aurora, and the entrepreneurial spirit grew to meet a growing demand.

In the early days, the east and west ends of Main Street were two distinct communities. In fact, the Village of Willink (on the west end) and the hamlet of East Aurora (on the east end) did not officially merge into one village until 1874. That translated into two distinct business communities. Mercantiles, groceries, meat markets, and hotels prospered on both ends of the village.

The entrepreneurial spirit is still alive and well in East Aurora. The village still has an independent bookstore, pharmacy, and family-owned 5 & 10 store. Today's proprietors have brought a modern touch to their businesses, expanding their outreach to webpages and online social media. However, they have not forgotten what makes their businesses special. More often than not, customers are still likely to find the owner greeting them at the door.

For some of East Aurora's oldest businesses, like the Globe Hotel and Larwood Pharmacy, new owners have successfully introduced modern amenities in an effort to remain competitive while also fostering an appreciation of nearly two centuries of history.

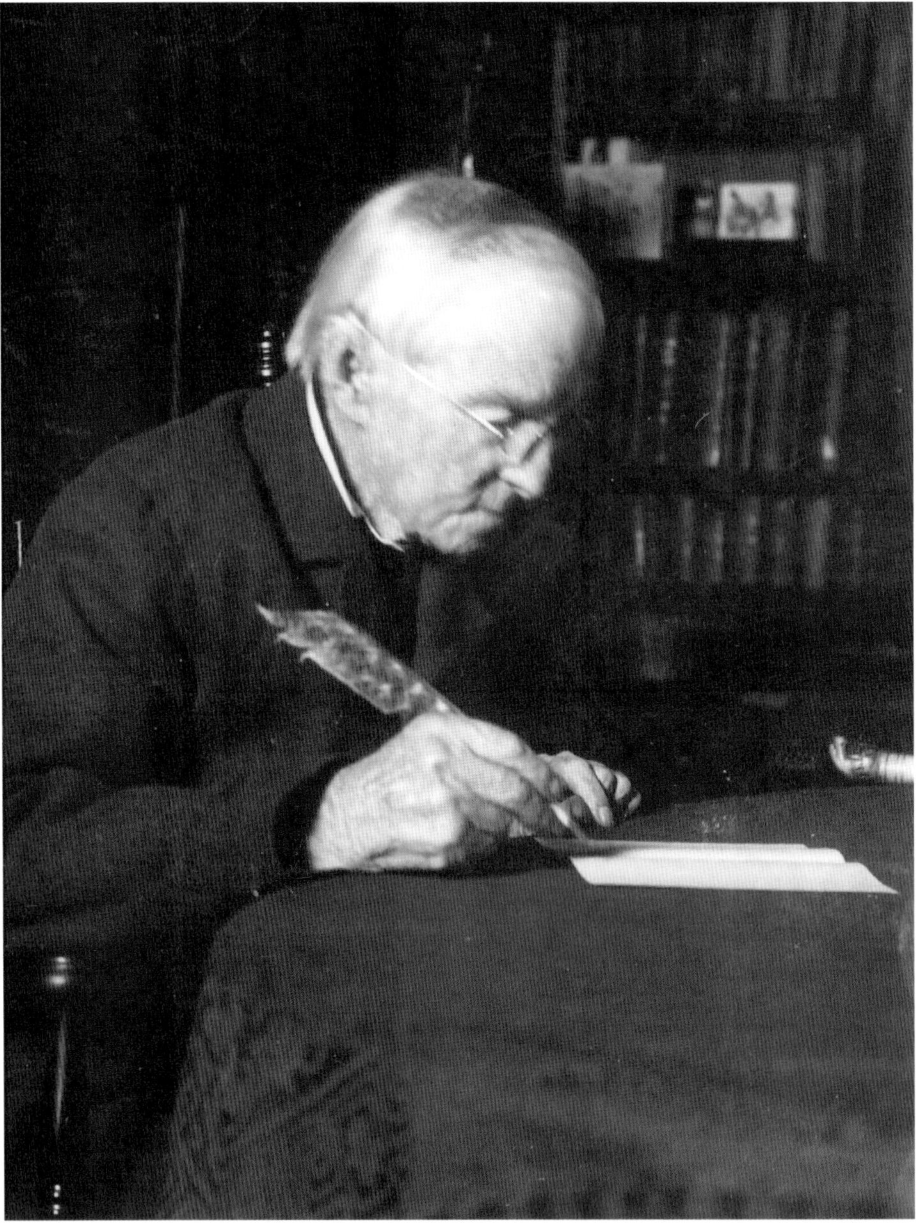

Big in Business

Gen. Aaron Riley, a veteran of the Civil War, was perhaps the most successful businessman the village has ever seen. During the second half of the 19th century, he was involved in nearly every successful business venture in the community. After coming to East Aurora in 1820, he was a law clerk for a short time for Millard Fillmore, who asked Riley to become a partner in his practice. Riley, however, insisted he would be better in business than in law. He was right. At one point, he controlled so much of the real estate in the village that some residents and business owners worried that he had too much power. He served as the tax assessor, was a trustee for the Aurora Academy school, was instrumental in developing the plank road between the village and Buffalo, and later, helped bring the railroad to the community. Riley credited his success "to attending to all matters of business with promptness and dispatch."

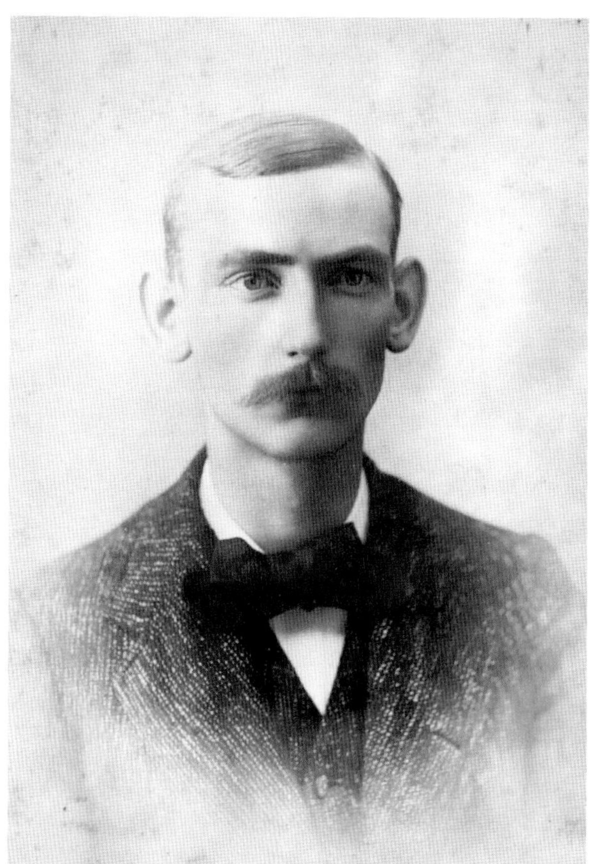

Quiet Philanthropist

Byron D. Gibson took over his father's general store on the Circle (pictured below) and operated it for more than 50 years. With his success, he quietly supported many civic causes. When he died in the early 1930s, Gibson's obituary noted, "Although not generally known, it is said Mr. Gibson did much in the community along philanthropic lines." Gibson also operated a store on the east end of Main Street with business partner Arthur Hammond between 1897 and 1914, and he served as Aurora town supervisor between 1895 and 1905.

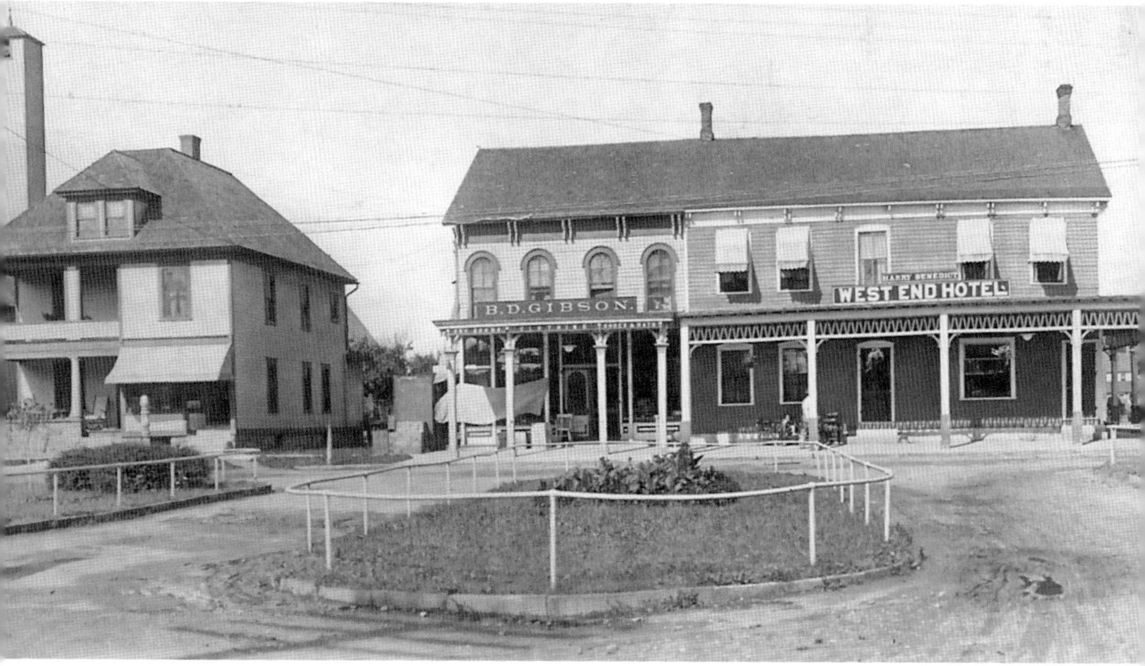

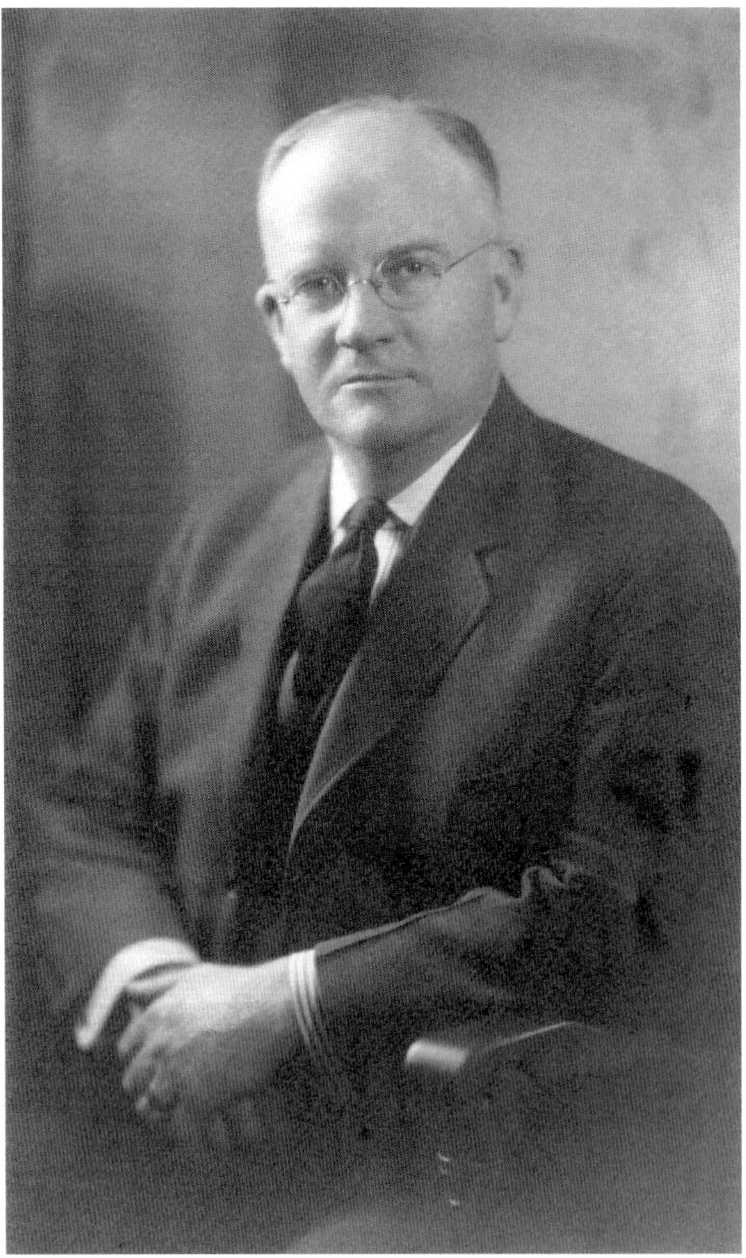

The Oldest Attorney

Wells W. Parker was the oldest practicing attorney in the village when he died in 1965 at the age of 91. Born in nearby Wales Hollow, Parker walked seven miles each day to East Aurora to attend high school. When he graduated in 1892, he was the only boy in his class. After graduating from the University at Buffalo Law School in 1896, he returned to East Aurora, where he maintained a successful law career for decades. He was village clerk for many years and headed the local draft board during World War I. "He was a familiar figure in Buffalo and East Aurora," his obituary noted, "always dressed in a dark suit, black tie, black shoes, black wide-brim hat and the same black brief case that he carried through his long career."

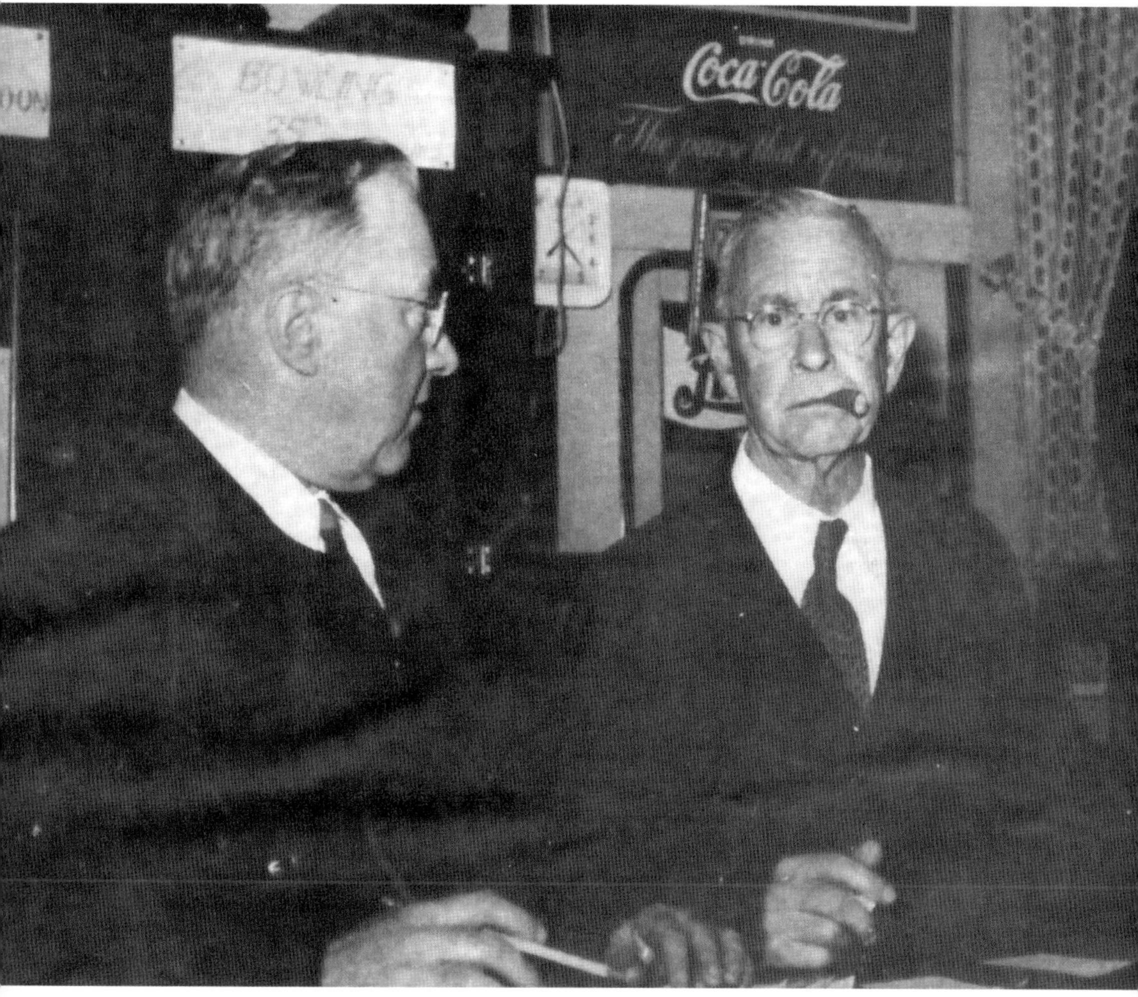

Bowling Family
Merritt H. Jackson (right) built Jackson's Bowling Alleys on Whaley Avenue in 1915. After his death, his son Cecil (left) continued to operate the bowling alley until 1958. In the early days, Jackson's had only two lanes, and high school boys were hired as pinsetters. Additional lanes were added, two at a time, until there were eight. Automatic pinsetter machines were installed in 1957. The business continued to operate as one of the oldest bowling alleys in the nation until the 2000s. The vacant building was torn down in 2012.

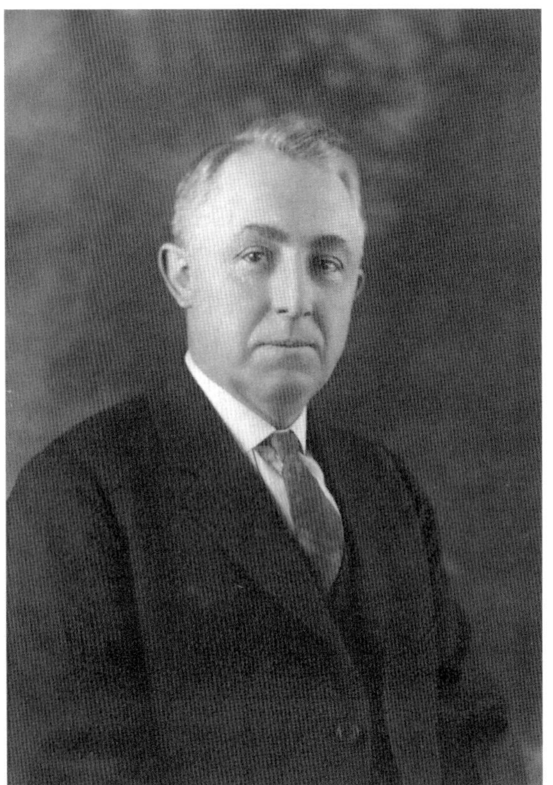

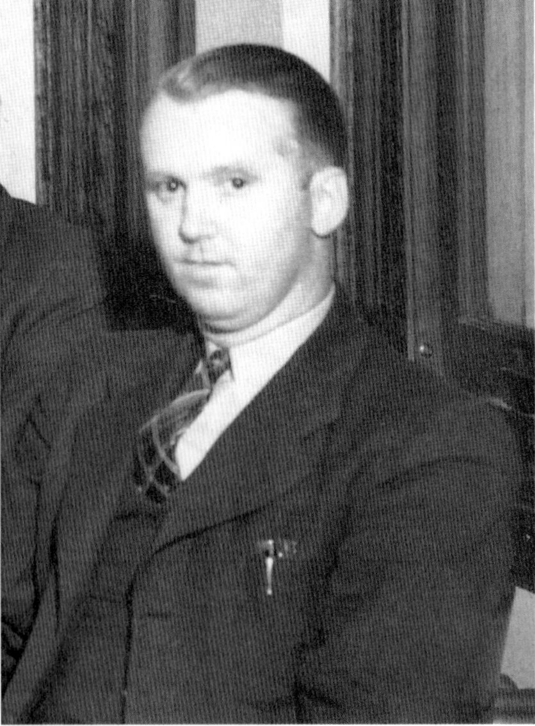

Town Hall Barbers

John D. Bradburn (top), a barber in the village and a town clerk in 1910, kept all the town files dating back to 1832 in his barbershop. Before the town bought him a safe, Bradburn kept the records in his desk. In 1929, the town began renting space for records storage and meetings in the new village hall at the corner of Main and Paine Streets, but Bradburn continued to conduct town business from his barbershop on the north side of Main Street near the Circle. Local residents could get a marriage license and a haircut at the same time! When Bradburn was struck by a car and killed in 1939, deputy town clerk Harry R. Hennessey (bottom), who had been Bradburn's apprentice in the barbershop, became town clerk. Under Hennessey, the barbershop continued to double as the town clerk's office until 1958, when the Town of Aurora purchased the former Roycroft Chapel from the Baptist church for use as the first town hall. The barbershop was later torn down to make room for a parking lot.

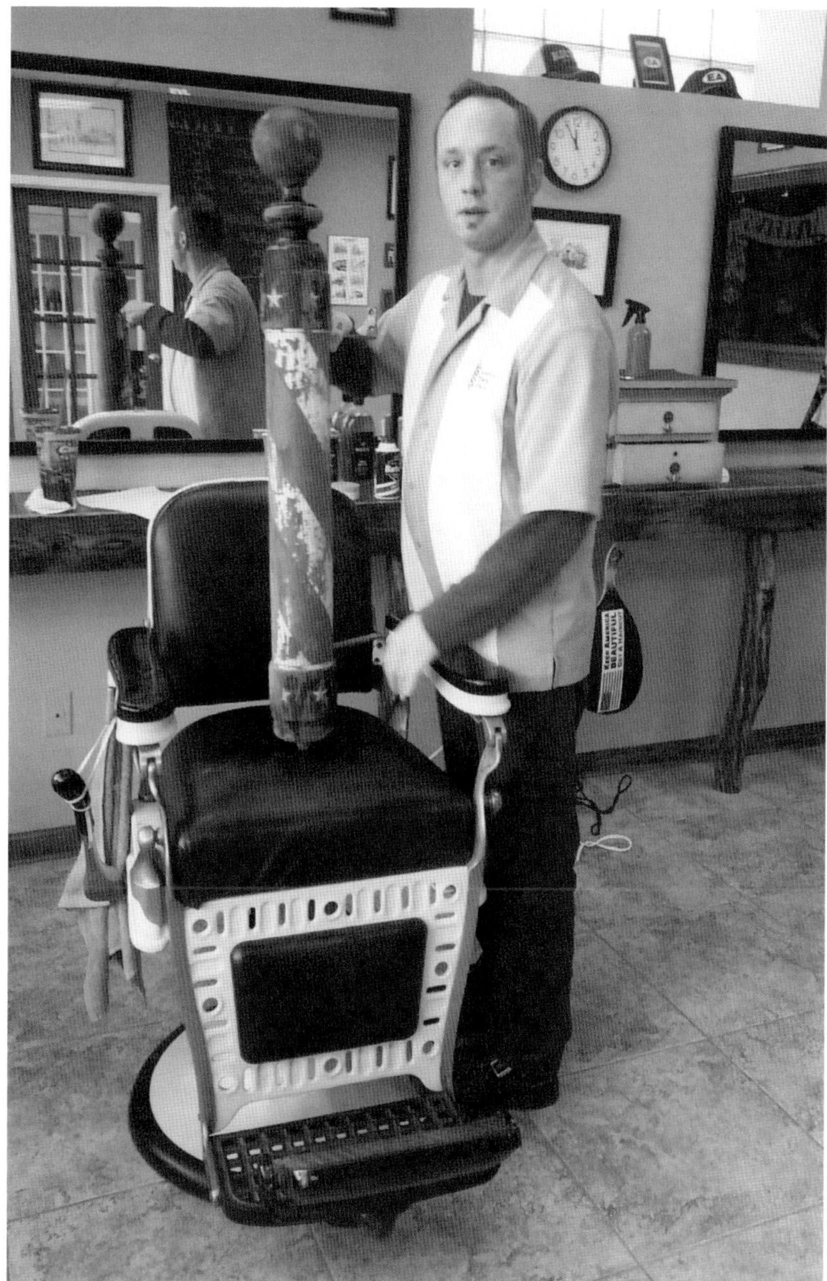

Newest Old-Fashioned Barber

C.J. Andrews displays the red-white-and-blue wooden barber pole that once hung on the outside of John D. Bradburn and Harry R. Hennessey's Main Street barbershop near the Circle. Ironically, in 2013, Andrews opened his East Aurora barbershop almost directly across the street from where the previous barbershop once stood. Andrews says he wants customers to experience an old-fashioned barbershop, much like they would have in Bradburn and Hennessey's day. The wooden barber pole is on exhibit at the Aurora History Museum, which is located in the Southside Municipal Center at 300 Gleed Avenue. (Courtesy of C.J. Andrews.)

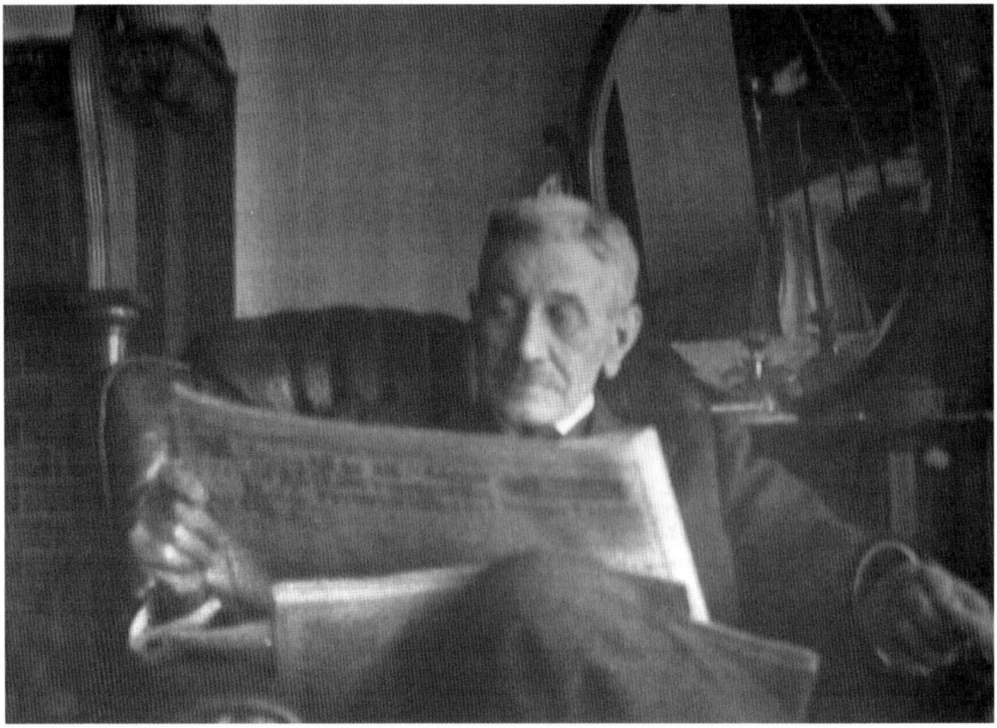

Griggs and Ball

Brothers-in-law Abbott S. Griggs (above) and Fay H. Ball (right) joined forces in the general milling business in 1893. The partnership was incorporated into the name Griggs and Ball Inc. Ball remained president of the firm for many years after Griggs died in 1917. Both men served as mayor of the village.

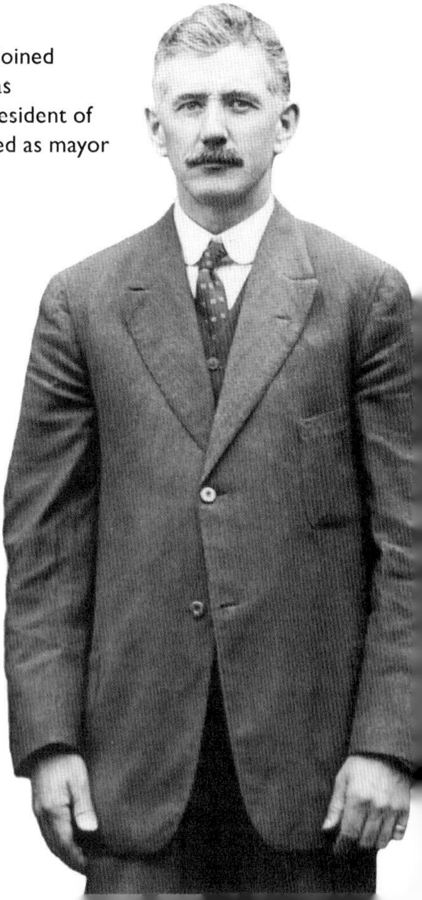

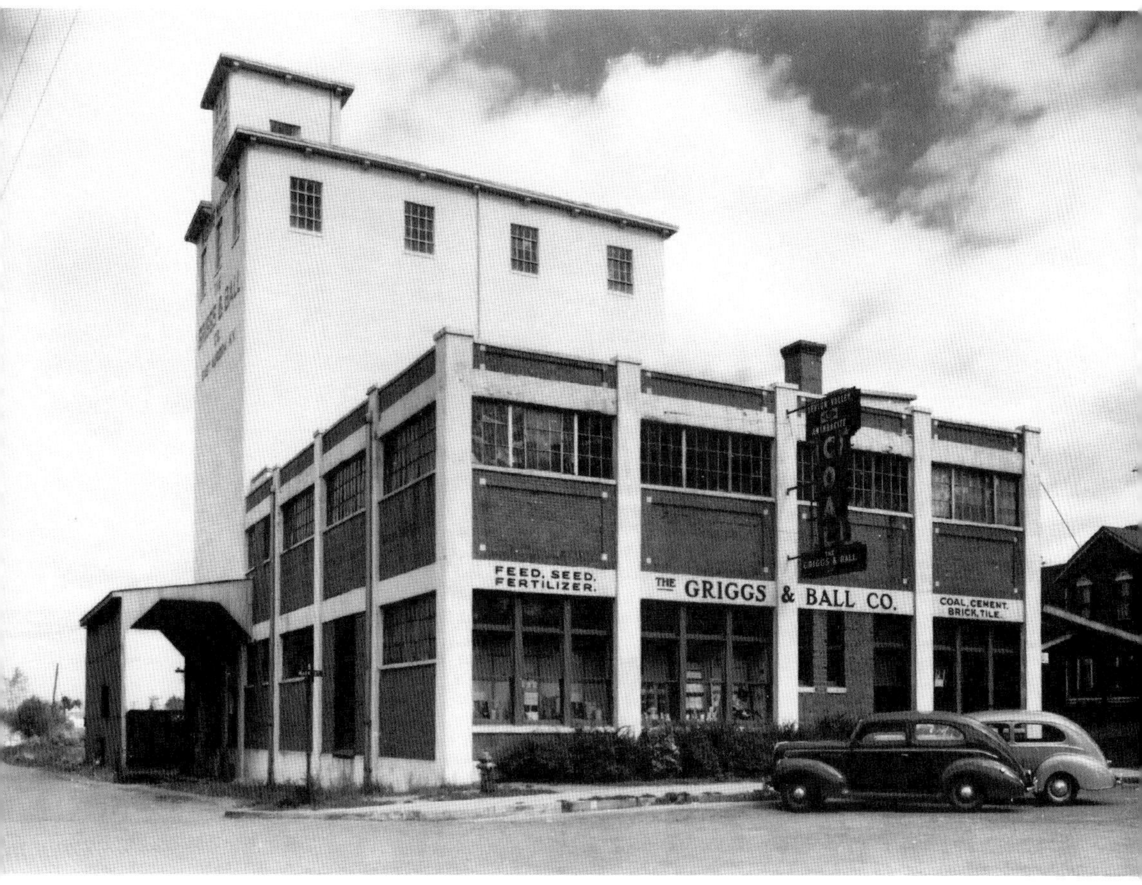

Griggs and Ball Building

Though restaurants and offices now occupy the building at Main and Riley Streets, many locals still refer to the former grain mill as the Griggs and Ball Building. Extensive renovations have allowed new uses for the building while retaining much of its historical character.

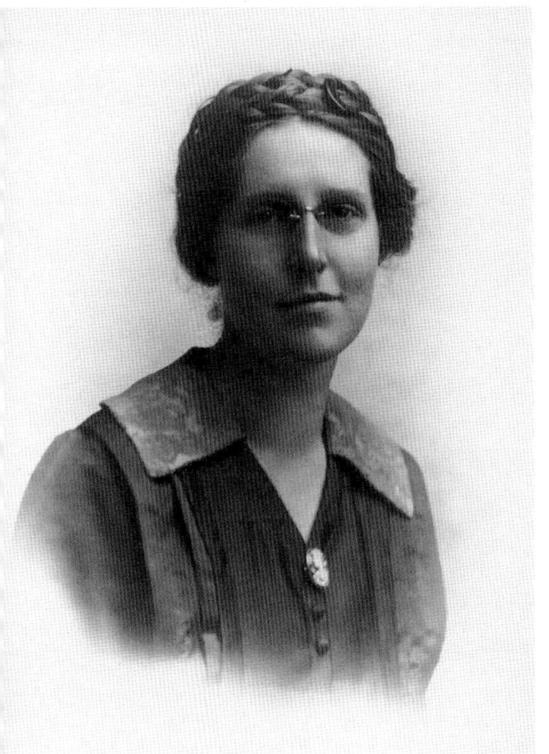

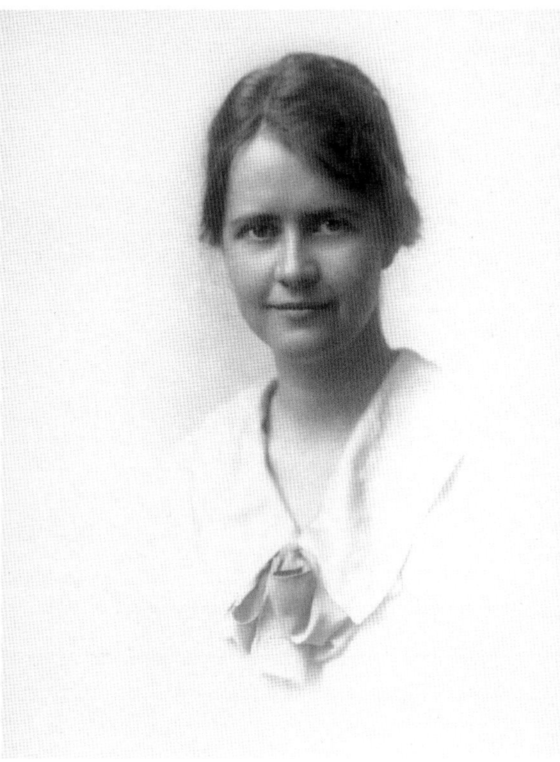

Seaman, Hood & Morey

In 1914, Roycroft workers Allene Seaman (left) and Beulah Hood (right) joined forces with Betty Morey to become businesswomen ahead of their time when they purchased a variety store on the north side of Main Street near Riley Street. Three years later, in January 1917, they faced the ultimate business challenge when the entire store burned to the ground. A new building was constructed, and within months, the store reopened under a new name, Seaman, Hood & Morey. The store was sold to a Buffalo firm in the 1950s. The building was later divided into several smaller stores.

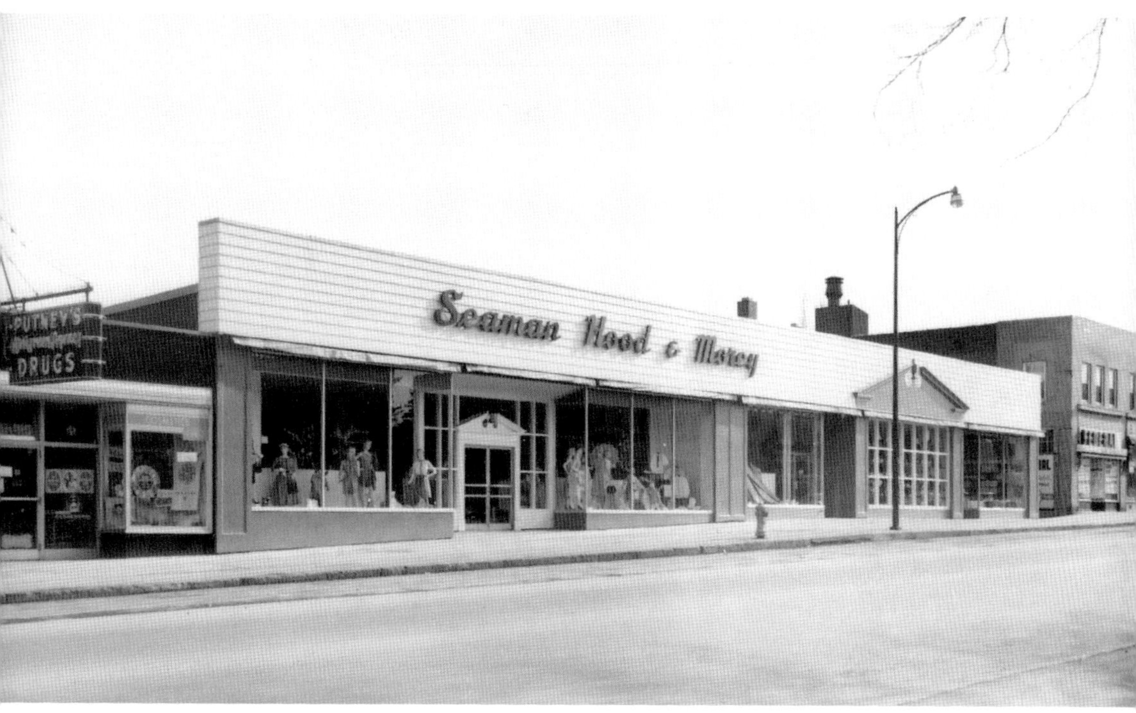

Seaman, Hood & Morey Building
The Seaman, Hood & Morey building was considered a "metropolitan department store" on the east end of Main Street for decades. Beulah Hood came back to cut the ribbon when a greatly enlarged and remodeled store was unveiled in April 1959.

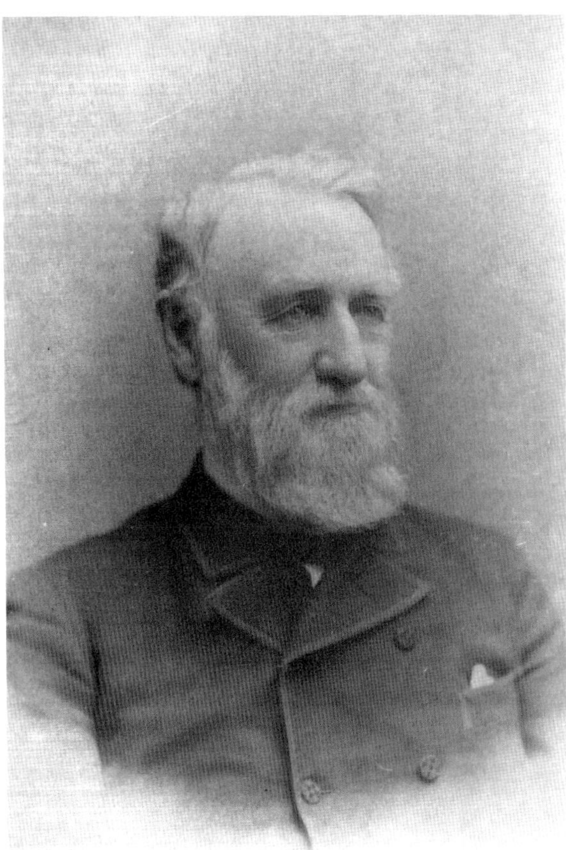

Provider of the Park

Cicero J. Hamlin gained worldwide fame for his Village Farm on the west end of Main Street, at which he bred champion racehorses. However, he left behind a more important local legacy on the other side of the village. When Hamlin caught wind in September 1899 of the village's plan to borrow money to buy Holmes Grove and some of the adjacent property for use as a recreational area, he quickly stepped up to save taxpayers the expense. "It has been my purpose to do something of a public character which would show my appreciation of my residence there and of the generous treatment of a holder of property in your village since I became a resident of Buffalo," Hamlin wrote in a letter to the village board. Hamlin put two conditions on the deal: the park shall always be open to the public for recreational purposes, and at least $100 must be spent every year on maintenance. In appreciation, the village immediately renamed the park in Hamlin's honor.

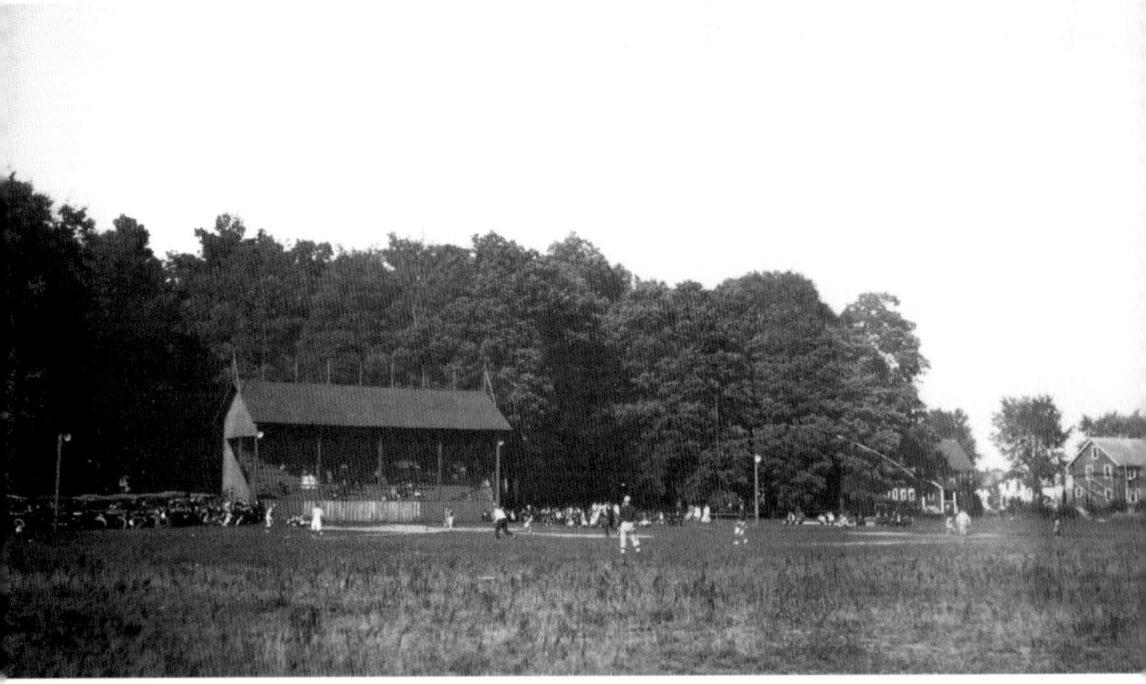

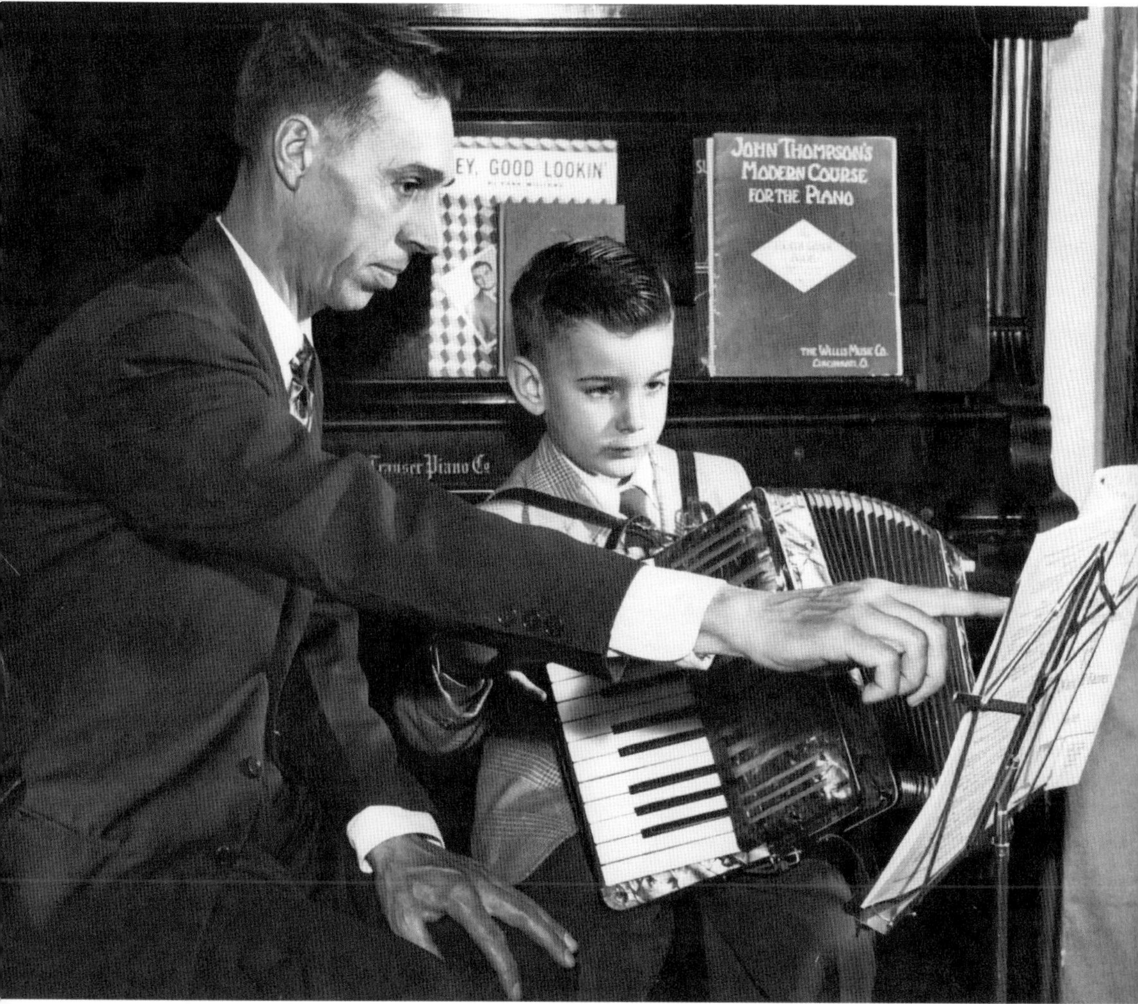

The Music Man

Noted guitarist Charles E. Nyhart Sr. established Nyhart Music Center in 1954 and is best remembered for the numerous instrumental lessons he gave to local schoolchildren over his 35-year career. When Nyhart, a graduate of East Aurora High School, retired in 1979, the store reopened as the East Aurora Music Center. (Courtesy of the Nyhart family.)

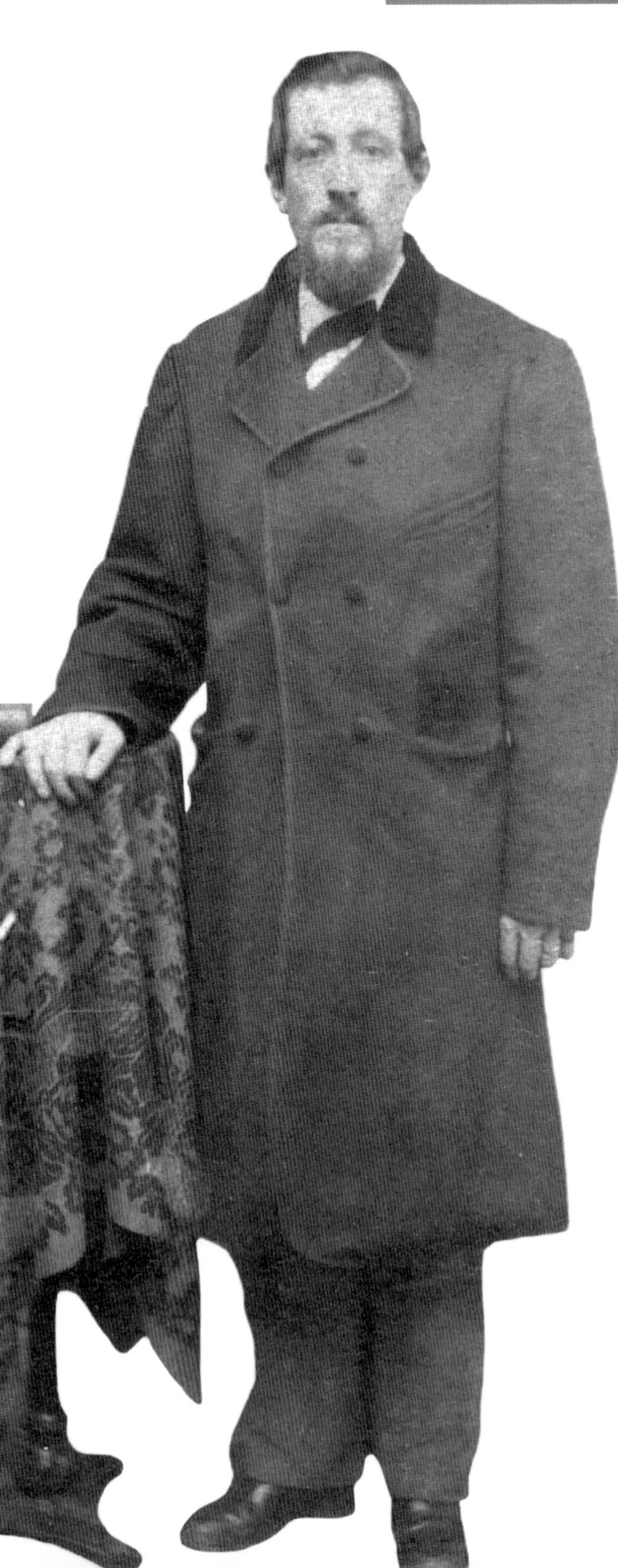

Civil War Postmaster
James F. Crandall was postmaster of Willink on the west end of the village between 1861 and 1868. It must have been a very interesting time to be in charge of the post office. Among his duties, Crandall, who also operated a store, would have handled letters home from Civil War soldiers and would have been one of the first in town to see newspapers detailing accounts of the battles.

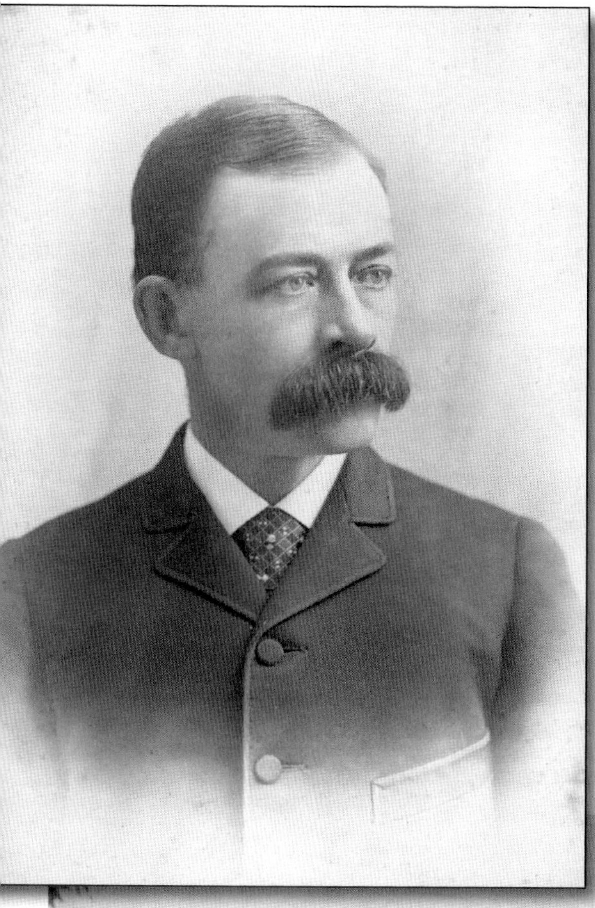

House History Keeper

The lack of reliable records makes it difficult to determine the dates that many houses were built. However, thanks to Dwight M. Spooner, it is known that 110 Pine Street was built in 1878–1879. Spooner kept a detailed diary of the construction process. "Sept. 5: Commenced digging cellar," one entry noted. "Sept. 16: Oscar Bowen started framing." The project hit roadblocks when two big snowstorms, on December 21 and January 2, blocked the trains for several weeks. According to Spooner's diary, he and his wife, Mary Bowen Spooner, finally were able to enjoy dinner in their new house on August 30, 1879. Dwight ran a hardware store with Mary's brother at the nearby corner of Main and Pine Streets. He died in 1918. The diary, which is now part of the town archives in the Town Historian's Office, was discovered in 1967.

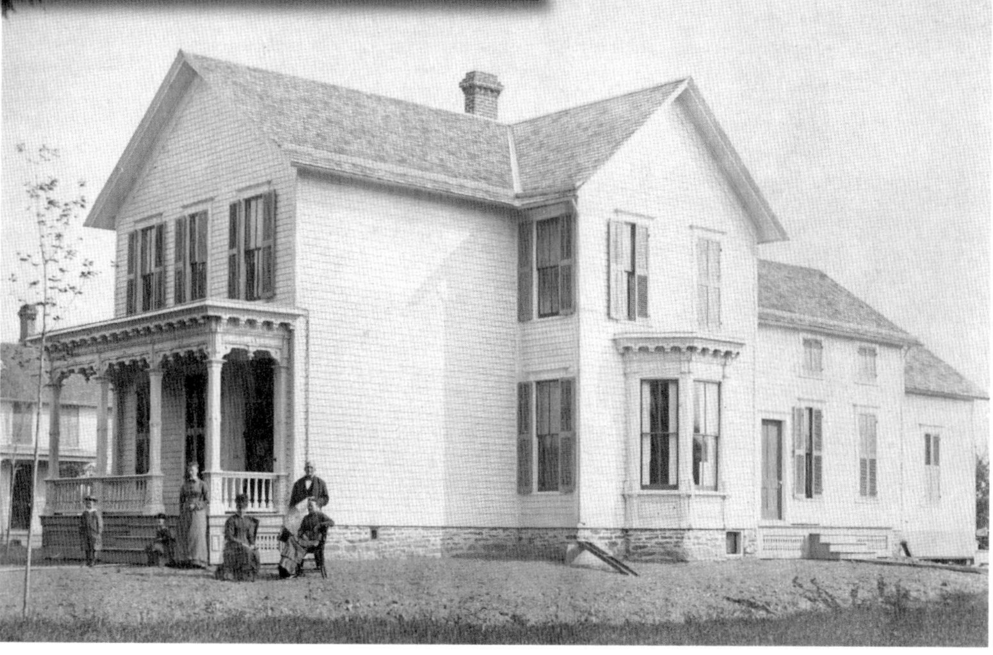

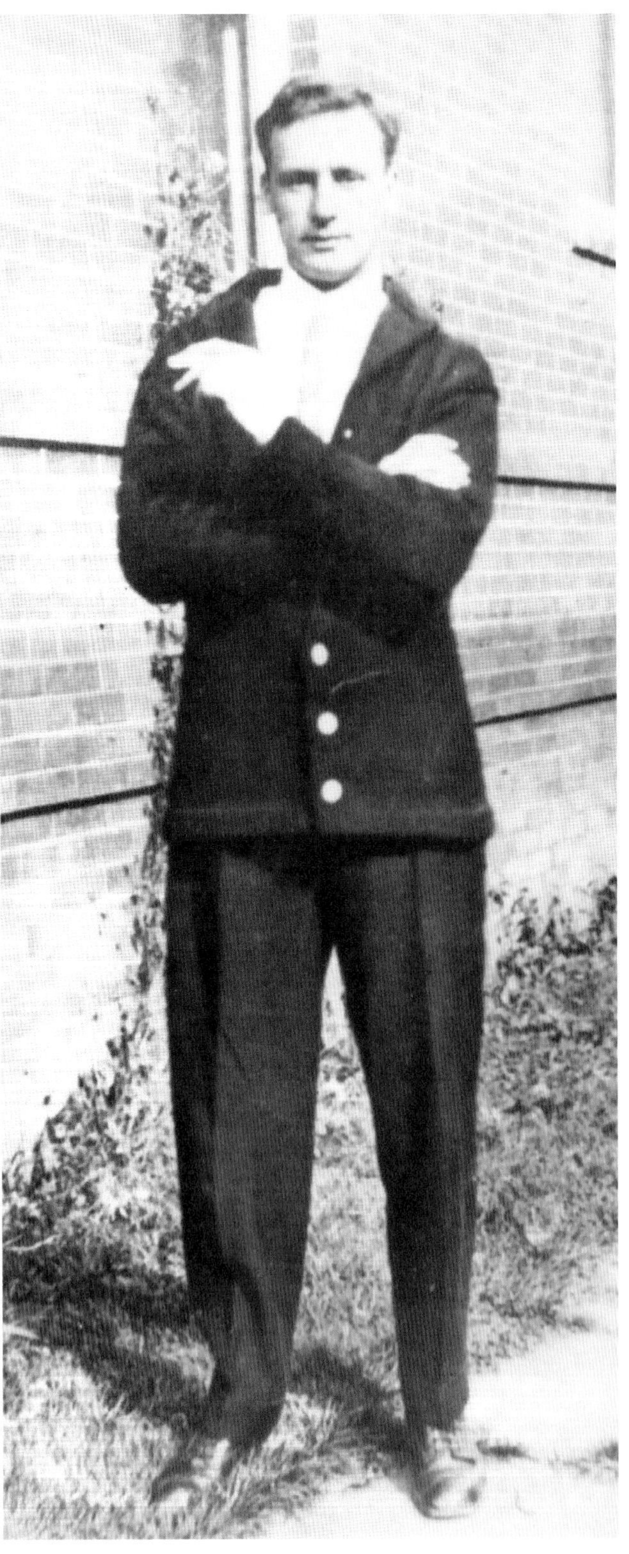

The First Mr. Vidler
According to local legend, Robert Vidler Sr. was prompted to open the Fair, a five-and-dime on Main Street, in 1930 after his mother-in-law complained that she had to travel all the way to Buffalo, 17 miles away, just to buy a spool of red thread. Vidler took a big risk by opening a store at the onset of the Great Depression. In fact, it is said that neighboring merchants took bets that the store would close in a few months. Vidler waited 15 years to change the name of the store to Vidler's 5 & 10, no longer worried about besmirching the family name with a failed business. Today, Vidler's still sells spools of thread, in red and almost every other color imaginable. (Courtesy of the Vidler family.)

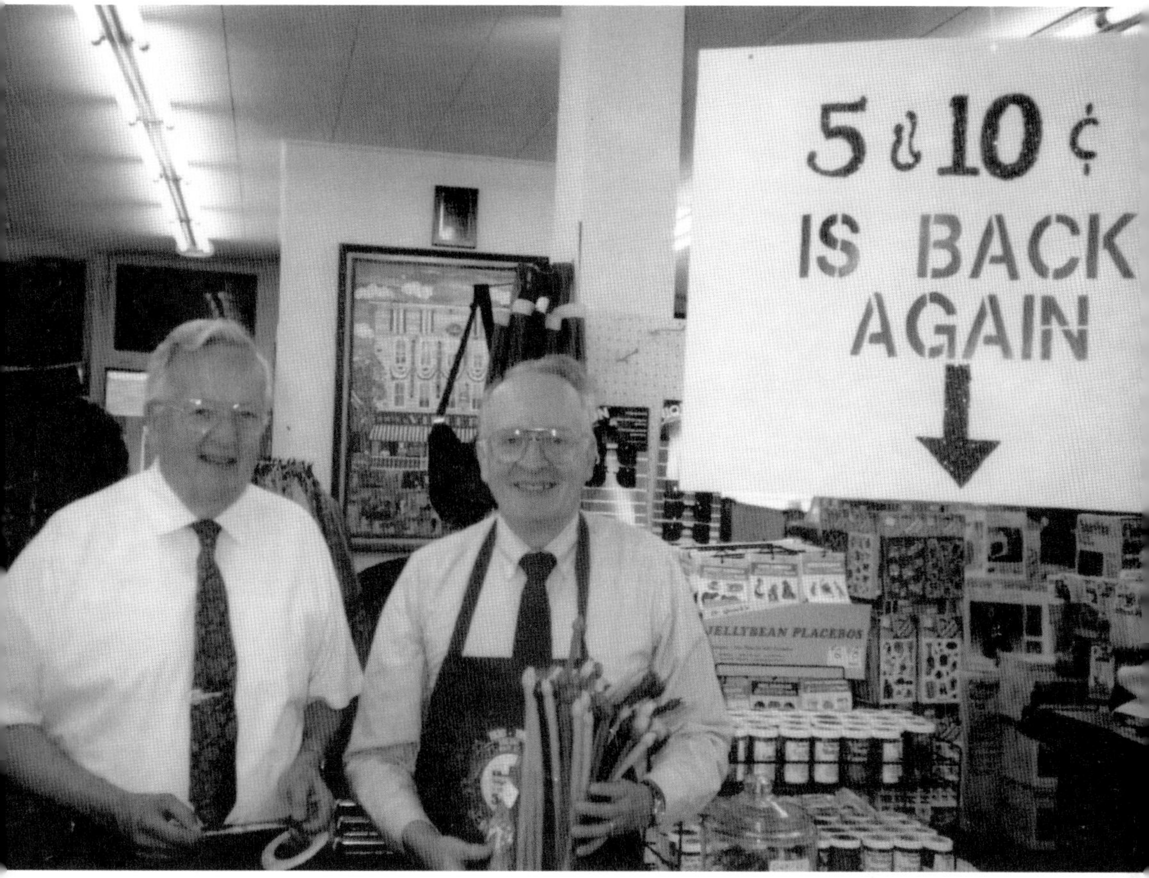

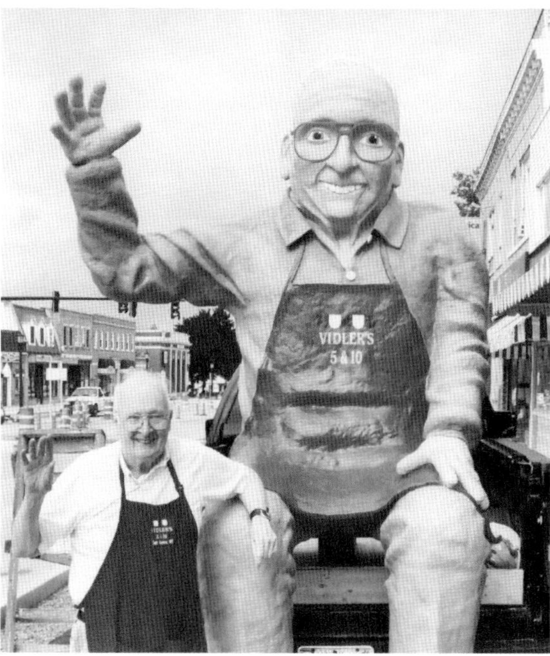

Second Generation
Brothers Robert Vidler Jr. (left) and Edward Vidler (right) took over the family business and transformed it into a nostalgic tourist destination. Their humorous appearances in television commercials in the 1980s brought wide attention to the store and turned them into regional celebrities. One commercial, which featured Edward on the roof of the store, led to a giant "Vidler on the Roof," which has become a conversation piece on top of the store ever since it was installed a few years ago. A third generation of the Vidler family is now in charge of day-to-day operations. (Left, courtesy of the Vidler family.)

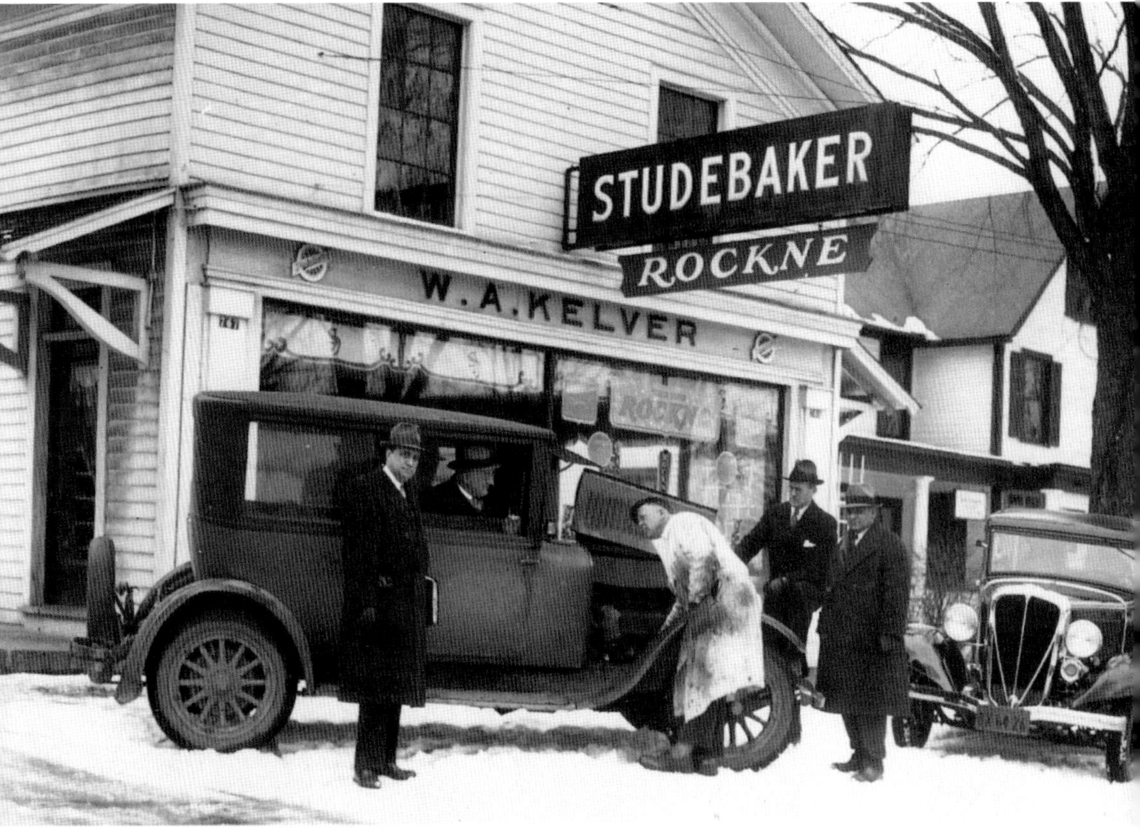

Oldest Studebaker Dealer

William A. Kelver, pictured sitting in the driver's seat, was the oldest Studebaker dealer in the country. He opened his first auto dealership in nearby Wales Center in 1911, the first year Studebaker began manufacturing cars. He moved the dealership to 765 Main Street in 1920 and continued working until shortly before his death in 1971. When Studebaker stopped making cars, Kelver switched to selling Fiats, but announced he would continue to service Studebakers "as long as one continued to roll." The short street near his former dealership, Kelver Court, is named in his honor.

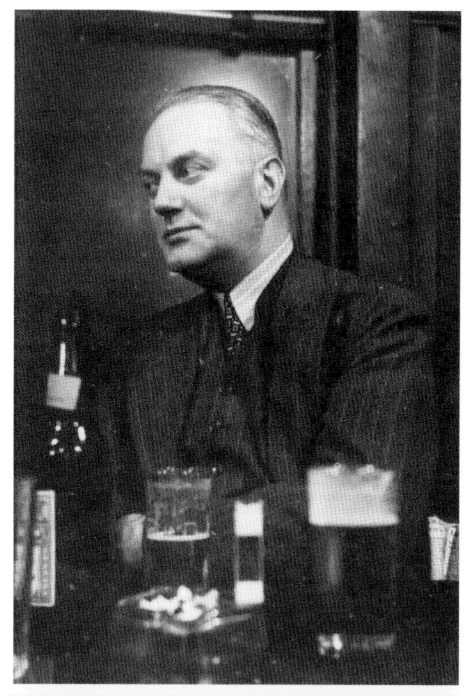

Keeping the Oldest Business Alive

For 74 years, members of the Balthasar family owned and operated the Globe Hotel and Restaurant, built in the early 1820s. It is East Aurora's oldest business still operating in its original location. Upon returning from service in World War I, Victor Balthasar (right) took over operations from his father, Henry, who had acquired the hotel in 1906. After Victor's death in 1975, his children took over. Rocco Sorrentino bought the business in 1981, shortly after a bank foreclosure threatened the landmark. "The deal happened very quickly," he recalled. While Sorrentino and his wife, Tara Woyton, pictured below, have been the official proprietors for more than 30 years, some have reported witnessing the friendly spirit of Victor Balthasar still stopping by to oversee operations at the restaurant. (Right, courtesy of Mae Kim Miller; below, photograph by the author.)

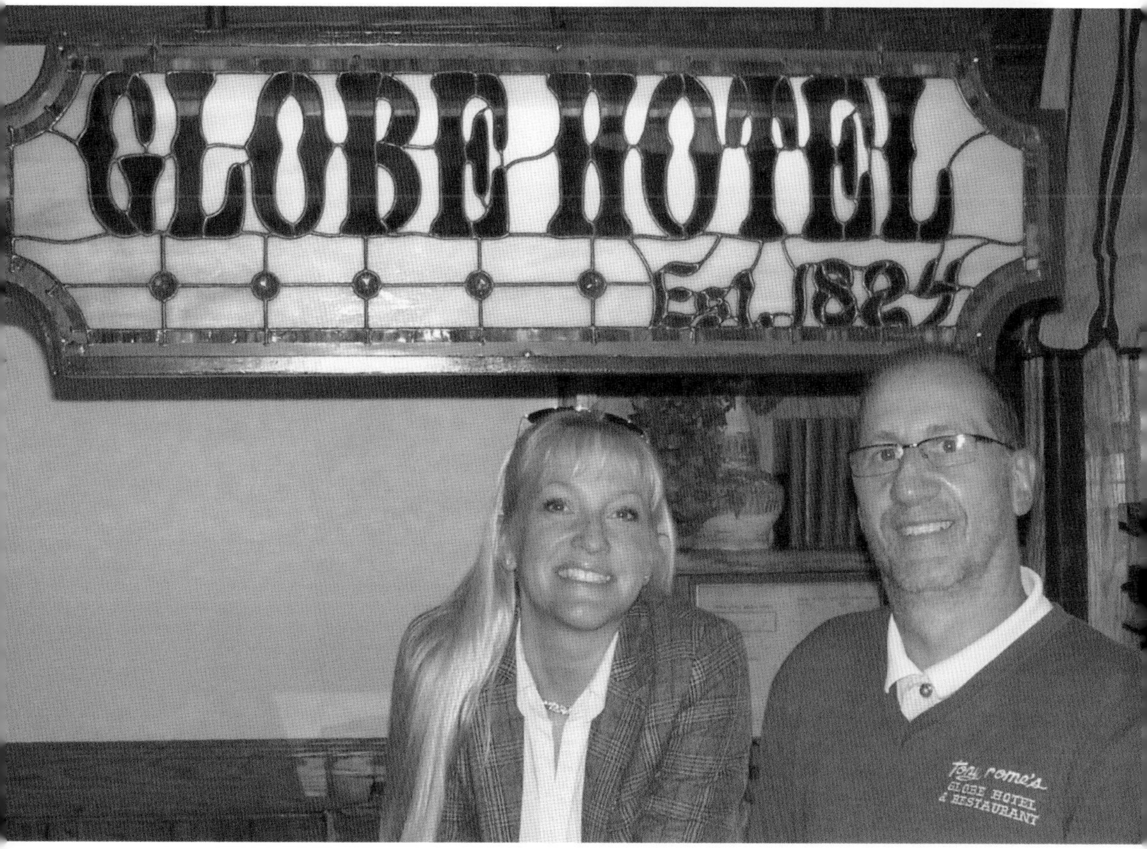

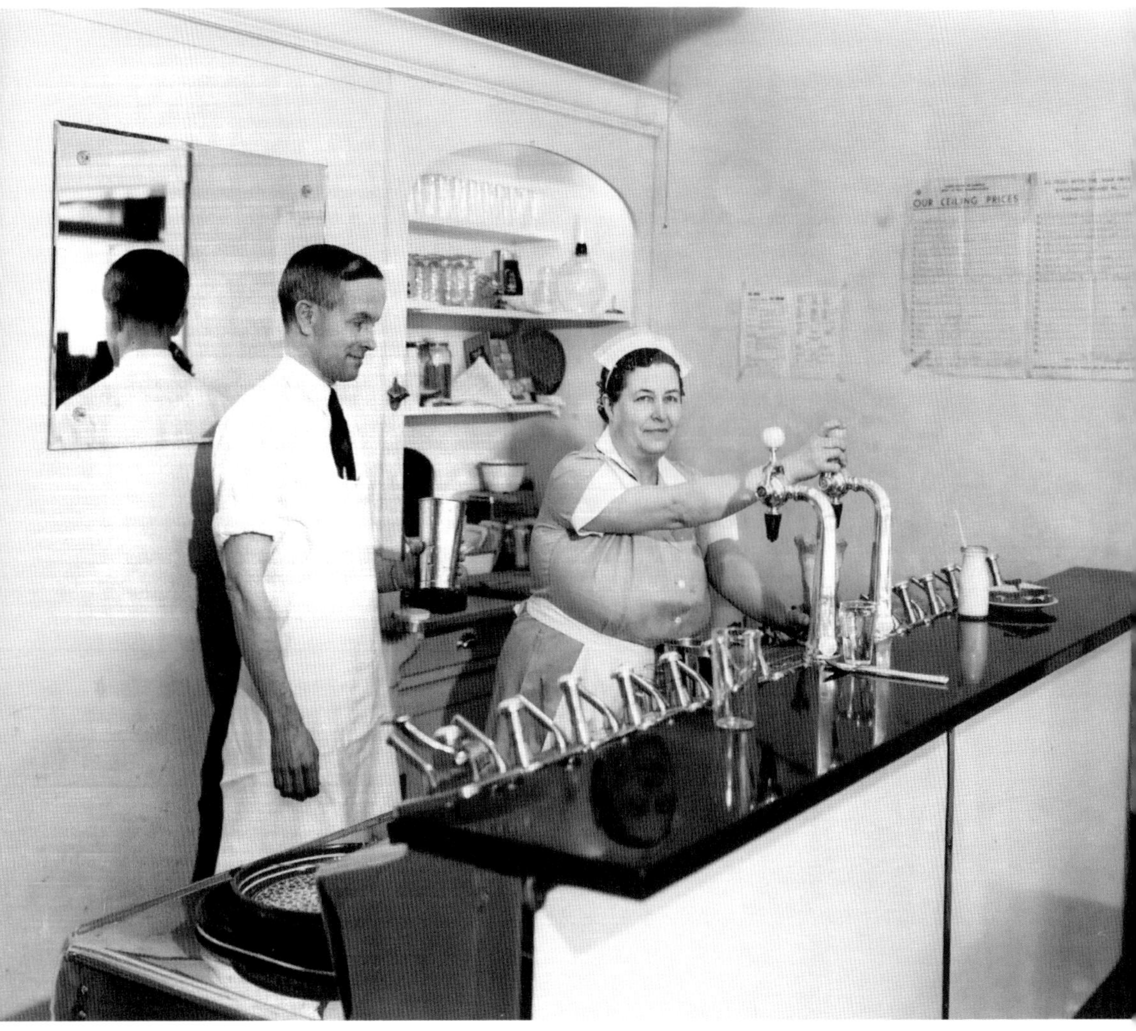

Ice Cream Couple

Stanley and Celina Rosenberg were the owners and operators of the Vel-Rose Ice Cream Parlor and Pharmacy, a popular after-school hangout, for several years in the 1940s and 1950s. The shop was originally located at 396 Main Street, across from Walnut Street and within a few steps of the high school. It moved to 703 Main Street in 1948. The original location later became Thomas Drugs.

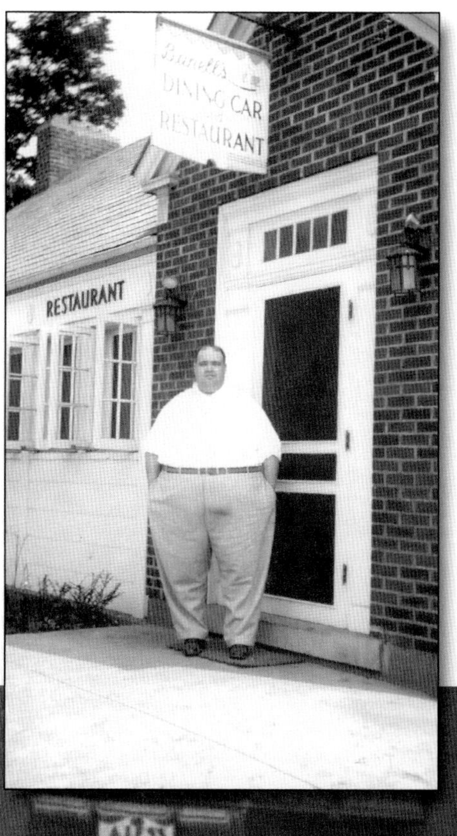

Popular at Lunch Hour

Sherman E. Bunell, pictured at left in about 1935, was the well-known owner and operator of a popular diner at the corner of Main and Riley Streets. He is pictured below behind the wheel drumming up business during the Fourth of July parade in 1936. Just two years later, he died of a heart condition at the age of 34. The diner was later known as the Village Kitchen, and in 1964, it was moved to the parking lot behind Griggs and Ball.

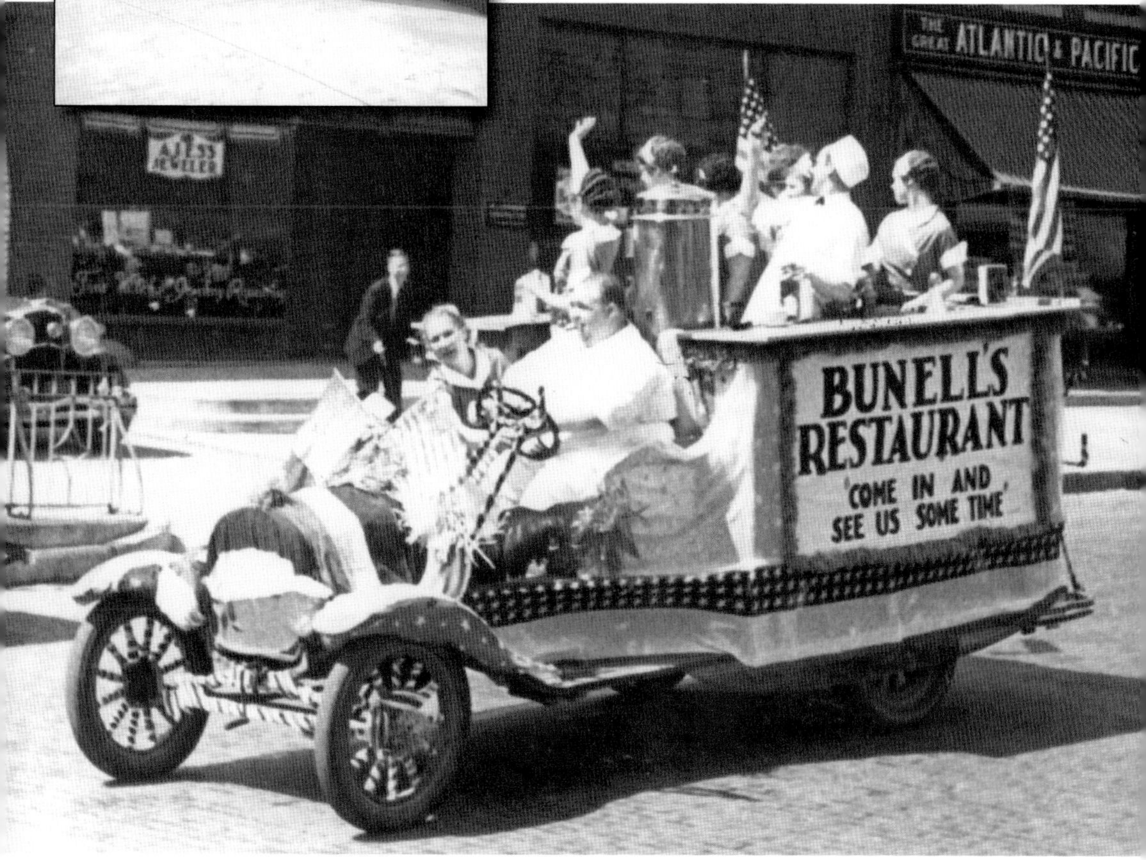

Pharmacy Team

The three longtime partners of Larwood Pharmacy, Nelson Smith, Robert Hillier, and Peter Schultz, are pictured behind the pharmacy counter in 1981. The trio purchased the store from its namesake, Loren Larwood, in 1967. They moved the store from Main Street to the Oakwood Square Plaza in 1974. Larwood Pharmacy traces its lineage to the community's first drugstore, which Dr. Jabez Allen opened on Main Street in 1834. Over the years, the business has changed names and locations a few times.

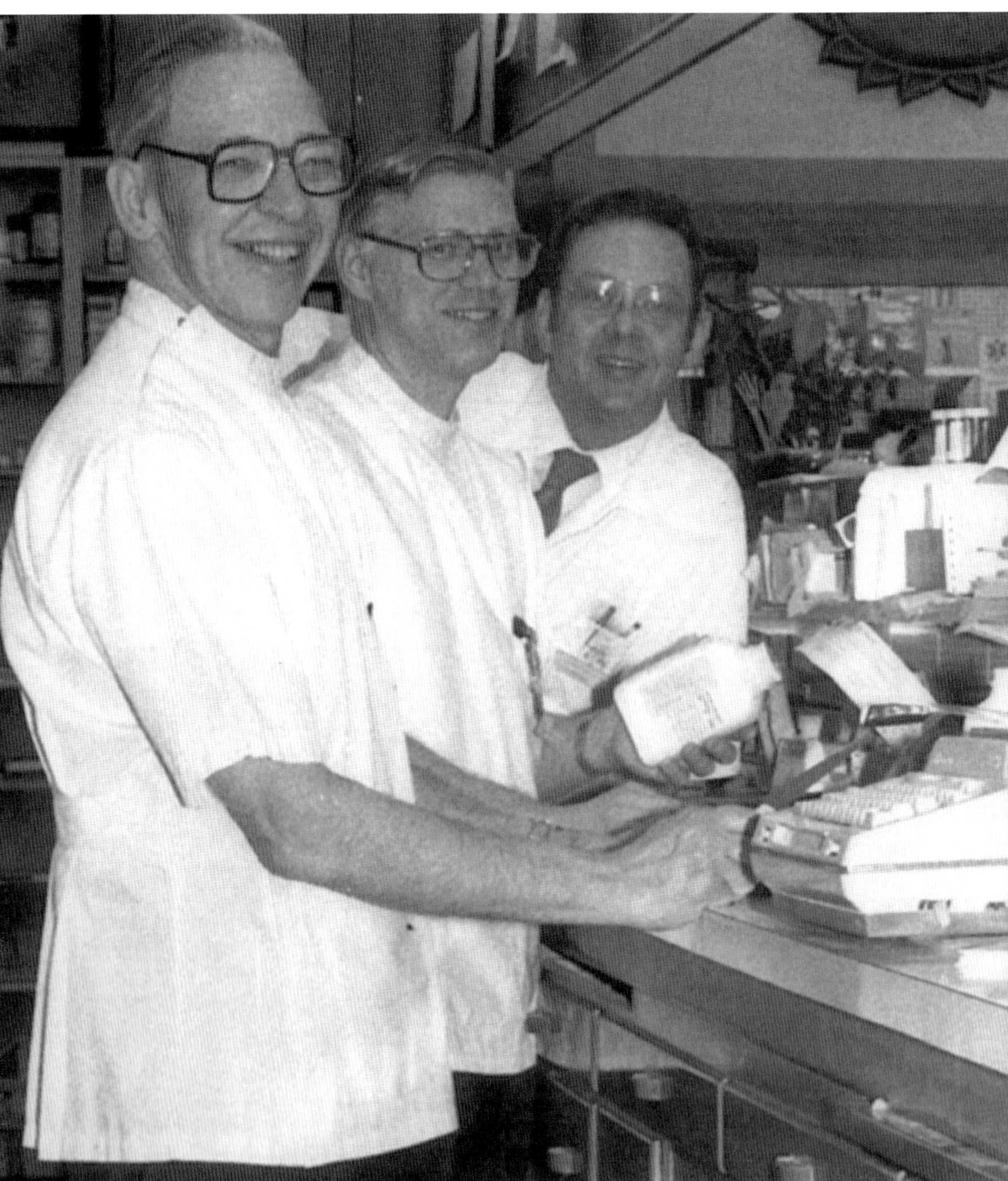

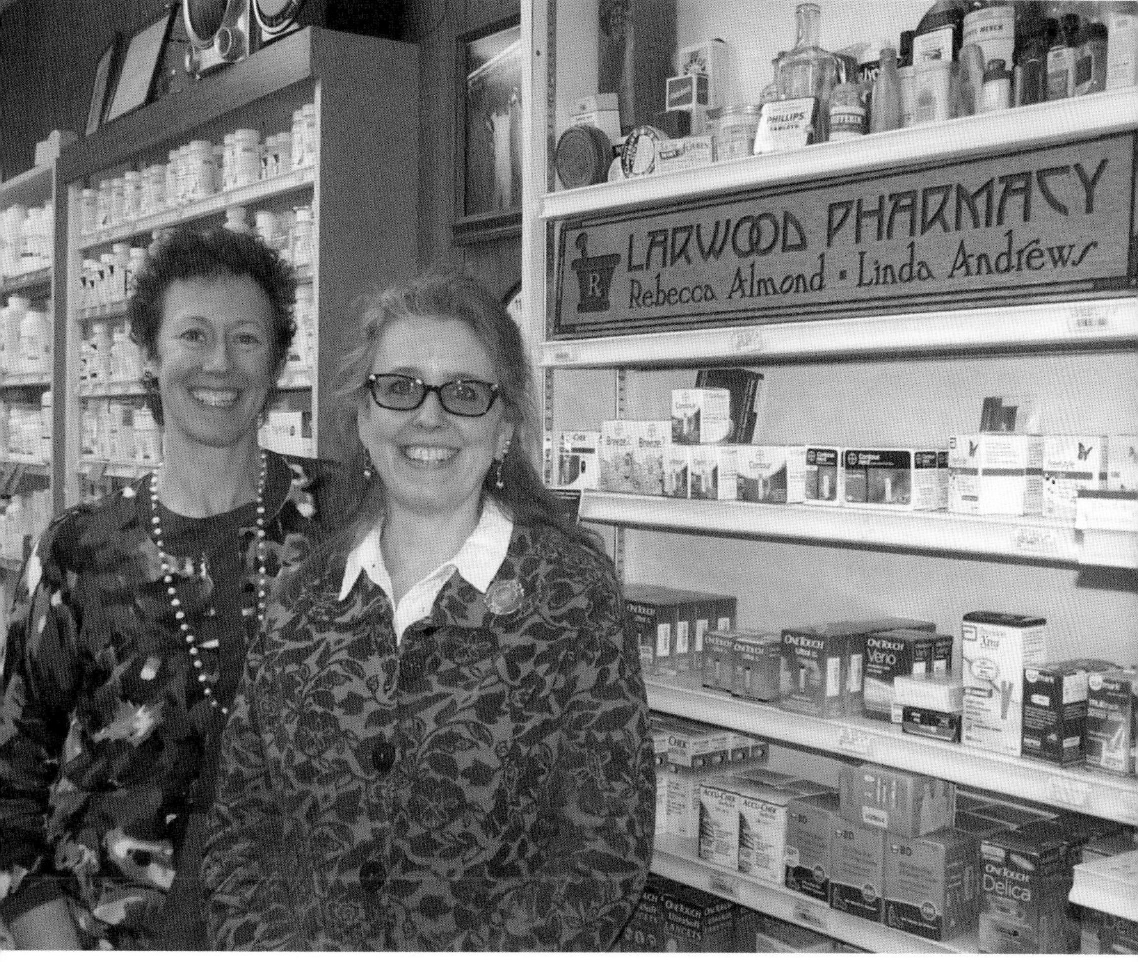

Maintaining the Independent Tradition
Linda Moden Andrews (left) and Rebecca Almond (right) started working at Larwood Pharmacy as interns when they were in pharmacy school. They became the owners in 2005. Larwood is one of only a few independent pharmacies in the area. Despite the competition from numerous chain drugstores, the owners maintain that great, individualized customer service keeps East Aurorans coming back. When other stores closed during a blizzard in 2014, Larwood employees battled through the snow and wind to deliver emergency prescriptions to their customers. "Our phone numbers are on the front door of the store, in case our customers need anything after hours," Almond says. "Sometimes we get emergency calls in the middle of the night, but that's what we do." (Photograph by the author.)

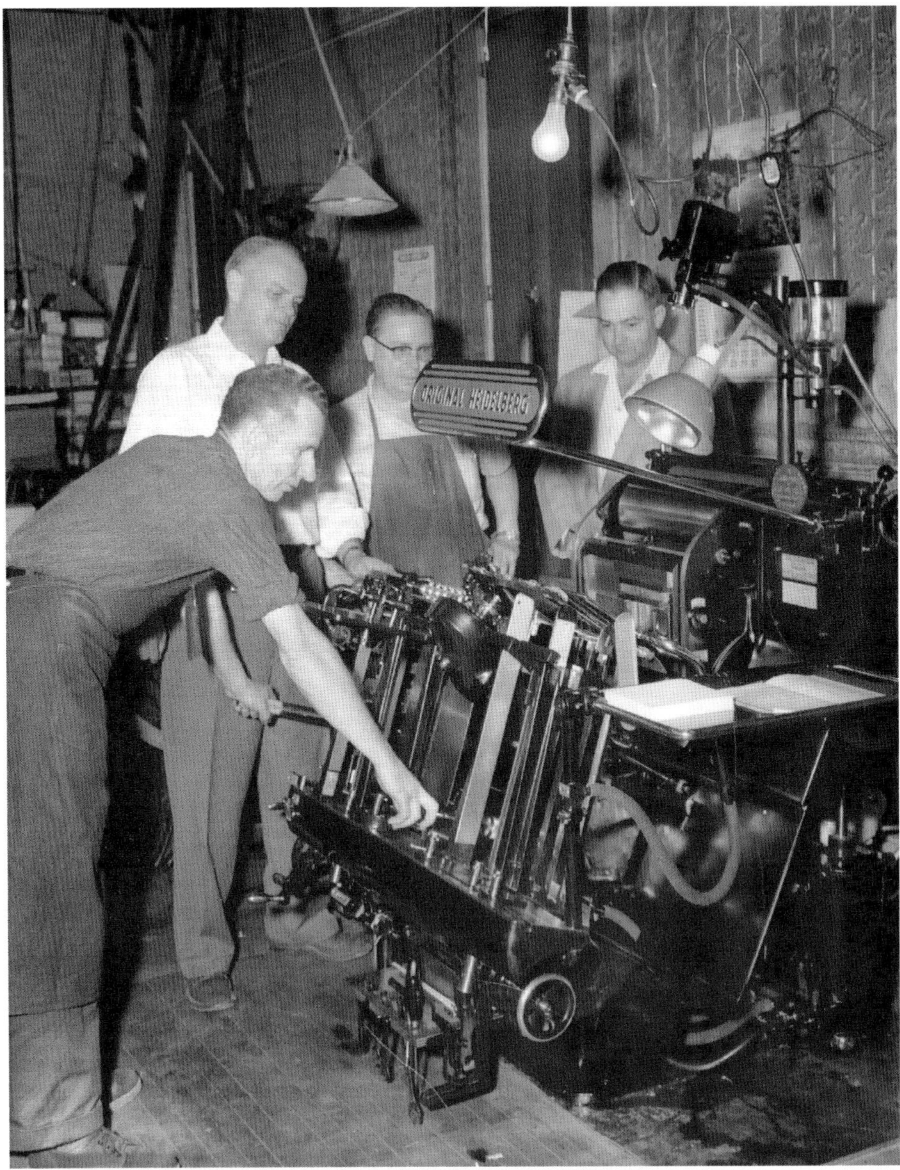

Keeper of the Community Record

Alfred P. Spooner (right) was publisher of the *East Aurora Advertiser*, the community's longest-running newspaper, for 47 years. He took over as publisher in his twenties when his father, R. John Spooner, died in 1935. The "Spooner era," which began in 1915, took the newspaper through two World Wars and the Great Depression. After overseeing nearly 2,400 weekly editions, Alfred Spooner sold the newspaper in 1981 to former editor Grant M. Hamilton, ending nearly seven decades of Spooner family ownership. In one of his first editorials as the new publisher, Hamilton wrote: "Al Spooner was not a flamboyant publisher that is the stuff of books and movies. What he did, however, was more important. He guided a newspaper through difficult times and times of incredible technological change. His legacy is a 47-year chronicle of our community history as it happened." Hamilton, who has guided the newspaper through even more technological change since 1981, remains publisher more than three decades later. (Courtesy of the *East Aurora Advertiser*.)

Ink Was in His Blood

Oliver E. Bailey worked as a printer at the Roycroft and a pressman at the *East Aurora Advertiser* before launching *The Shopping Guide* in 1938. The publication was the first of its kind in East Aurora, providing more space for advertising than news articles. In 1957, he incorporated under the name S-G Press, which was later operated by his son Clayton Bailey and grandson Tim Bailey. In a diary, Oliver E. Bailey recorded details of his service in France during World War I. In one of his entries, he wrote, "Right after going over the top, a big German shell exploded, burying my buddies and me. I was saying the 91st Psalm when the burst came. We dug ourselves from under the loose earth, and no one was hurt."

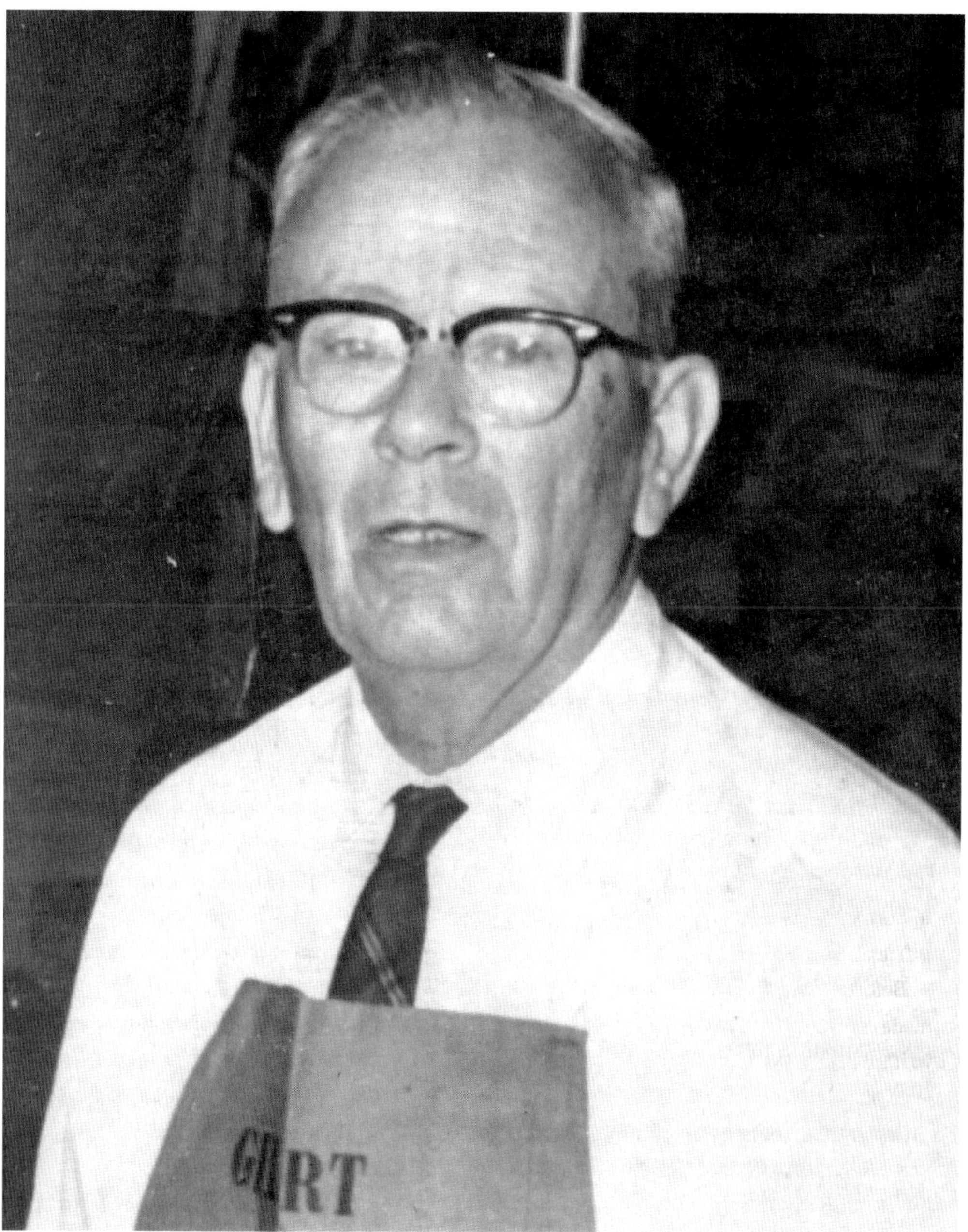

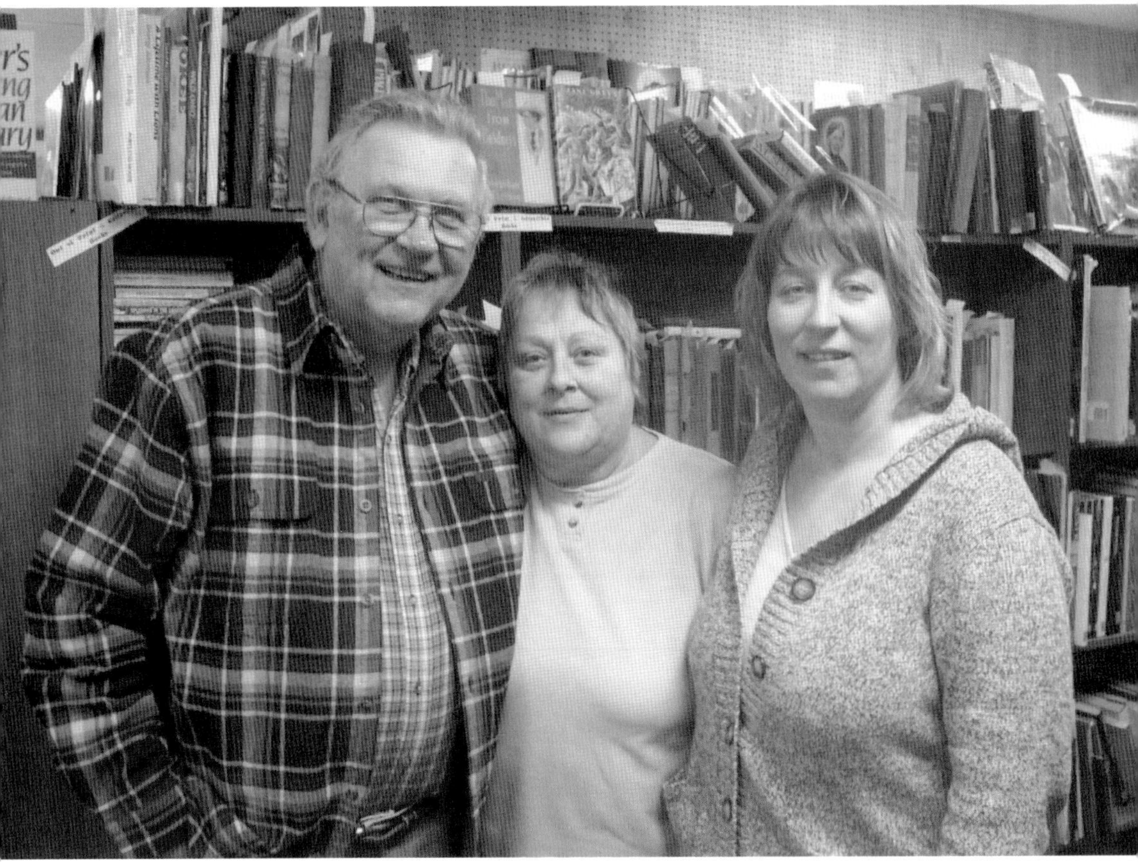

Keeping Readers Happy

Since 1986, Jerry and Judy Heaton (left and center) and daughter Jen Reisdorf have maintained a unique niche as operators of one of the few remaining independent bookstores, the Bookworm. Judy Heaton was substitute teaching when she had the urge to try something else. "I said, 'The only other thing I would want to do is own a bookstore.' " When another discount bookstore opened in the area, she thought she had lost her chance. "I went in, and the owner said, 'Well, it's for sale.' I bought it and the rest is history."

After outgrowing their space and moving twice, the Bookworm owners have settled in the former Aurora Bottling Works building at the corner of Elm Street and Millard Fillmore Place. In an age of online shopping, the owners say they stay competitive by offering books and gifts that people cannot find anywhere else. They also host book signings with local authors and special themed events when new titles are released. Throughout the years, they have also embraced a paperback trading policy, which allows customers to exchange books they have already read for other titles. "We were 'green' before it was popular." (Courtesy of the Bookworm.)

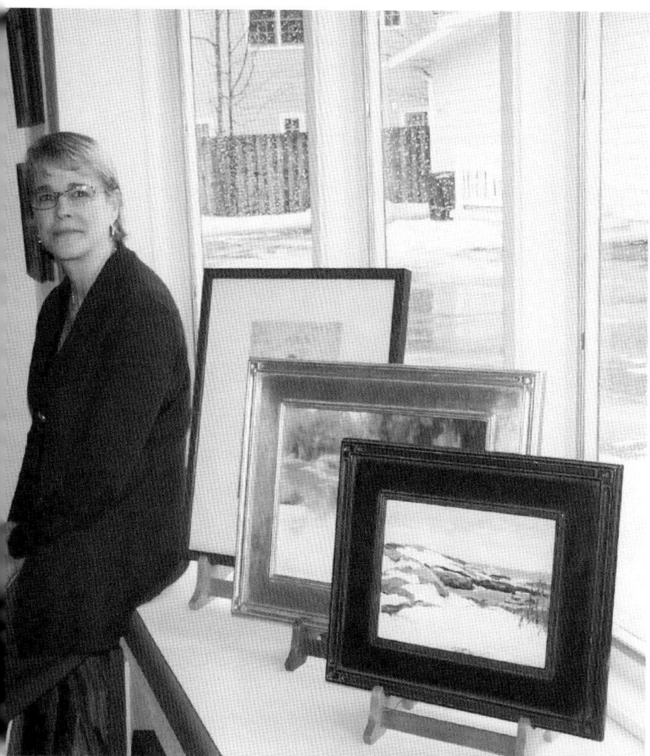

Three Generations of Fine Art
Grace Meibohm is successfully growing the art gallery that her grandfather started more than a century ago. Carl H. Meibohm, a photographer at the Pan-American Exposition, opened The Art Shop on Connecticut Street in Buffalo in 1901. After Carl and Pearl Meibohm died, their son Walter N. Meibohm (below) and his wife, Betty, moved to 478 Main Street in East Aurora, to set up a specialized business in oil paintings and custom framing. "He's the reason I am in East Aurora," notes Grace Meibohm. Through many civic efforts, Grace Meibohm actively promotes local artists and history while continuing the family tradition of custom framing, paintings, and prints. (Left, photograph by the author; below, courtesy of Grace Meibohm.)

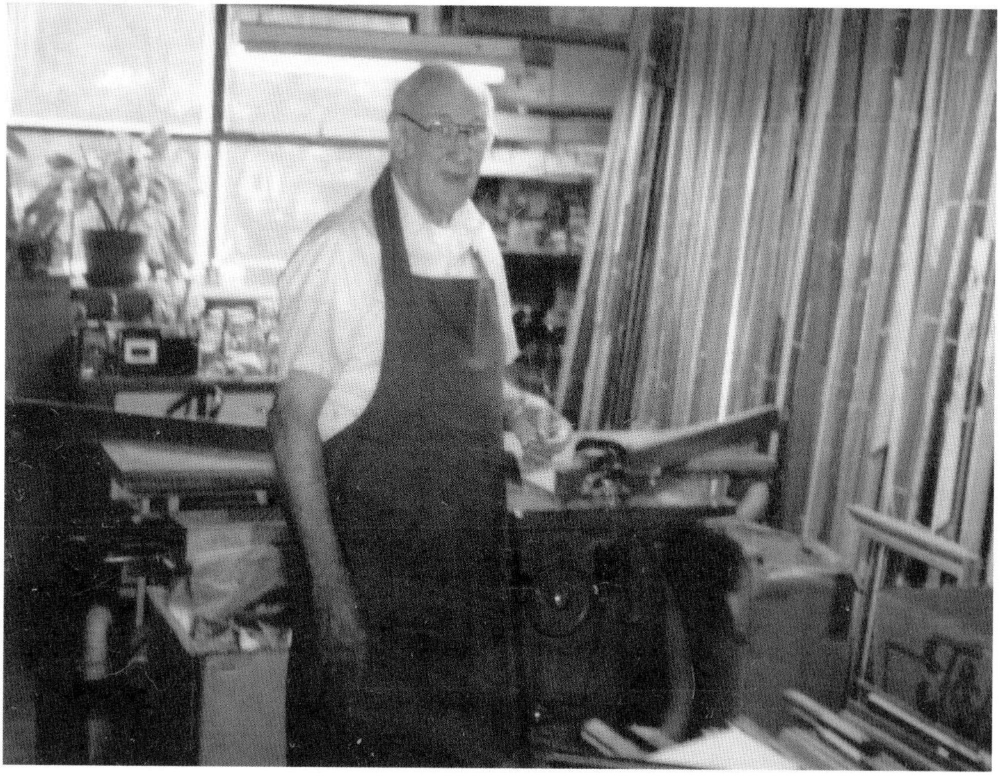

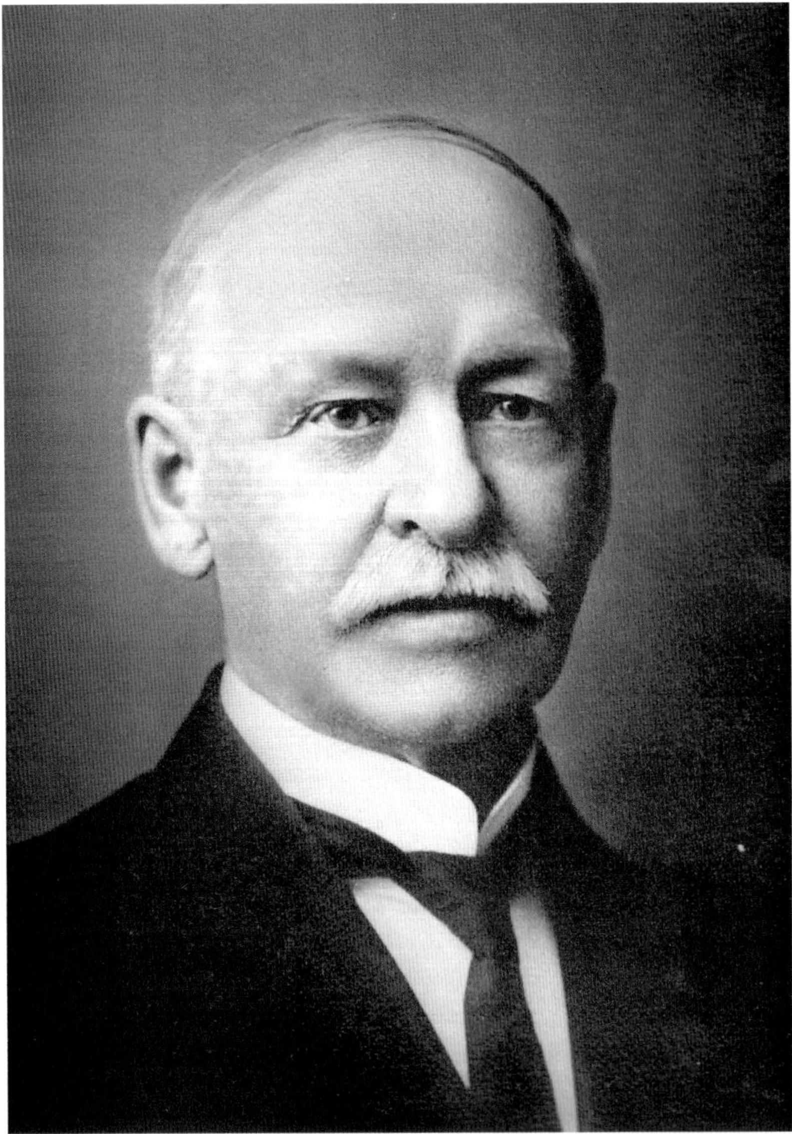

The Big Cheese

Harvey W. Richardson made a fortune on cheese. He and business partner Wellington Beebe took advantage of the many dairy farms in the area. The operation was headquartered on Elm Street, in the building now home to Redfish Art Studios and Gallery. Remnants of Richardson's name can still be seen on the north side of the building. In September 1885, Richardson claimed to have made the largest block of cheese ever produced up to that point. It reportedly weighed in at 3,300 pounds. In addition to his cheese business, Richardson also owned a great deal of land in the village, including lucrative plots on the banks of Cazenovia Creek. He played a major role in bringing electricity to East Aurora, and he was president of the East Aurora Land and Improvement Company, a development firm that controlled much of the land around Hamlin Park in the early 1900s. Richardson's company developed many of the houses on Sycamore Street, Linden Avenue, Walnut Street, and South Grove Street. Richardson used his wealth to further several community causes. In 1911, he made it possible for the First Spiritualist Temple to build its church on Temple Place. He was president of the church at the time.

CHAPTER TWO

Public Servants

Nearly every dictionary defines a public servant simply as "government employee." However, most public servants are more than that. Throughout East Aurora's history, there has been a wide variety of citizens who have served the public in one way or another. For some, including the police chiefs, school principals, and superintendents, public service was a career. For others, including the firefighters, being a public servant meant countless hours of unpaid volunteer service. Political advocates, including members of the local abolitionist movements, served the public good by pushing for social change when it was not always politically popular. Of public service, Pres. Harry S. Truman once said, "If you can't take the heat, get out of the kitchen." He was referring to federal government employees, but even local public officials have felt the heat from time to time.

Due to the nature of their positions, public officials are often the most well-documented people in the history books. However, little is known about East Aurora's earliest elected officials. In fact, due to lost records even the identities of the first village mayor and town supervisor are unknown. That is a shame, because government leaders by nature are often legendary for reasons other than their public service.

Behind their public faces are some of the community's most interesting and least known stories. When Millard Fillmore lived in East Aurora, he was the community's only lawyer. He was also the only US president to build his own house.

The village's longest-serving mayor paid homage to his last name with a collection of clowns. While most conductors on the Underground Railroad kept their activities secret out of fear of being arrested, an abolitionist with ties to East Aurora wrote a detailed diary of his life. As a result, he preserved a unique perspective of the antislavery movement for future generations.

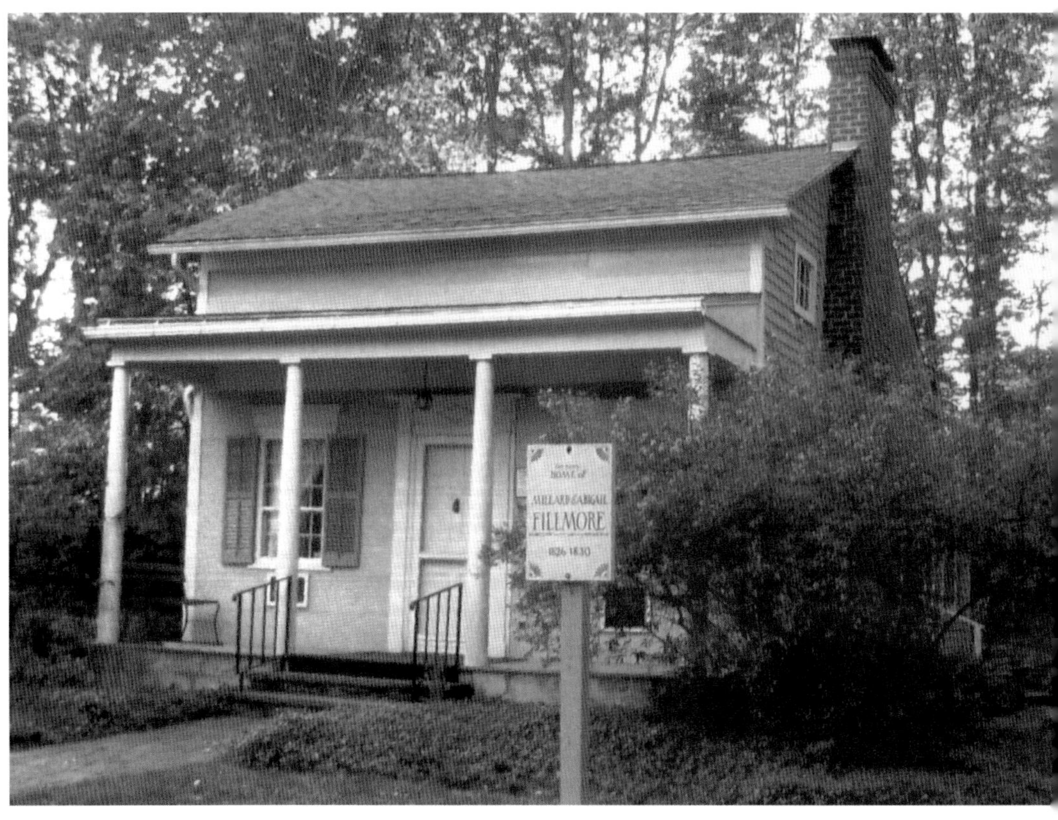

Least-Known President

The most well-known public servant from East Aurora was Millard Fillmore, who launched his political career with a seat in the New York State Assembly while practicing law on Main Street in the 1820s. Fillmore went on to become vice president and, upon the death of Zachary Taylor in the summer of 1850, president of the United States. His home, the only house built with a president's own hands, is a National Historic Landmark museum owned and operated by the Aurora Historical Society. Due to his brief time in office, Fillmore is considered one of the least-known presidents. His signing of the Compromise of 1850, which included the controversial Fugitive Slave Law, postponed the Civil War for a decade, but angered Northern abolitionists. The Whig Party denied him the presidential nomination in 1852. However, he left his mark in Buffalo with several philanthropic endeavors after his presidency.

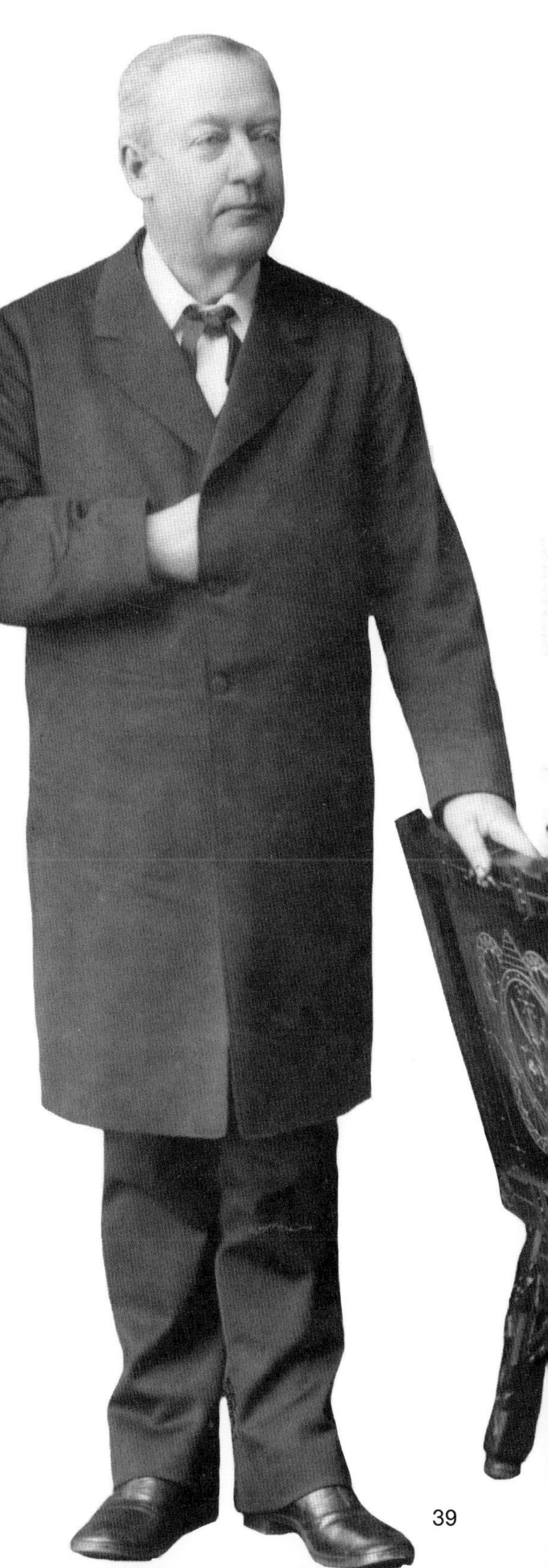

Forgotten Fillmore
Although he was also a lawyer, Millard Powers Fillmore never became as famous as his father. Born in East Aurora April 25, 1828, "Powers" studied law with his father and attended Harvard. He served as his father's private secretary in the White House. After the death of his mother, First Lady Abigail Fillmore, Powers failed to warm up to his father's second wife, the wealthy Caroline Carmichael McIntosh. Following his father's death in 1874, Powers engaged in a bitter battle with his stepmother over the will. He died of apoplexy in Buffalo in November 1889. He never married, and his only sibling, Mary Abigail, died of cholera at the age of 21 in East Aurora. As a result, there are no direct descendants of the 13th US president. (Courtesy of the Millard Fillmore Presidential Site.)

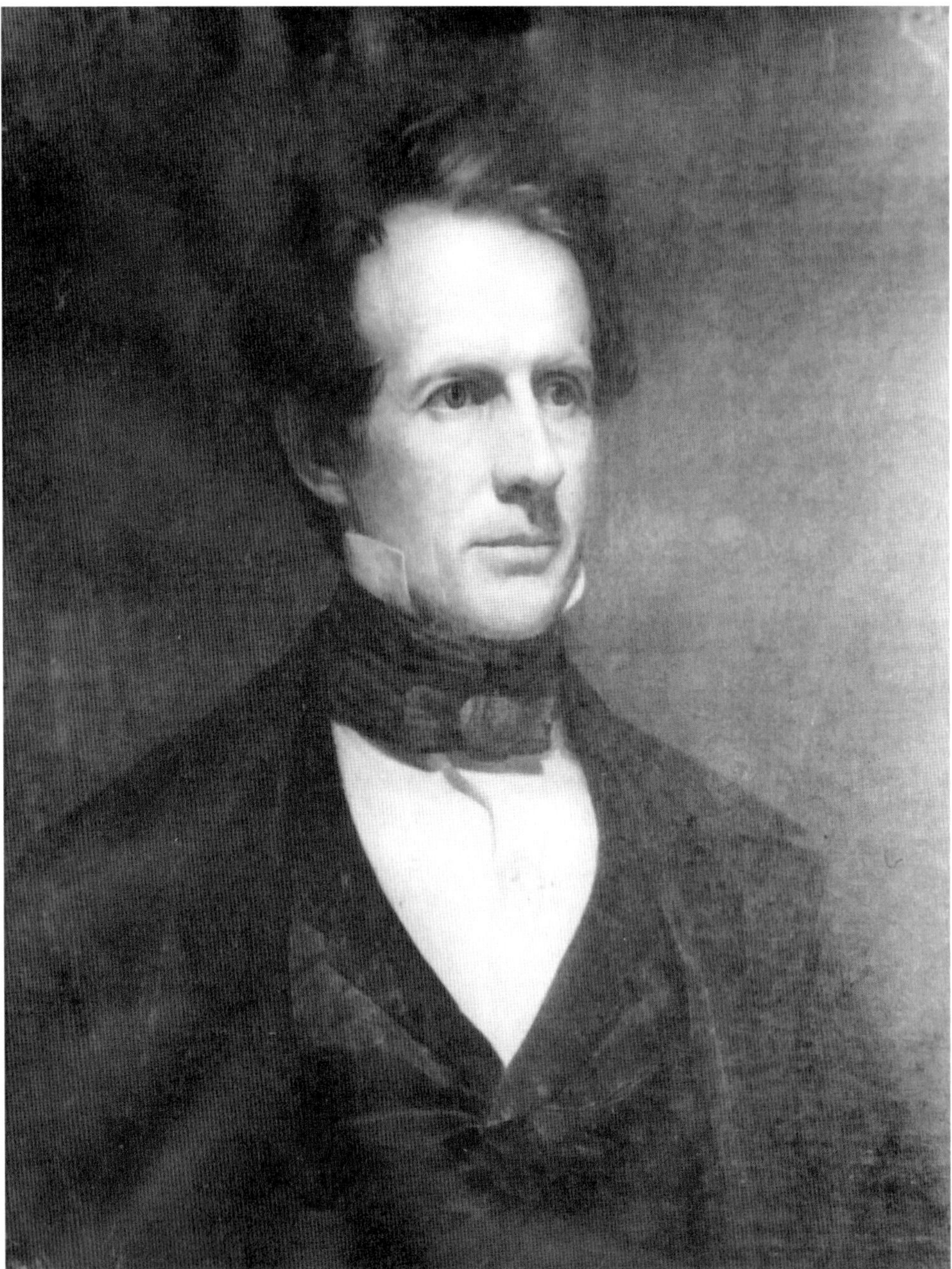

Underground Railroad Leader
George Washington Jonson supervised the schools and taught classes in Aurora between 1828 and 1832. After leaving Aurora, he studied law with Millard Fillmore in Buffalo for many years. While Fillmore took a more moderate stance on the abolition of slavery, Jonson was a staunch advocate of abolishing the institution. He was involved in the early abolition meetings in the area and was an organizer of the Underground Railroad in Western New York. Jonson is best known for keeping a detailed diary of every single day of his life in Buffalo, from the 1830s through the 1870s. The diaries offer a unique glimpse into the day-to-day life of the city and the region's anti-slavery activities.

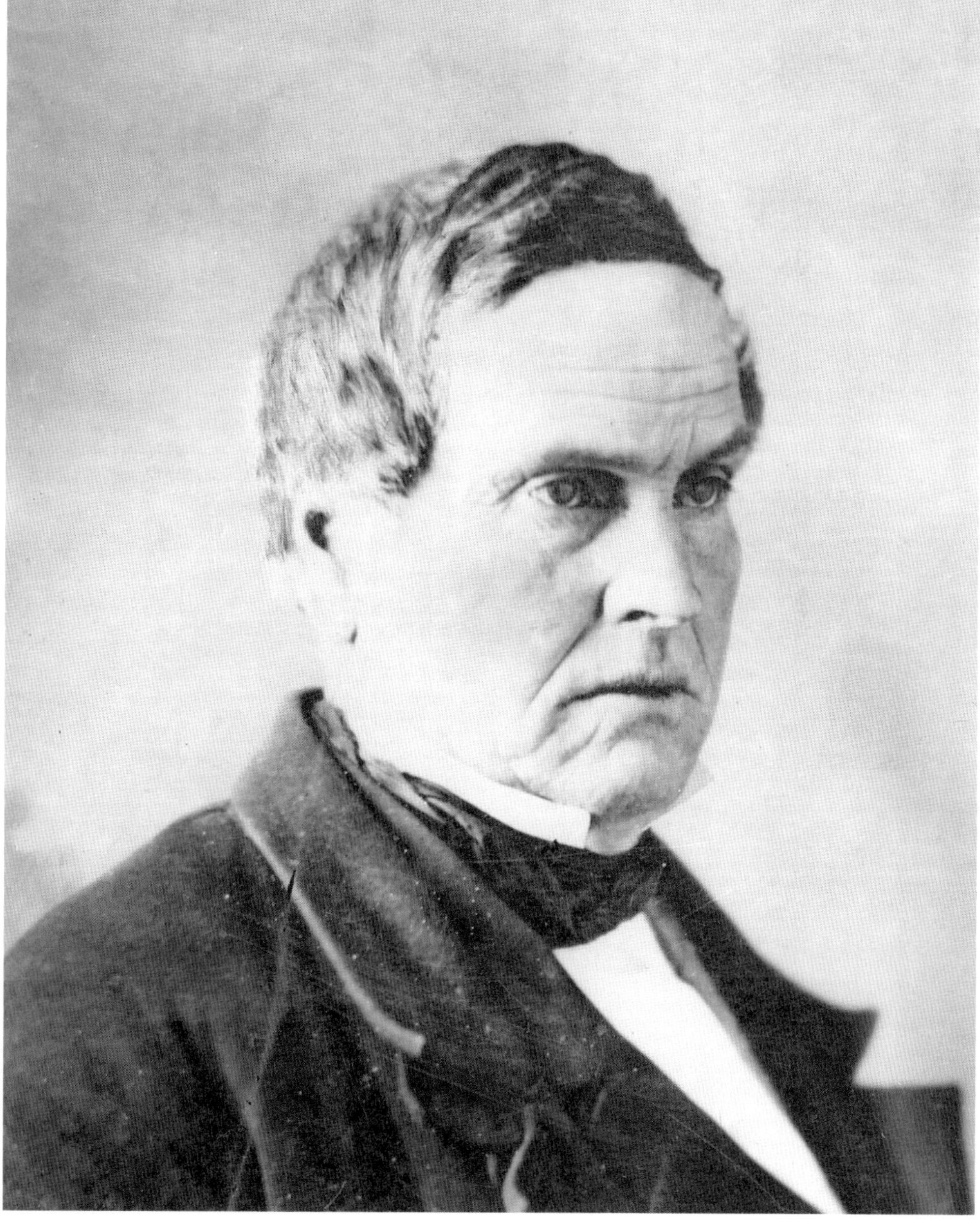

Never on the Fence

Edward Paine served as Aurora town supervisor in 1857 and 1858 and was elected county judge. One of the community's most prominent citizens, Paine was known for his strong views, on both political and social matters. "The judge was not neutral on any subject," one profile of Paine noted. "He was either on one side or the other side of the fence." At one point, he left the Democratic Party and joined Free Soil, a short-lived third party founded in Buffalo that opposed the expansion of slavery into Western territories. Paine died in 1872 at the age of 82.

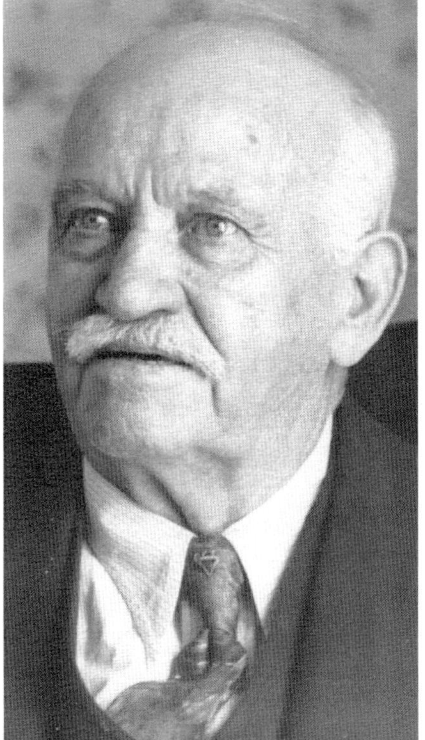

Ready to Serve

William Henry Geib bought a coal and wood business in the late 1890s and set up shop on Elm Street, near Oakwood Avenue. He also established a hardware store and kept a team of horses and mules in barns on the property in order to deliver oil, coal, and wood to surrounding towns on a moment's notice. Geib also lent out his horses to the nearby fire department, Chemical Engine Co. No. 1, to pull the equipment when the fire alarm sounded. He is pictured below holding the reins of horses John and Nell outside the fire hall at the corner of Oakwood Avenue and Elm Street.

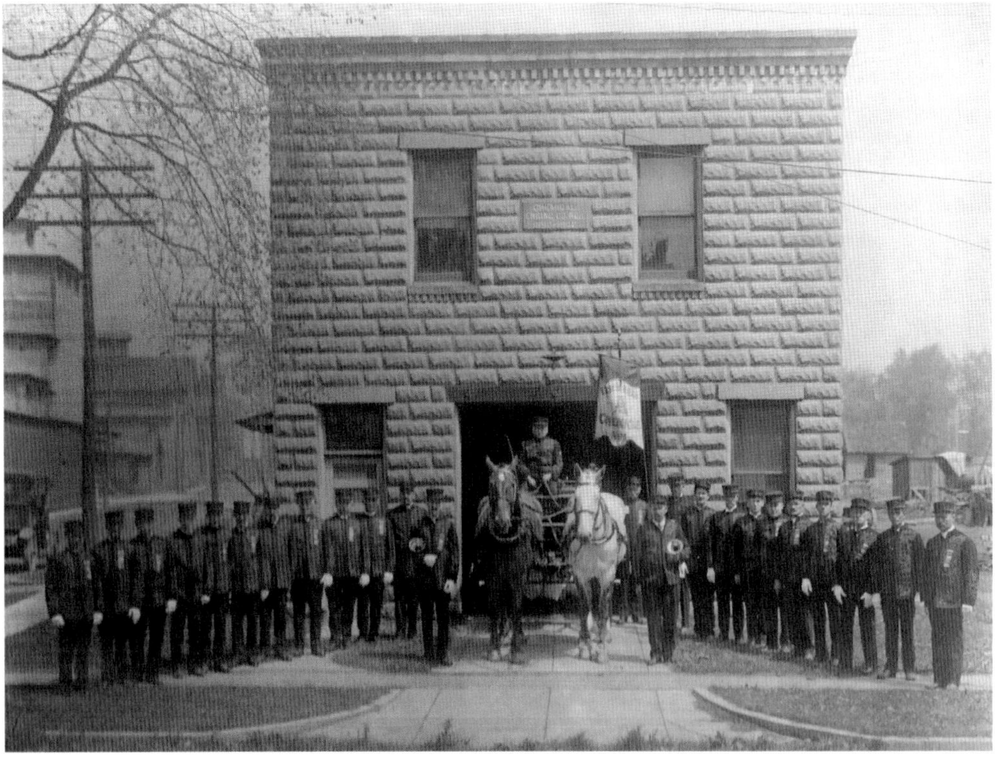

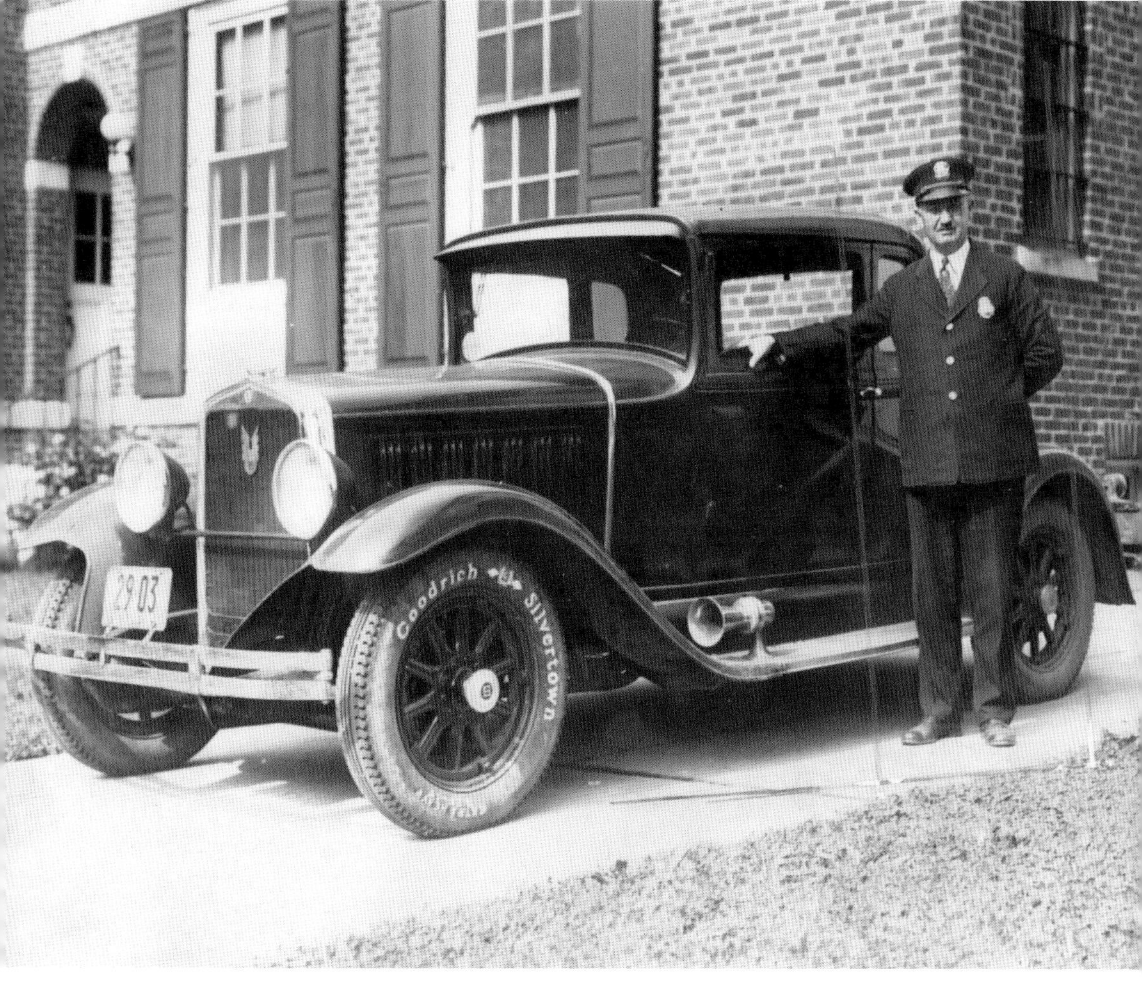

One-Man Police Department

Robert O'Neil became East Aurora's one-man police force when he was appointed the village's officer in 1910. With the appointment of additional officers, he was named police chief in 1917, and held the position for nearly three decades, until his retirement in 1945. "Mr. O'Neil saw the force grow from a one-man department to a swift-acting, radio-controlled mobile force patrolling the entire Town of Aurora," his obituary noted in 1958. Prior to joining the police force, O'Neil was a veterinarian and horse enthusiast. (Courtesy of the *East Aurora Advertiser.*)

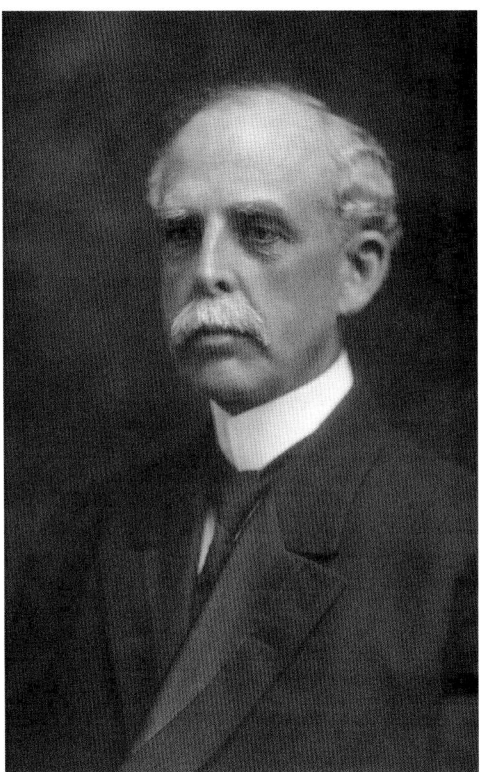

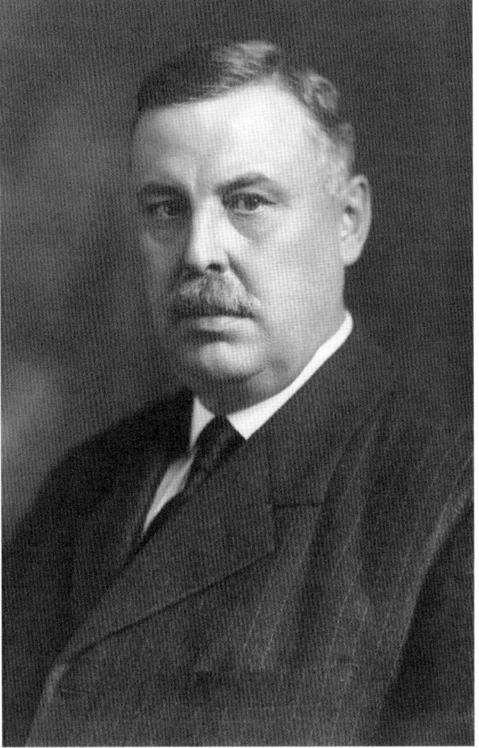

Brothers in Justice
Brothers Edward Kellogg Emery (top) and Asher Bates Emery (bottom) both served as justices of the New York State Supreme Court. In addition, a third brother, Albert, was also an attorney. They followed in the footsteps of their father, Josiah, who was a successful trial lawyer and justice of the peace before it became necessary to be admitted to the bar in order to practice law. As county judge in 1901, the oldest brother, Edward, oversaw the grand jury trial of Leon F. Czolgosz, assassin of Pres. William McKinley. He won election as Supreme Court justice in 1907, a post he held until his death in 1919. Three years later, Asher Emery was named to the same position after the retirement of another judge. He subsequently won election to the post.

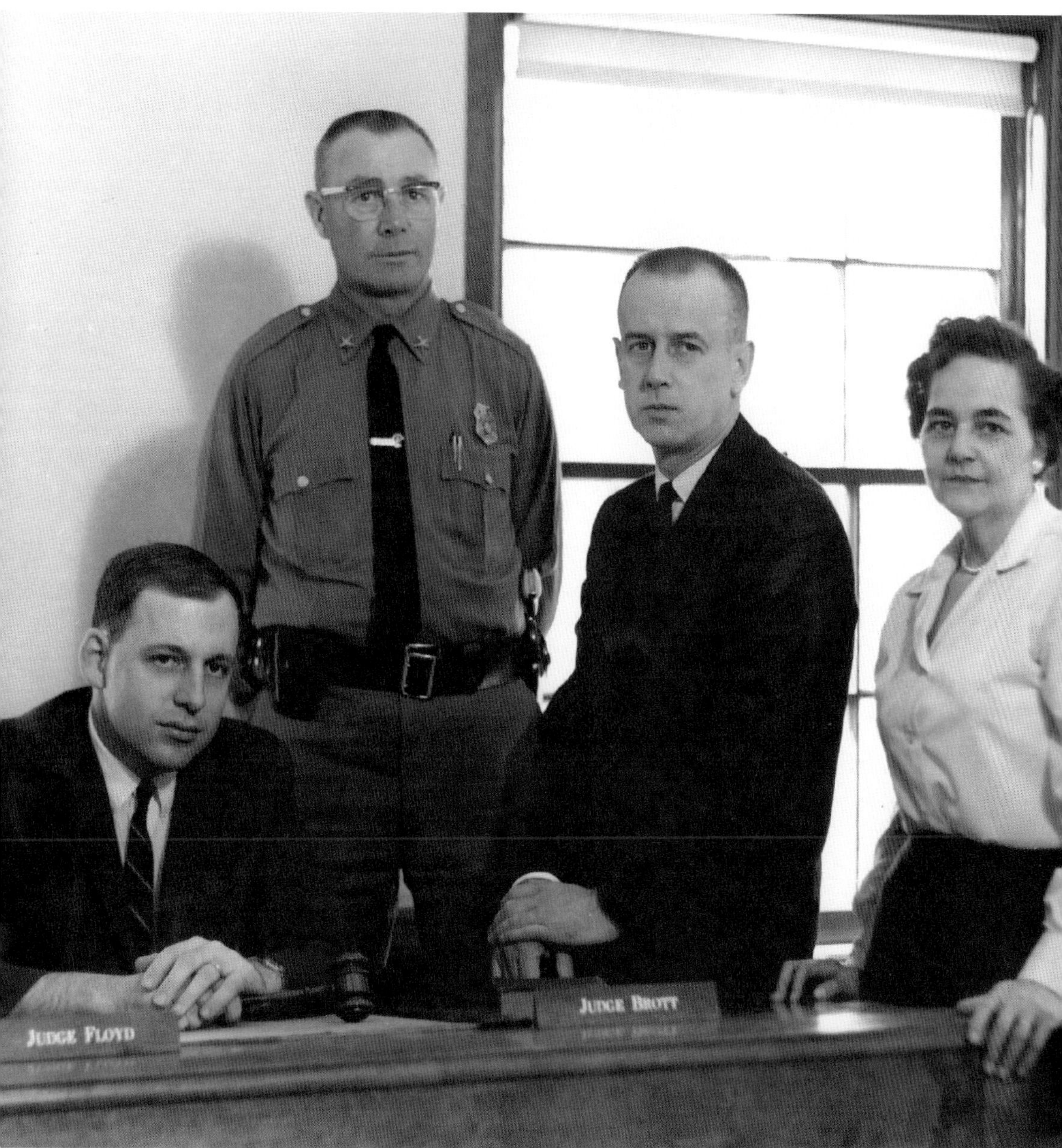

Judges for Three Decades

Justices David Floyd (left) and Irving Brott (second from right) had an unprecedented six decades of combined service on the town bench when they both retired from their posts in the mid-1990s. Brott had presided over cases for 28 years, and Floyd retired after 31 years. They are pictured in 1968 with police chief Kenneth Hartman and court clerk Edyth McCabe.

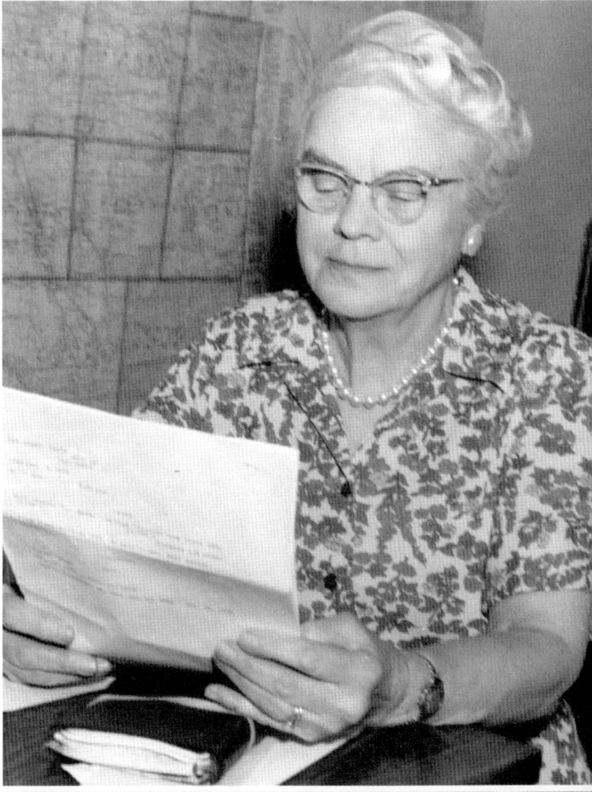

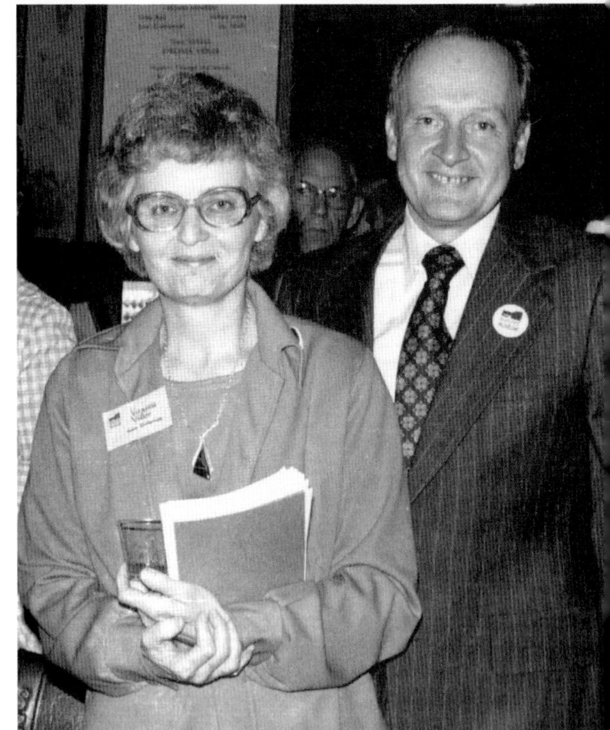

The Town Historians

Of the eight people who have served as Aurora town historian since 1919, two were women. Amy Adams Forden (top) was the great-great-granddaughter of Joel and Lydia Adams, who were among Aurora's first settlers. During her tenure as town historian between September 14, 1959, and March 1, 1974, she championed a number of local causes, most notably the restoration of the Pioneer Cemetery on Oakwood Avenue near Olean Road. Her successor, Virginia Dawson Vidler, pictured with her husband, Edward, was the author of several books on antiques, a noted researcher of Native American history, and helped establish the Aurora History Museum in 1978. She died in office on December 21, 1986.

Mr. East Aurora

Edward Godfrey (left) earned the nickname "Mr. East Aurora." A descendant of the community's earliest settlers, he championed numerous efforts to preserve local history. He quietly purchased several artifacts related to the Roycroft and Pres. Millard Fillmore and donated them to the Aurora Historical Society. He also played a pivotal role in the restoration of President Fillmore's house in the 1970s. He is pictured in the late 1970s serving from Millard Fillmore's punch bowl with Barbara "Bobbie" Kelly and East Aurora mayor Robert Kelly. Godfrey donated the punch bowl to the Aurora Historical Society, and it is on exhibit at the Millard Fillmore Presidential Site.

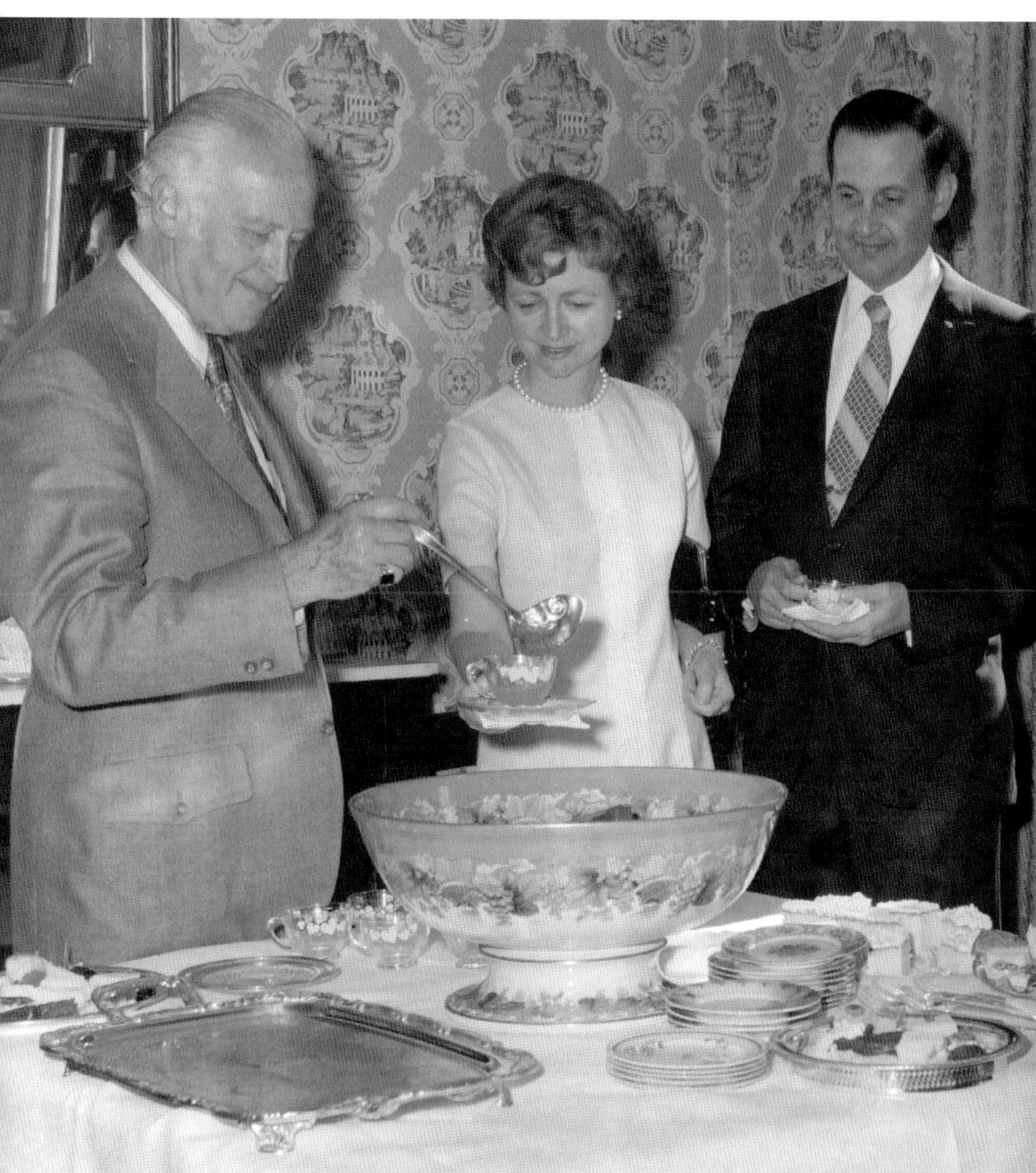

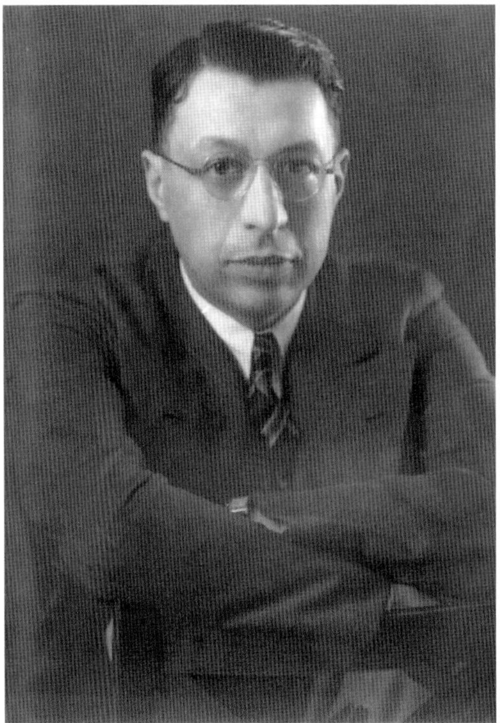

Education Expert

After 20 years as a member of the East Aurora High School faculty, the last 12 as principal, Dr. Joseph E. Barber resigned at the end of the school year in 1946 to become a vocational counselor for the US Veterans Administration, to help local service members after their return from World War II. Considered an expert on education, Barber contributed articles to dozens of magazines. He later went to Washington, DC, where he became a consultant in the US Office of Education.

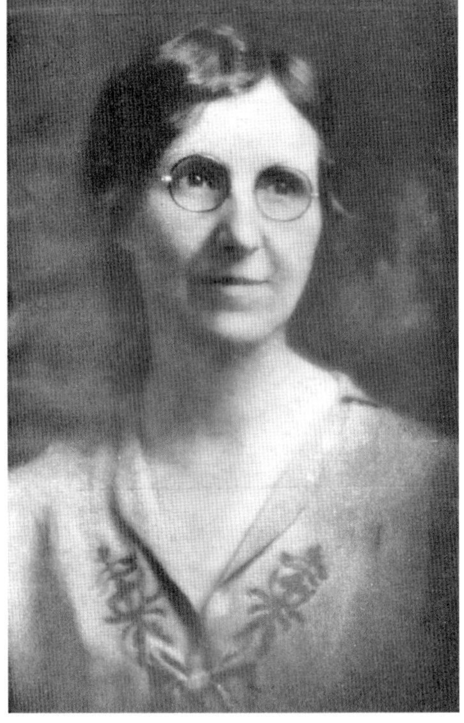

Dean of Girls

Classes were cancelled at East Aurora High School for Mable Reed's funeral in January 1929. Reed taught mathematics from 1905 until shortly before her death and served as the high school's dean of girls, when such a position existed. The classes of 1928 and 1929 erected a plaque at the school in her memory.

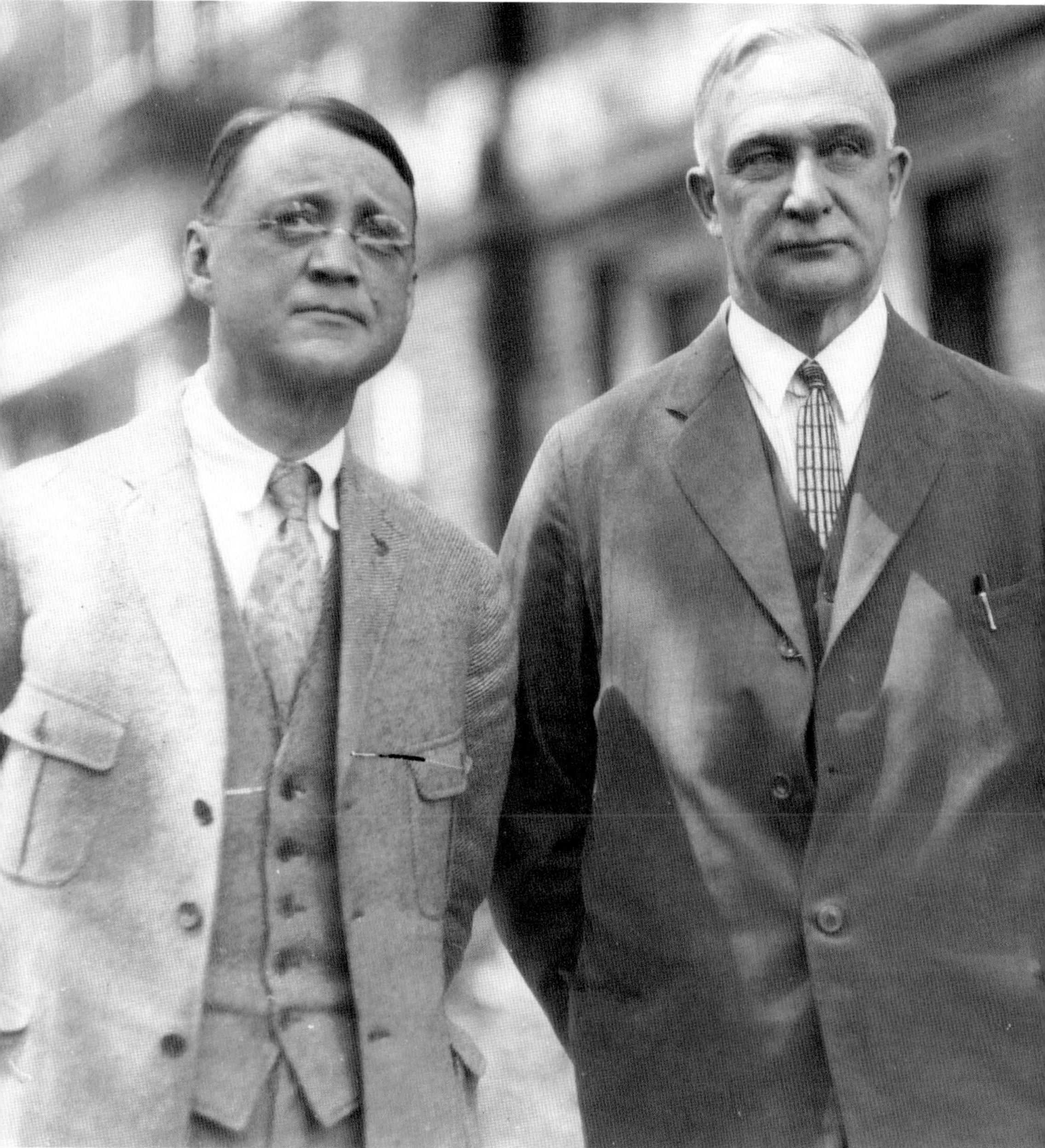

Longtime Leaders
Harry W. Mead (left) and William E. Pierce (right) were both longtime school superintendents. Mead served as principal from 1905 until 1927, when he became superintendent. He served until October 7, 1933, when he died of a heart attack while attending a high school football game. He was known for his clear-cut and direct approach to students and teachers alike. Pierce served as the superintendent for the third supervisory district of Erie County, overseeing schools throughout the area. A former insurance man, he was well known in education circles throughout the state. He was a member of a state committee that developed plans for centralized schools. He was described as a "just and kindly man, always looking for things to commend."

30 Years at the Helm

Walter L. Bumgardner (right), pictured with School Board member Dr. Arthur E. Nield, served as East Aurora School superintendent for nearly 30 years. He had been serving as the high school principal since 1927 when he was appointed superintendent upon the unexpected death of Harry Mead in 1933. A Virginia native, World War I veteran, and 50-year member of the East Aurora Kiwanis Club, Bumgardner once said he valued providing as many opportunities, especially in the area of athletics, for all students. "Every educator dreams of developing each pupil's abilities," he said. "In our school, that dream is realized."

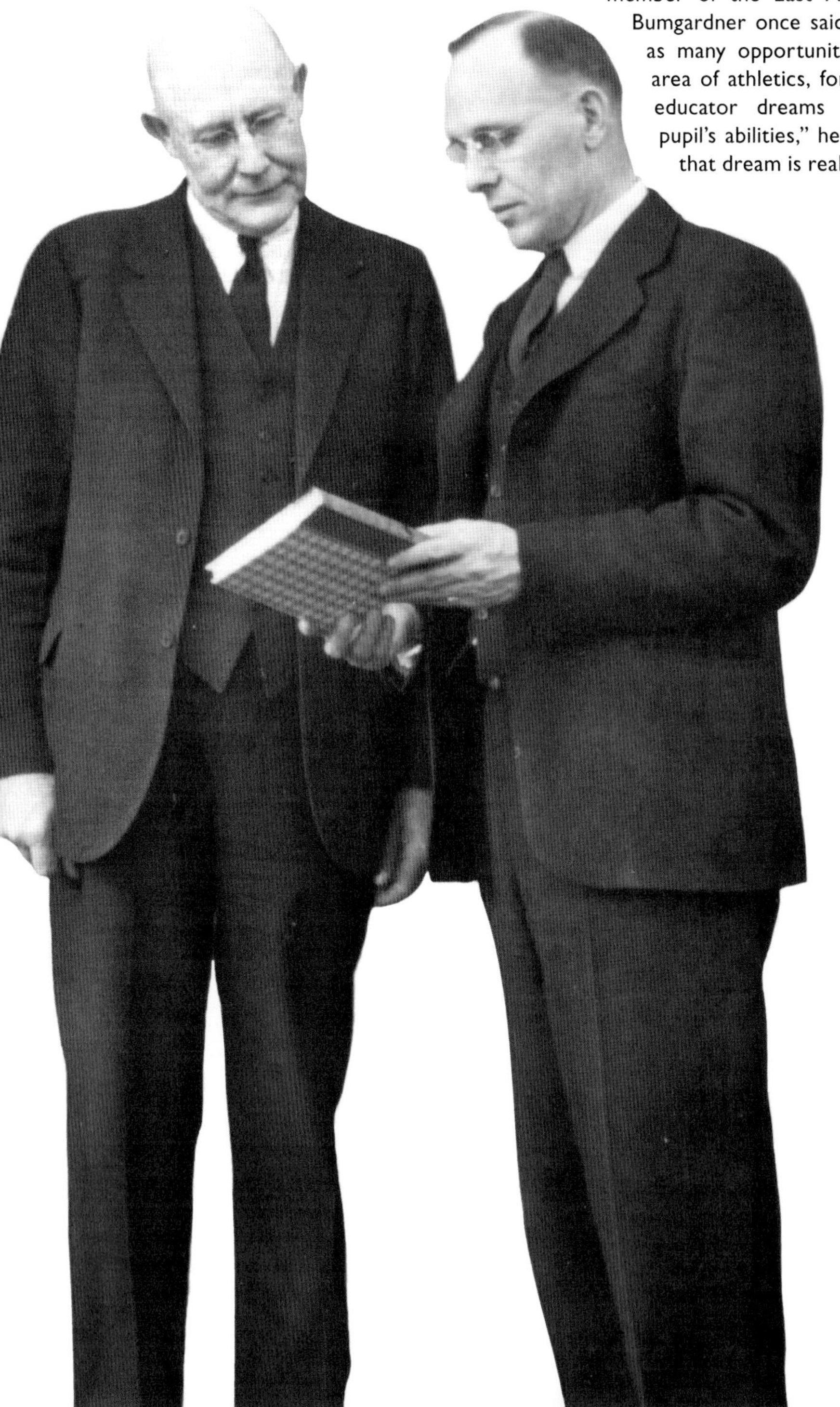

Longest-Serving Supervisor

Abbott Henshaw (right) served as Aurora town supervisor for longer than anyone else in the town's two-century history. He was on the town board for 34 straight years, the last 18 as town supervisor, when he retired in 1983. However, his service record was almost interrupted. He tried to resign as councilman when recalled to military service for 17 months during the Korean War in 1951. His colleagues on the board refused to accept it. "I guess (the town supervisor) just stuffed it in his coat pocket," Henshaw later said, "because when I came back to town, he called me up and said my seat was still waiting for me." Henshaw spent most of his workdays split between town hall and the hardware store his father had purchased in 1922.

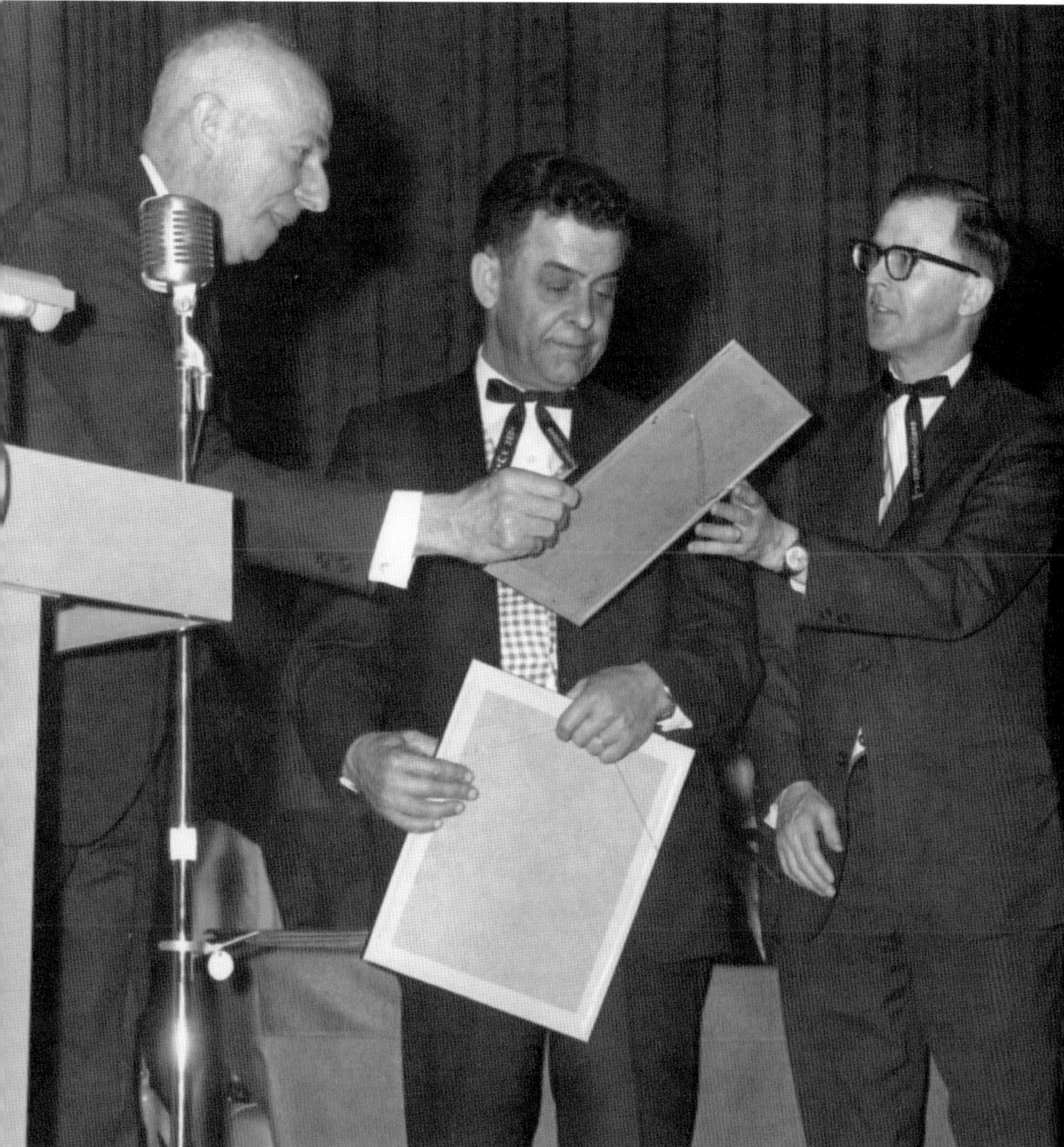

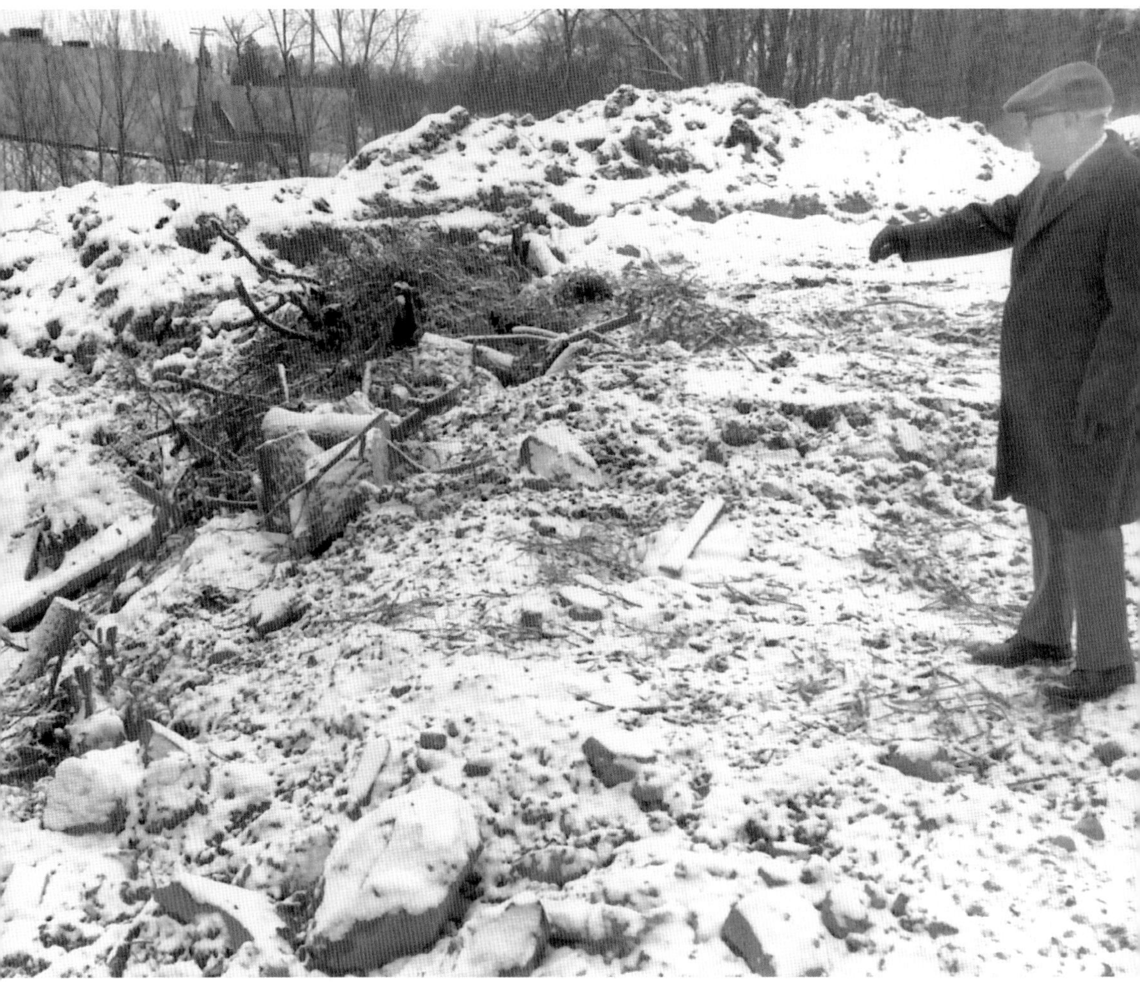

Aurora's Nitpicker

A self-proclaimed nitpicker, Jay P. Nicely made no apologies for ruffling feathers during his service on the East Aurora School Board and Aurora Town Board. Born near Knoxville, Tennessee, in 1910, Nicely was a combat veteran of World War II and traveled extensively around the world as a corporate executive for the National Gypsum Co. It did not take him long to immerse himself in civic organizations after moving to Quaker Road with his wife in 1960. One of his more controversial posts was serving as chairman of the local draft board during the Vietnam War. He joined the school board in 1963, and in an unprecedented move, after he was elected to the town board in 1974, he served on both boards simultaneously for three years. He was known for fighting for causes that were most important to residents of the more rural areas of the town. When he caught wind of a plan to reduce hours at the West Falls library, he snapped, "There would barely be enough time to open a dictionary." Nicely was also known for his warm side. He often arranged for Santa to visit local children at Christmastime, and he grew evergreens on his Quaker Road property, which he donated to local civic groups. After more than 30 years in public service, Nicely was denied the Republican nomination for reelection to the town board in 1993. He said he looked forward to traveling again in retirement. However, he never got the chance. He died just weeks before the end of his term. His town board colleagues renamed the town park in West Falls in his memory.

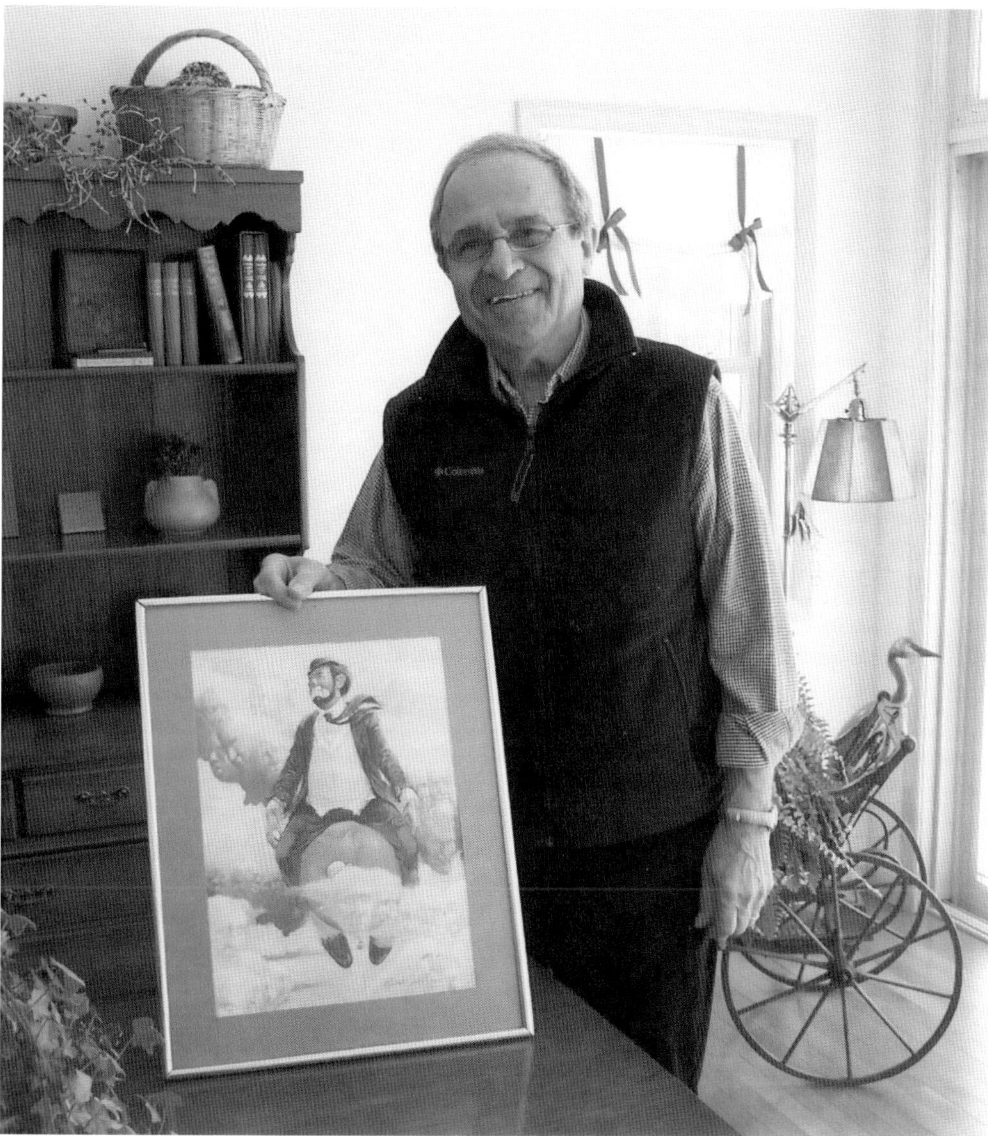

Clowning Around
John V. Pagliaccio served as East Aurora's mayor longer than anyone else, from 1984 to 2002. Pagliaccio decorated his village hall office with photographs, marionettes, and statues of clowns because, he said, "In Italian, Pagliaccio means clown, so I collected clowns." The decor helped lighten the mood when things proved challenging. Pagliaccio, who retired after working more than 44 years at Moog, said the best part of being mayor was "meeting the people," but he was also the village's leader during the debate over whether or not to allow Walmart, one of the most divisive periods in the village's history. "That got national attention," Pagliaccio says. "I was called every name in the book. It was really nasty, but we came through it as a village." (Photograph by the author.)

Making History

After retiring from teaching at the high school, Donald Dayer served as town historian from 1996 through 2006. In the early 1950s, he and his wife, Jayne, a well-known kindergarten teacher who died in 2009, bought the home on Linden Avenue where William C. Moog launched the Moog manufacturing company in the basement just a few years earlier. Today, Moog's sprawling facility is located on Jamison Road. Jayne Dayer's extensive gardens at the home were the talk of the town, and for many years, she led the Abigails, a group of crafters that sponsors the annual Christmas sale at the Millard Fillmore Presidential Site to benefit the Aurora Historical Society.

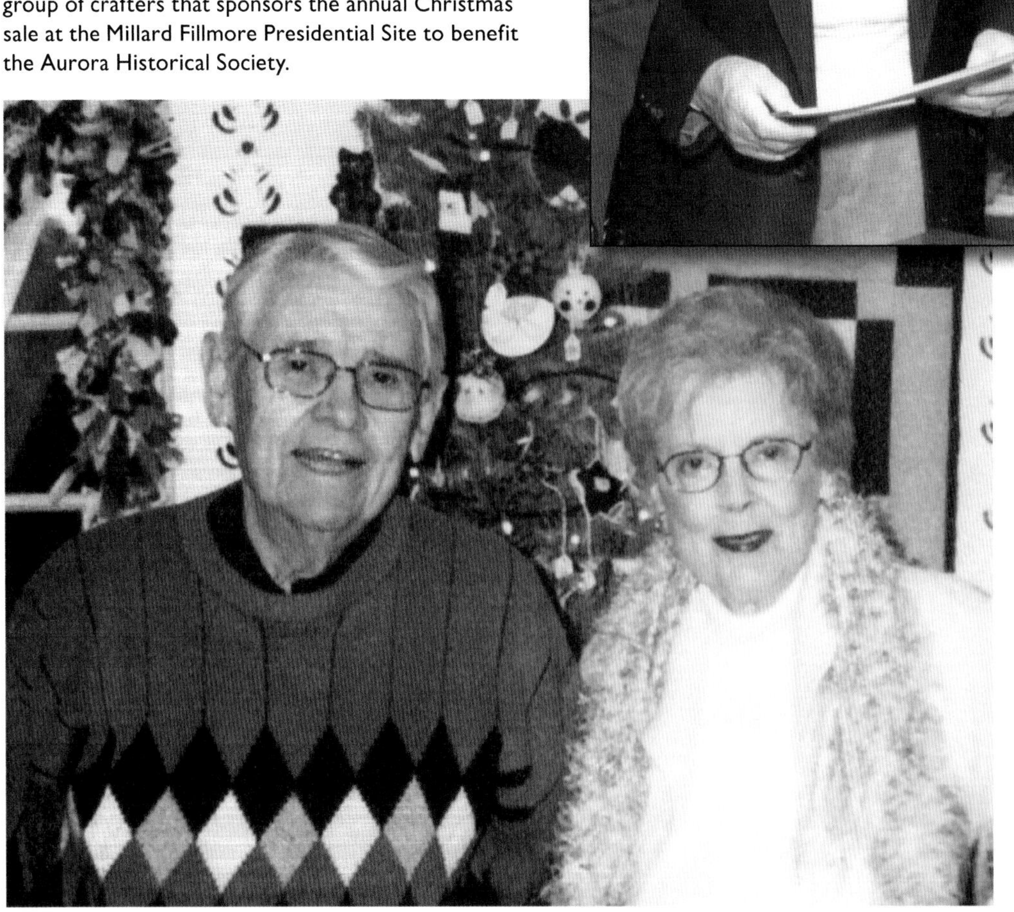

CHAPTER THREE

Good Sports

Sports have always played an important role in the social fabric of East Aurora. The baseball diamond in Hamlin Park has hosted games since the 1800s, making it one of the oldest continually used baseball fields in the region. In fact, the sport was so popular in the village that in order to make room for all the spectators, the Roycrofters constructed a massive wooden grandstand behind home plate in 1902.

Throughout its history, East Aurora has had several star athletes. Most notably, brothers Wally and Bobby Schang, who were born in the nearby town of Wales and played on the Hamlin Park baseball diamond in the early 1900s, both went on to successful careers in the Major Leagues. Both have been widely featured in previous books about East Aurora's history. Names of the fastest runners and highest scorers fill the record books at East Aurora High School. Many East Aurora High School graduates continued their athletic success in college, and several records have remained unbroken for decades.

However, the success of sports in East Aurora cannot only be measured by the number of broken records. Some of the local sports legends never even came close to shattering a record. Many excelled in—and brought attention to—sports that were less popular than the big three, football, basketball, and baseball. Many of the true local sports legends made their biggest mark long after they hung up their own jerseys. Some have passed on their athletic skills to the next generation as coaches. Others have spent countless hours making sure the field has been ready for the next game or raising funds to keep valuable athletic programs alive. Still others have meticulously documented the successes of young athletes in the newspaper or volunteered their time to ensure the success of sporting events, including tennis tournaments and horse races, which became important annual traditions in the community.

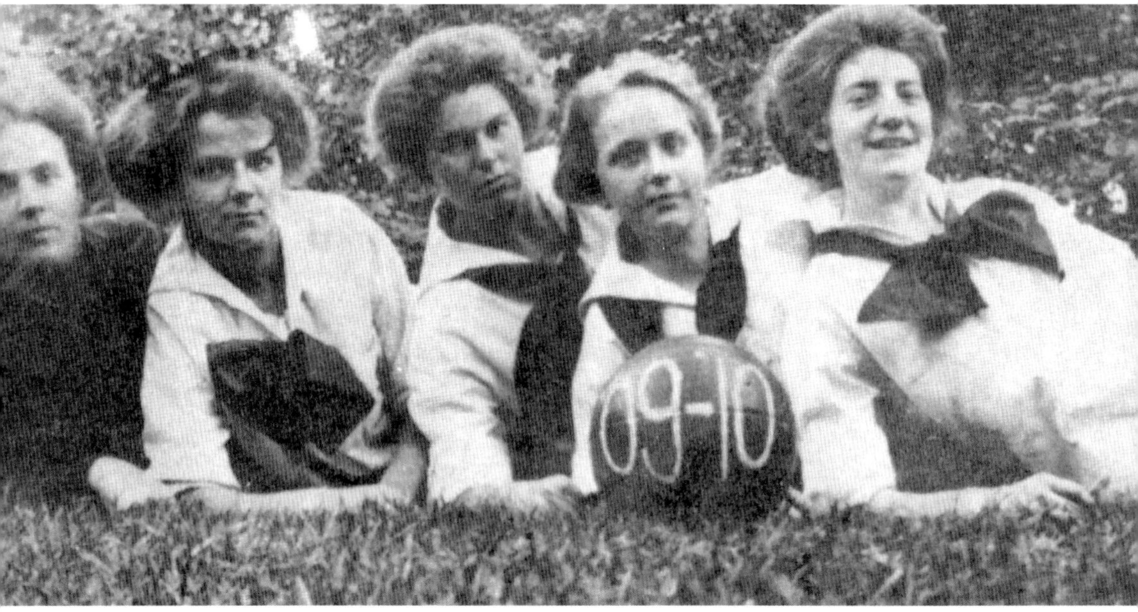

Sports Pioneers
Long before Title IX guaranteed equal athletic opportunities for female athletes, East Aurora had a competitive girls basketball team. The five girls in the photograph above were champion basketball players in 1909–1910. Known as the Roycroft team, they played by the so-called "boys' rules" and practiced with the boys' team. When they competed against Hamburg, one of the only other girls' squads in the area, they often traveled by sleigh. Pictured are, from left to right, Helen Marie Tanner, Irene Eldridge, Polly Stock, Mable Knight, and Ann Green. Pictured below are unidentified members of the 1920–1921 team.

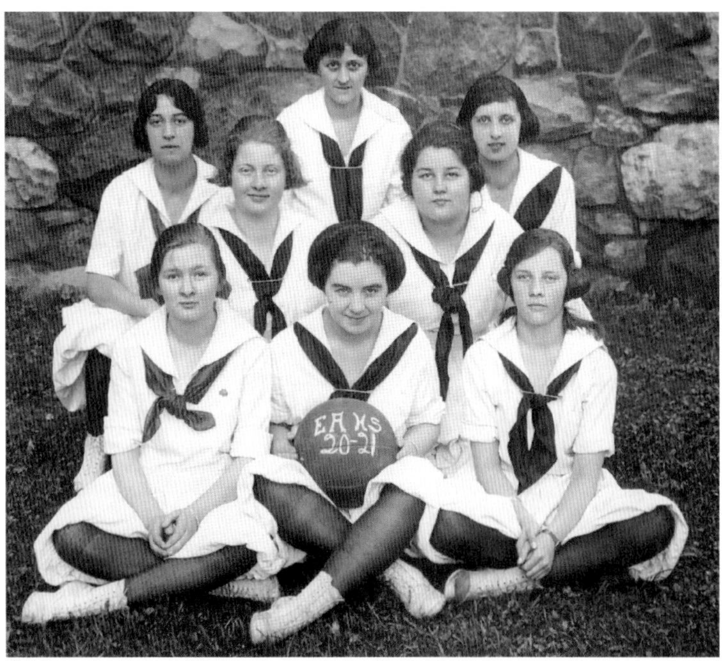

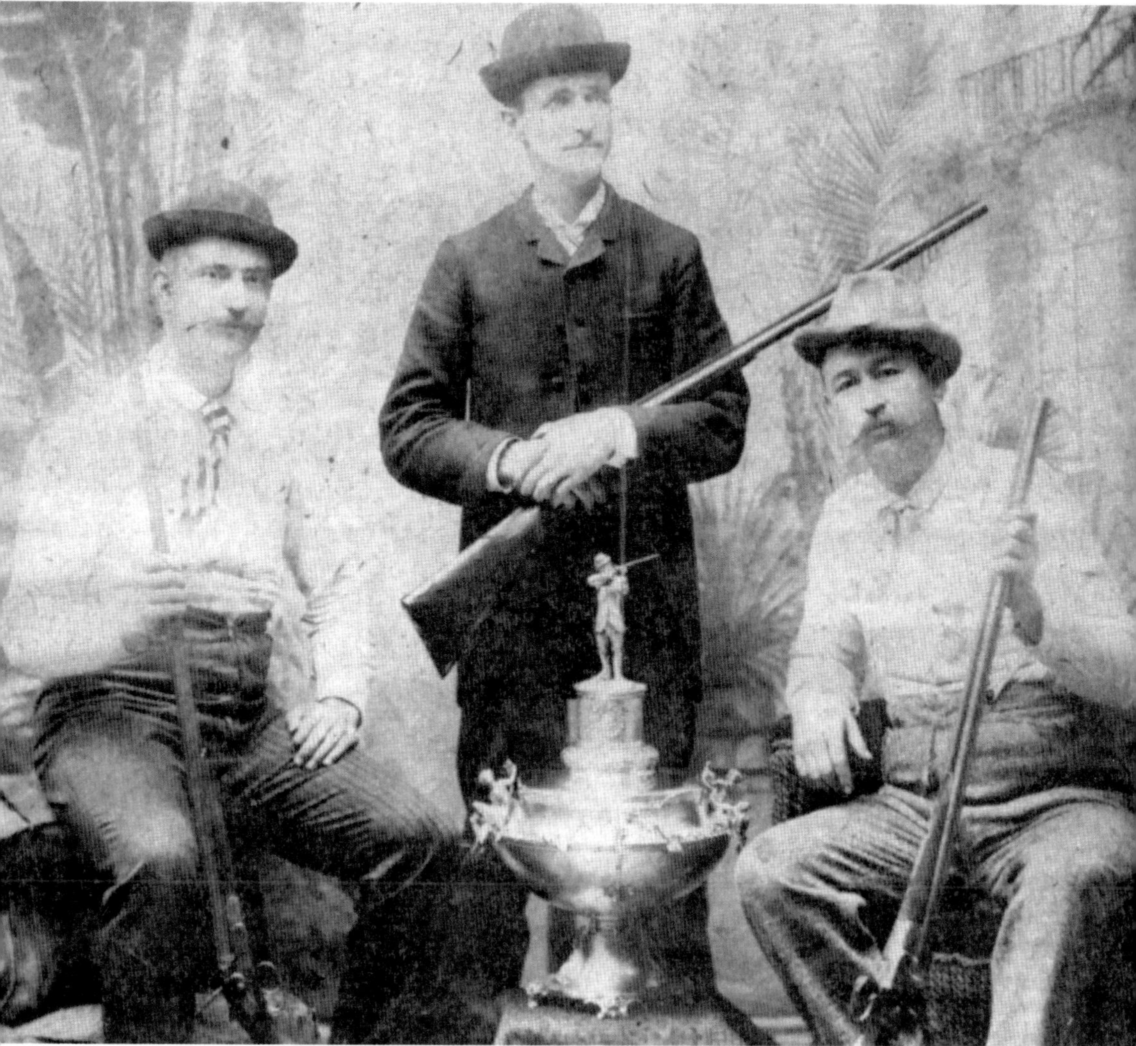

Sharp Shooter

Frank D. Kelsey, shown in the middle with two unidentified men, was the national trapshooting champion for two years in a row. For five years, he held the New York state title. Born February 23, 1855, in nearby Marilla, Kelsey became a jeweler in the village of East Aurora in 1880. At the time of his death in 1933, he was the oldest active merchant in the village. Two days before he died unexpectedly of a heart attack while walking to his store on Main Street, Kelsey took part in a shoot at the Buffalo Trap and Field Club. His son, Walter, took over the jewelry business, which is now Rahn Jewelers.

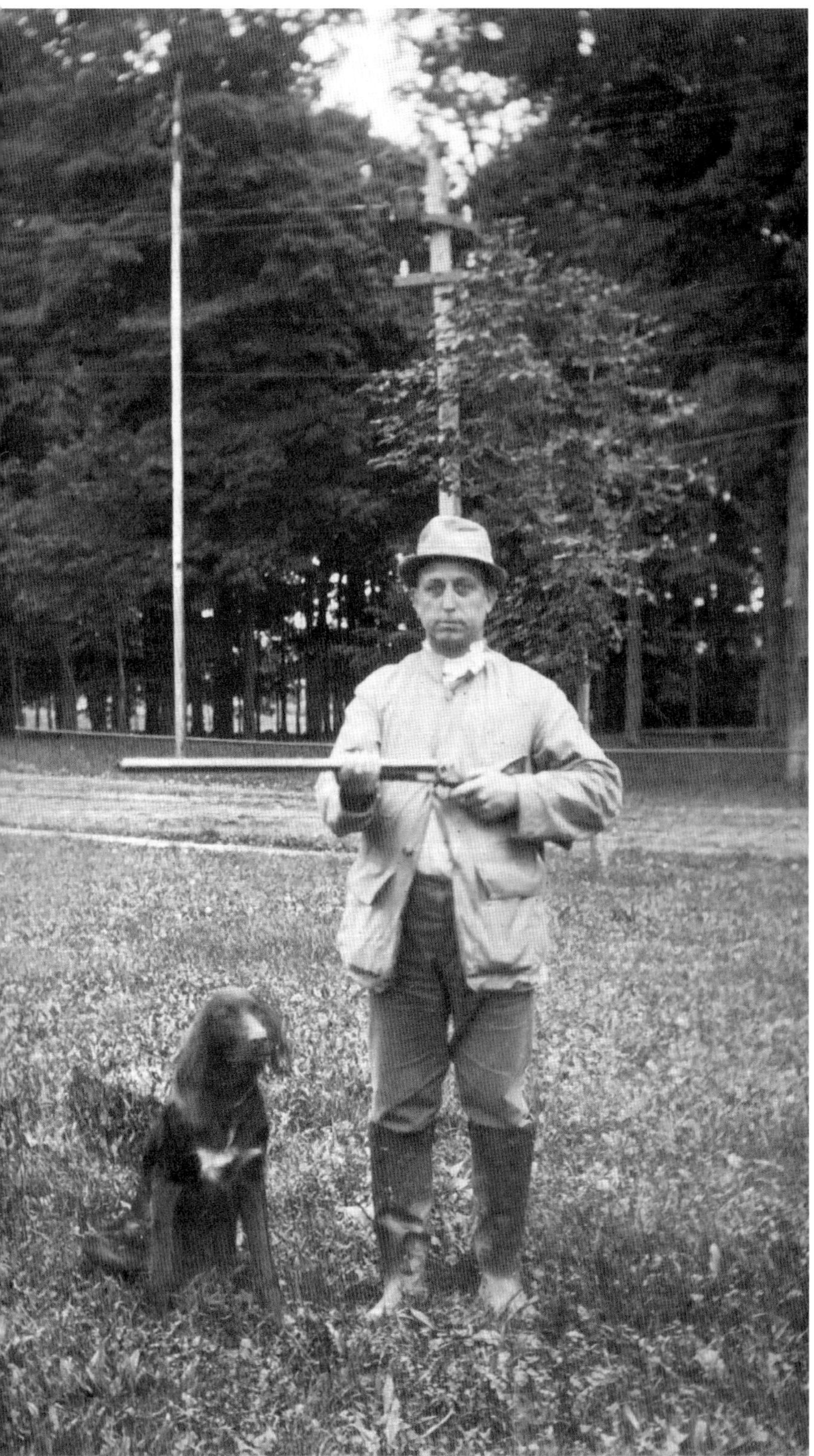

Crack Marksman
W.B. Moore was a Main Street barber for many years, but he was also described as a "crack marksman" during his time in East Aurora in the late 1800s and early 1900s. He is pictured on a Prospect Avenue front lawn across from Hamlin Park.

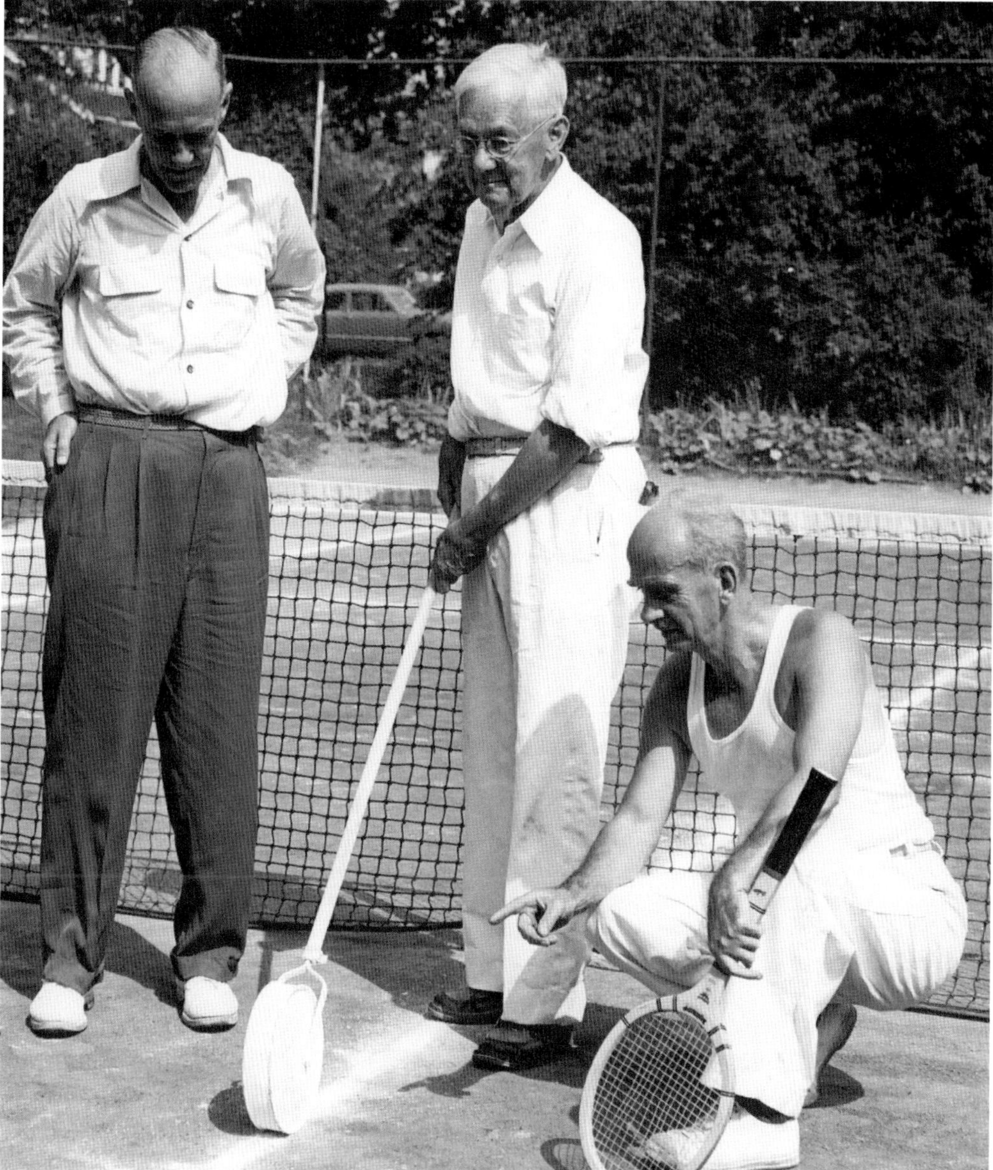

Tennis Tradition

Richard S. Persons Sr., pictured in the center, was best known for his public service. Over the years, he served as town supervisor, town historian, and Erie County comptroller and was president of a local bank. However, in local sports circles, he was legendary for his contributions to tennis. In 1921, Persons and a few of his neighbors gathered for an informal tournament on the clay court he and his three sons had constructed in their yard. "It's been a self-perpetuating thing ever since," Persons said more than 40 years later, when he served as one of the official groundskeepers. "Without any real planning, the tournament has become somewhat of an institution in East Aurora." The annual, informal tennis tradition continues today.

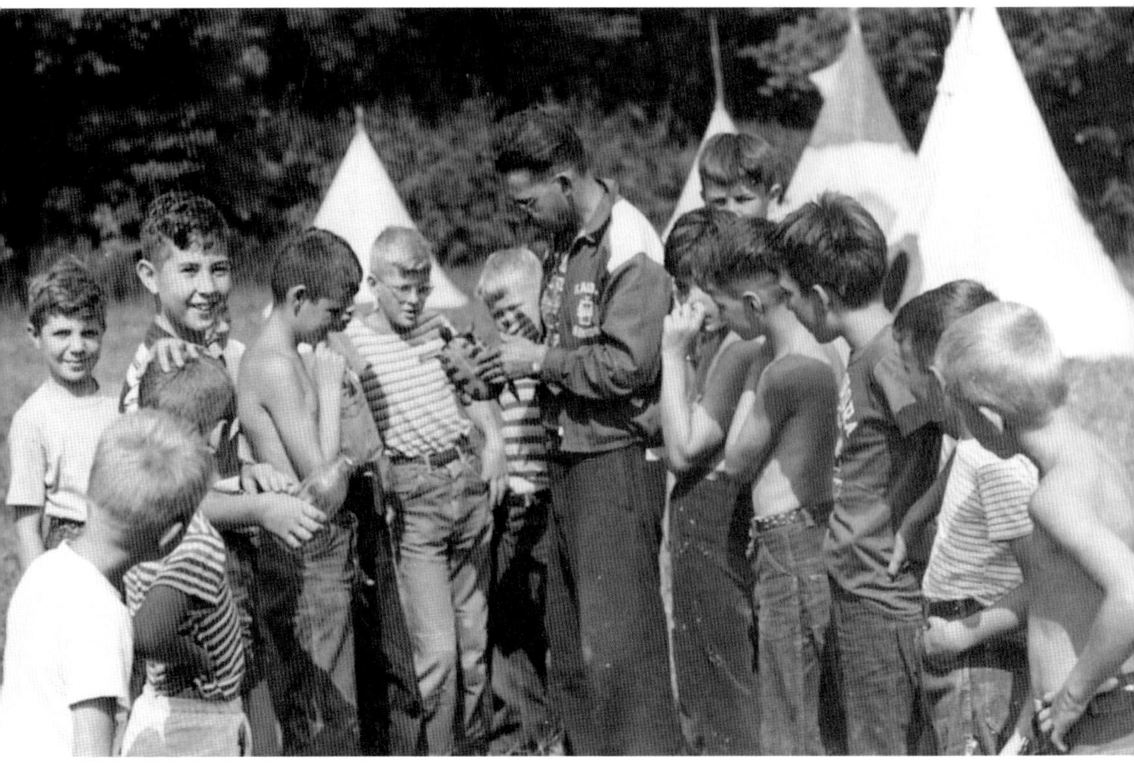

Mr. Boys Club

In his more than 25 years as director of the East Aurora Boys Club (later the Boys and Girls Club), H. Kenneth Whitney, also known as "Whit" or "H.K.," helped shape the lives of countless boys and young men who participated in the club's programs and camps. When speaking of the Boys Club in 1968, Whitney said: "It has been said that all that is needed to stop all crime is to make each individual feel important all the time. This, of course, is impractical and impossible. However, helping the individual develop his personal skills and create in him a knowledge of his own worth is a step toward a socially acceptable identity." An annual basketball tournament at the club was named in Whitney's honor.

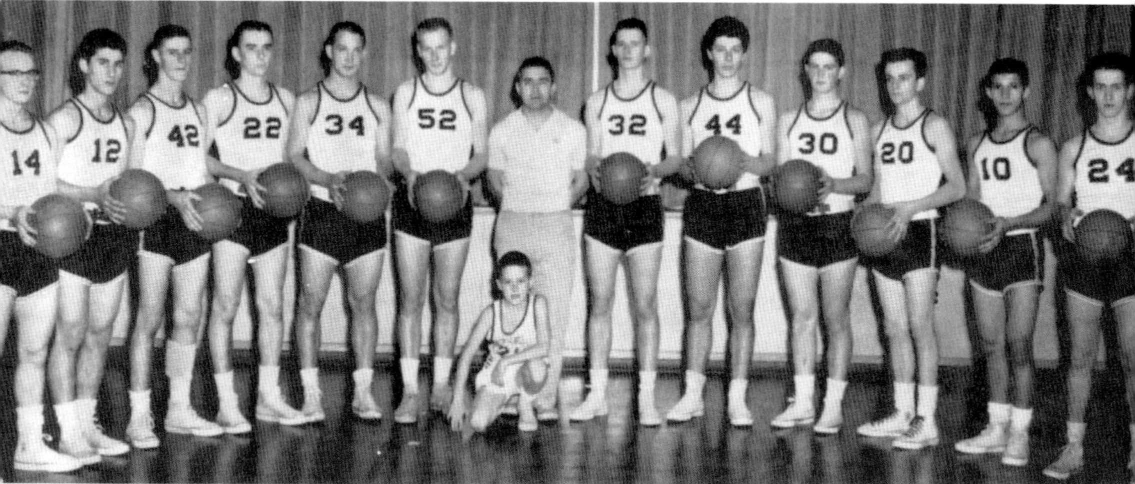

Coach Bowen

Bert Bowen spent more than 45 years in the East Aurora School District as a student, athlete, coach, and teacher. After serving with the 57th Airborne in World War II and graduating from the University of Buffalo in 1951, Bowen spent his life working with the community's youth. He served as the athletic director of the Boys Club, and later as the playground director for the Town of Aurora Recreation Department in the 1950s and 1960s. He was also player-manager of the Aurorans baseball team in the 1950s. According to his obituary in 2001, the highlight of Bowen's career was the East Aurora High School's 1964–1965 basketball season, during which the team, including his son Jeff, captured the divisional and sectional championships. In addition to sports, Bowen enjoyed history. He was a member of the Aurora Historical Society and the American Legion.

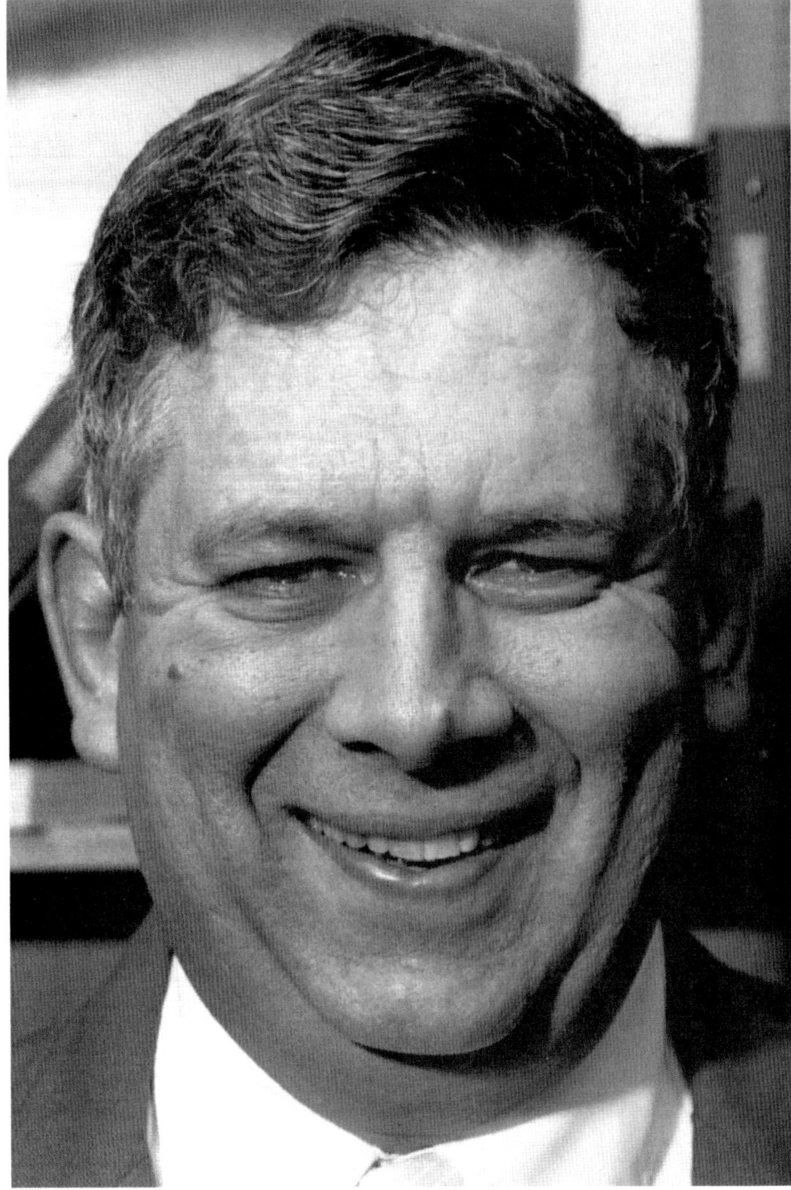

Athletic Advocate

Raymond Kron Jr. was inducted into the East Aurora High School Sports Hall of Fame in 1993 for his years of dedication to local athletics. A 1954 East Aurora High School graduate, Kron played football, basketball, and volleyball. His most lasting achievements, however, came later in life. Kron, who died in 2000, coached the local town baseball team for more than 25 years. He was often seen preparing the baseball diamond in Hamlin Park before each game. He also launched fundraisers for the football, wrestling, and cheerleading squads and served as a scorekeeper and statistician for several teams. After retiring as a state trooper, Kron worked part-time as a carpenter and school bus driver. He ran several times for town justice and for a seat on the school board. He never won, but he remained an outspoken community advocate at municipal board meetings, especially when it came to promoting projects for East Aurora's youth.

Grandpa Fones

Kenneth Fones, a longtime owner of a car dealership in East Aurora, developed an interest in stock cars at a young age, but also trained and rode horses. He has the distinction of participating in all 18 Racing Day competitions. He also had the biggest cheering section in his quest to win the coveted Aurora's Cup each year. "Grandpa's Groupies" gathered at the finish line to cheer him on and provide a little tongue-in-cheek persuasion of the judges. The trotting races, which were first run down Main Street and later down Girard Avenue, were part of Racing Day, which celebrated East Aurora's horse-racing heritage. The horse races were discontinued in 1993 due to safety concerns. (Photograph by the author.)

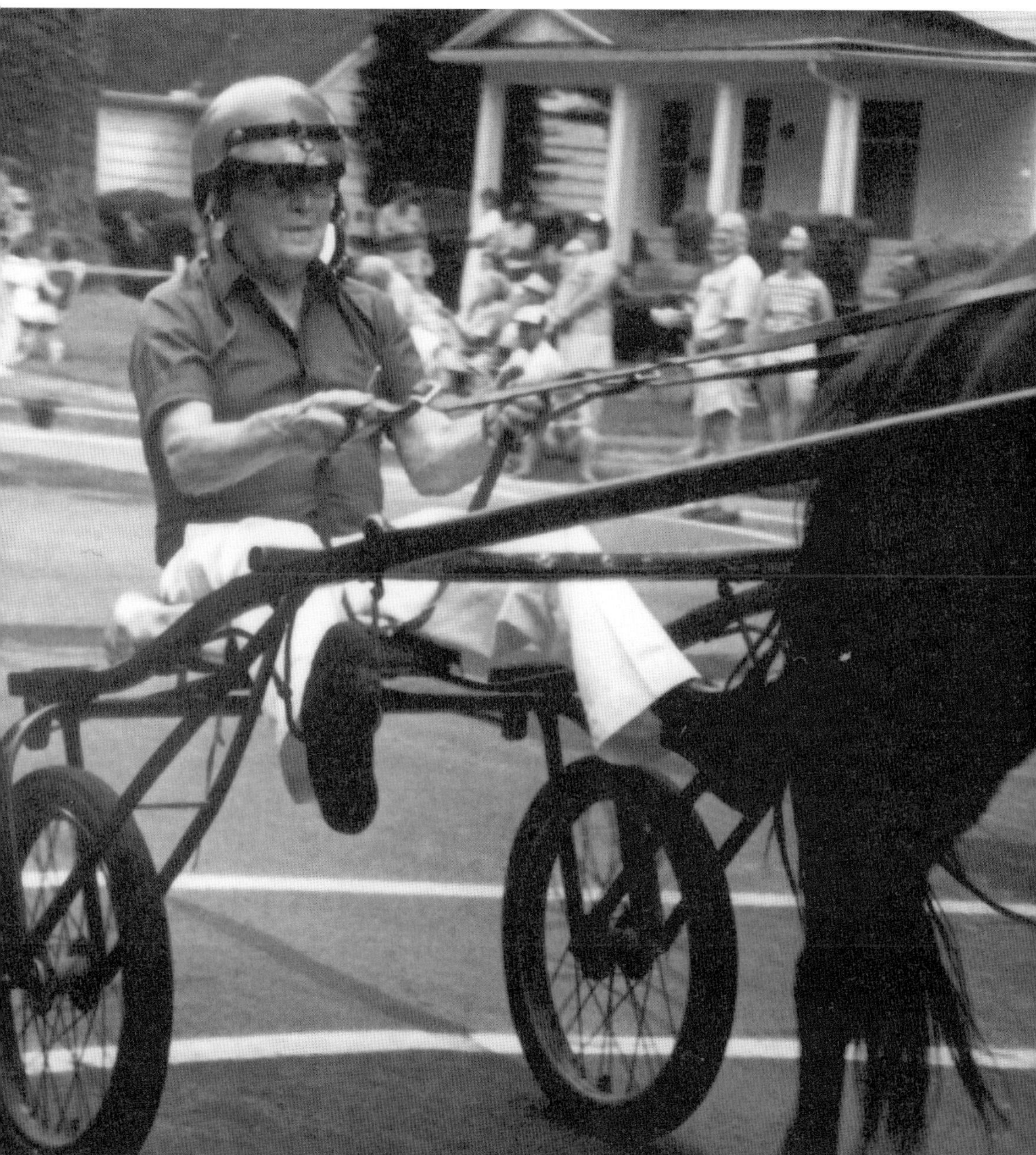

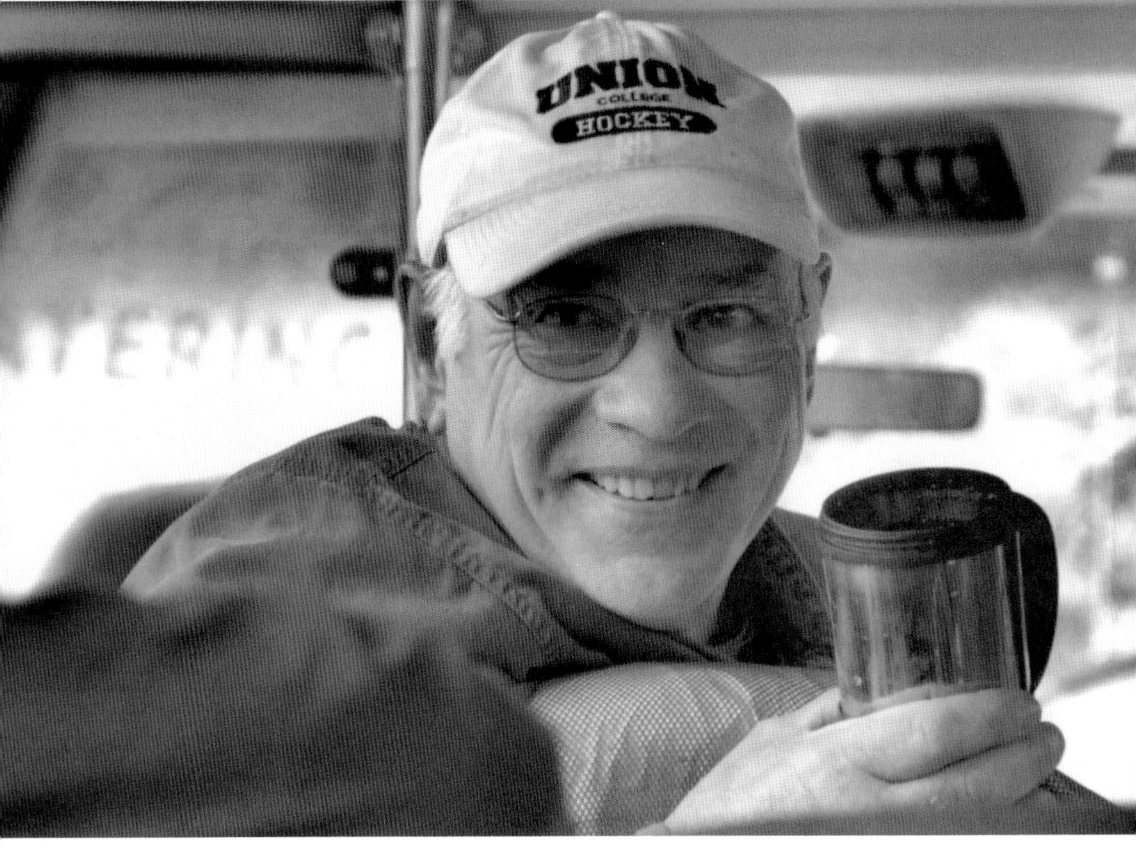

Small-Town Storyteller

Through his award-winning newspaper column, "View from Right Field," Rick Ohler highlights not only the unique sports accomplishments of area athletes, but also the intricacies of small-town life. His stories have already filled two books, *Have You Lived Here All Your Life? ". . . Not Yet"* and *Are You Still Here? Only 'Til I Run Out of Stories*. In awarding him first place in the 2013 New York Press Association contest, the judges correctly observed of his newspaper column: "One gets the sense that he's out on the streets, getting to know the community intimately." In all, Ohler has reported on 13 different sports in recent decades. "I like to say that I'd rather watch a high school game live than watch a pro game on TV," he says. Some of Ohler's more notable efforts have included researching obscure tidbits of local sports history. For example, he has attempted to identify and measure the farthest home run ever hit from the plate at the Hamlin Park baseball diamond. It is not an exact science, but the easygoing Ohler gives the nod to Lenny Mazurkiewicz, who is said to have hit a home run beyond the tennis courts in the 1970s. "I measured it with my GPS device and got 487 feet," Ohler says. "Not deadly accurate, but good enough for local lore." (Photograph by David M. Green.)

CHAPTER FOUR

The Roycrofters

Elbert Hubbard attracted hundreds of creative types to his Arts and Crafts community on South Grove Street at the turn of the 20th century. Some, like famed artist Alexis Fournier, were invited. Others simply showed up, in the hopes of landing a job at the Roycroft, a place where putting "head, heart and hand" into one's work in equal measure was encouraged in a world otherwise dominated by the assembly-line mentality of the Industrial Revolution.

"His shop became a place of pilgrimage to men and women who were interested in the handicrafts, and who dreamed of a greater idealization of common life," wrote one of Roycroft's most famous visitors, Henry Ford.

Hubbard struck a chord with many of these dreamers, who took the train to East Aurora after reading the Roycroft founder's thoughts on religion, work, and politics in one of his widely circulated magazines. "All kinds came to the Shops," one Roycrofter, Felix Shay, later wrote in his book, *Elbert Hubbard of East Aurora*.

When Elbert Hubbard went down with the sinking of the *Lusitania* in May 1915, his son Elbert II took over operations, bringing a new generation of Roycrofters to the campus. Like a college campus, the Roycroft was in many ways its own community. It had its own bank, fire department, Sunday school, baseball team, and band.

Though the Roycroft went bankrupt in 1938 as a result of the Great Depression, the creative energy is still alive in East Aurora. There has been a major effort to revitalize not only the buildings on the campus, but also the Roycroft spirit. Artisans still work in the tradition of "head, heart and hand;" the simple Roycroft style is still evident in local architecture; Hubbard's descendants are still active in the community; and the major philosophical questions of the day are debated in the same rooms in which similar discussions took place more than a century ago.

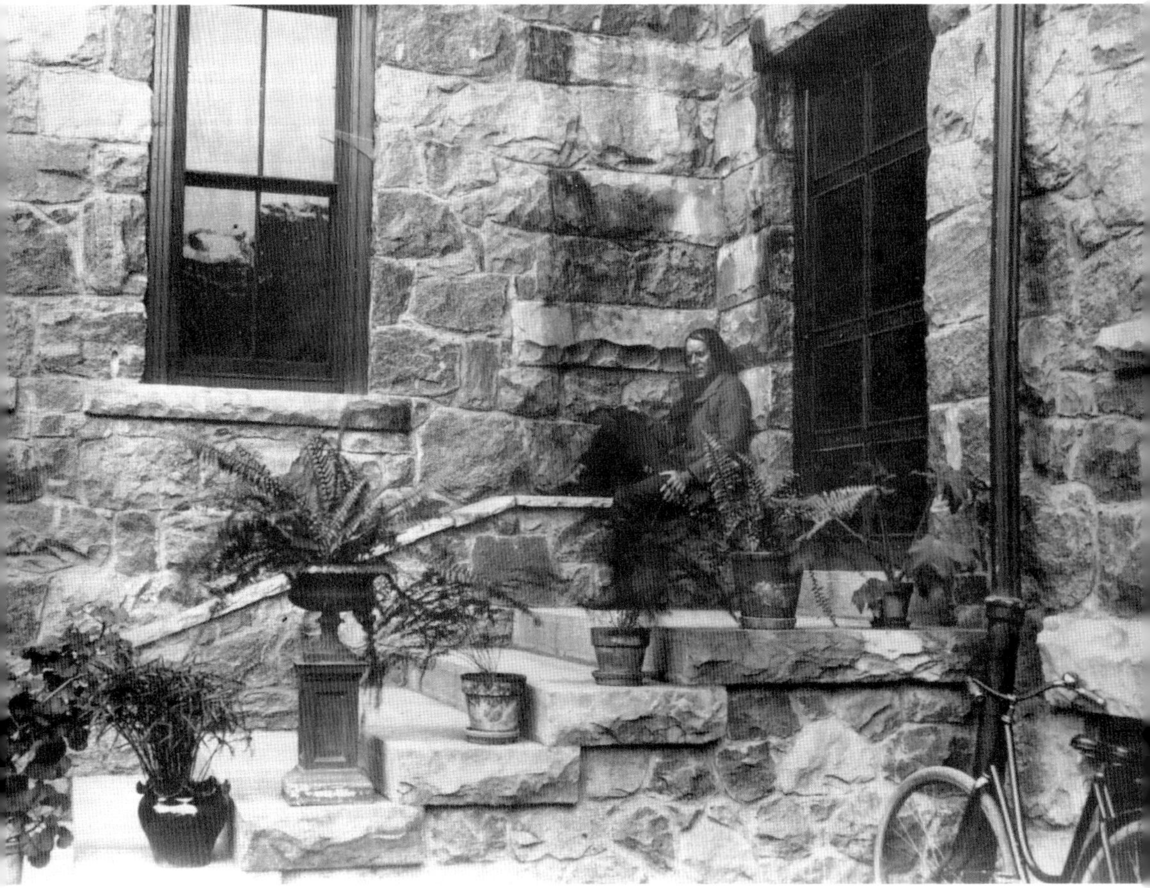

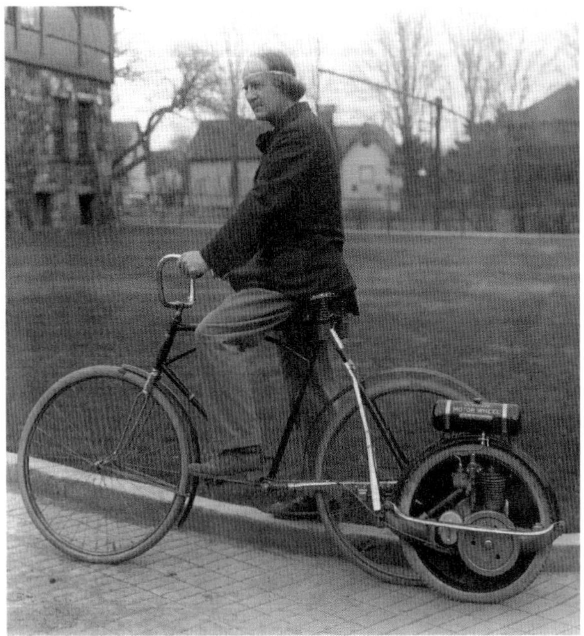

The Sage of East Aurora

Elbert Green Hubbard was probably the most eccentric person in the history of East Aurora. After a successful sales career with the Larkin Soap Co., he launched the Roycroft in 1895. It started out with magazines, in which Hubbard garnered a wide audience for his views on everything from politics to work ethic. Soon, his Arts and Crafts colony of medieval-looking buildings evolved on South Grove Street, where craftsmen were invited to ignore the Industrial Revolution and create furniture, books, copper, and leather. Hubbard, who reveled in the title "Sage of East Aurora," was often seen around the Roycroft campus with a signature shoestring holding back his long hair, which can be seen at left as Hubbard tries out a motorized bicycle.

Elbert Hubbard II

When his father and stepmother went down with the RMS *Lusitania* in May 1915, Elbert Hubbard II became leader of the Roycroft. "Bert," pictured later in life admiring the Jerome Connor sculpture of his father, was less eccentric than Elbert I. Unlike his father, who was often at odds with village leaders over his eccentric personality and political views, Bert Hubbard was embraced by the community. In fact, he was even elected mayor. Bert Hubbard steered the Roycroft ship for more than two decades; the Great Depression, however, took its toll in 1938, when the Roycroft declared bankruptcy. A few decades later, Bert Hubbard helped launch the Roycroft Renaissance movement that is still active today.

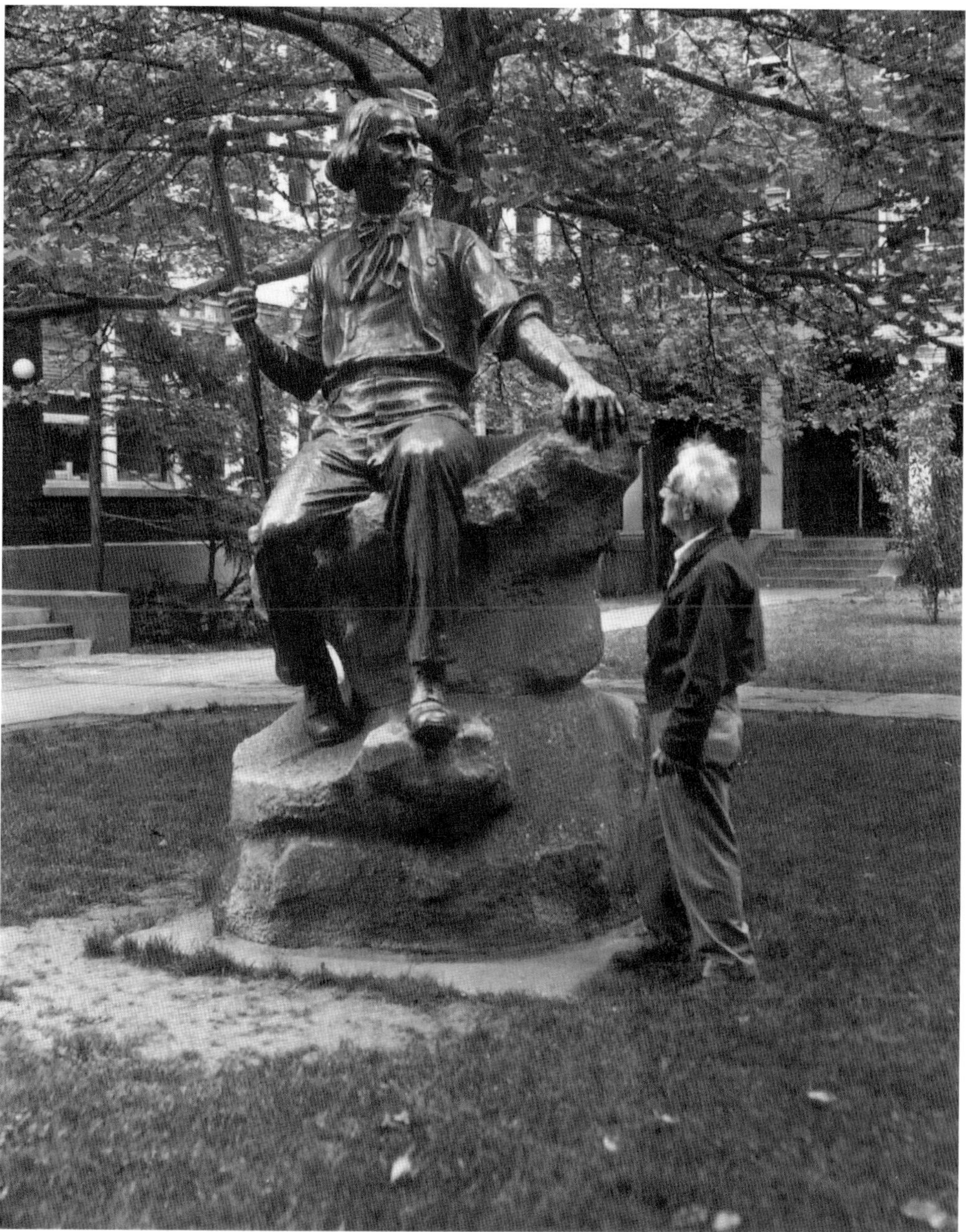

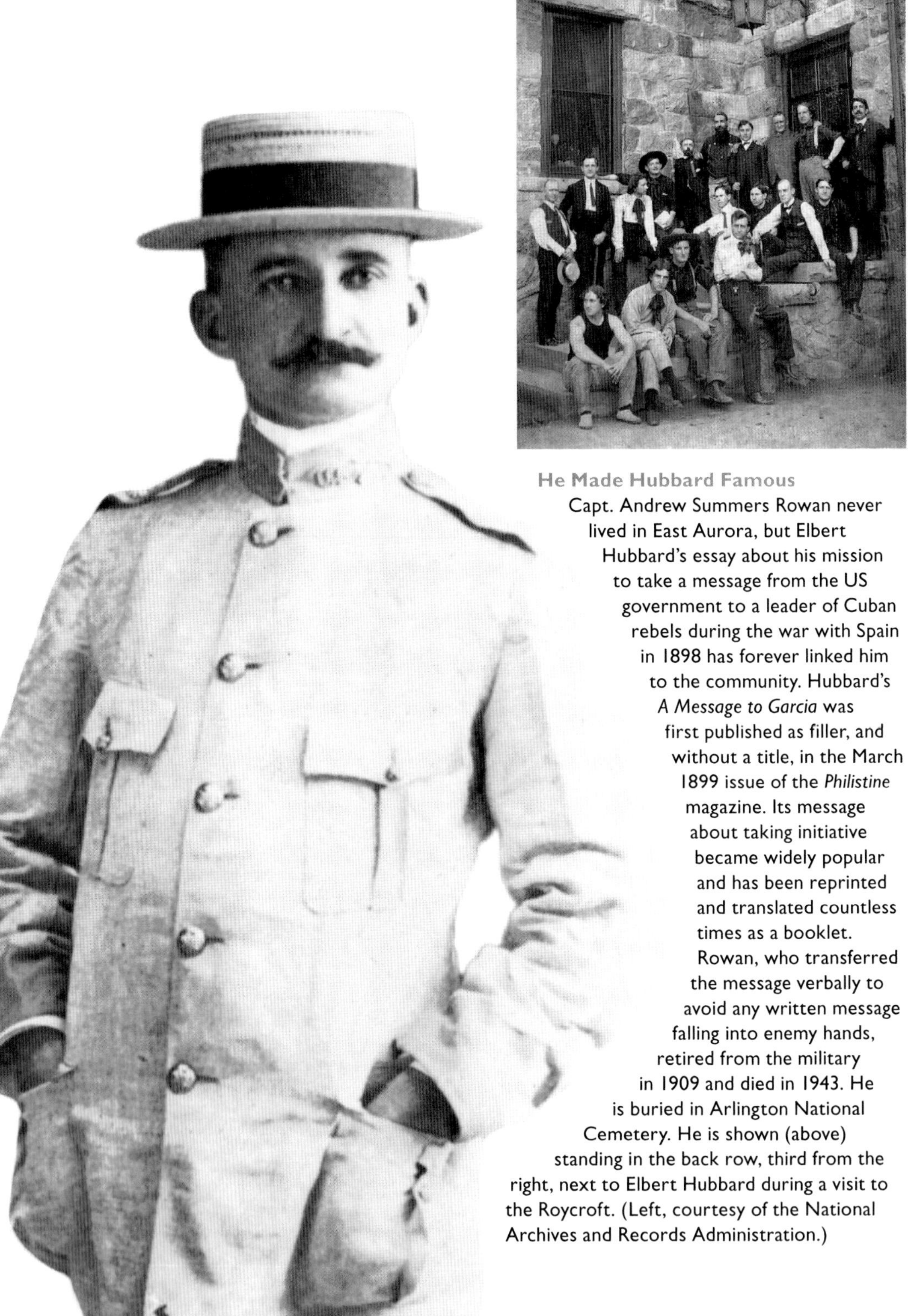

He Made Hubbard Famous
Capt. Andrew Summers Rowan never lived in East Aurora, but Elbert Hubbard's essay about his mission to take a message from the US government to a leader of Cuban rebels during the war with Spain in 1898 has forever linked him to the community. Hubbard's *A Message to Garcia* was first published as filler, and without a title, in the March 1899 issue of the *Philistine* magazine. Its message about taking initiative became widely popular and has been reprinted and translated countless times as a booklet.

Rowan, who transferred the message verbally to avoid any written message falling into enemy hands, retired from the military in 1909 and died in 1943. He is buried in Arlington National Cemetery. He is shown (above) standing in the back row, third from the right, next to Elbert Hubbard during a visit to the Roycroft. (Left, courtesy of the National Archives and Records Administration.)

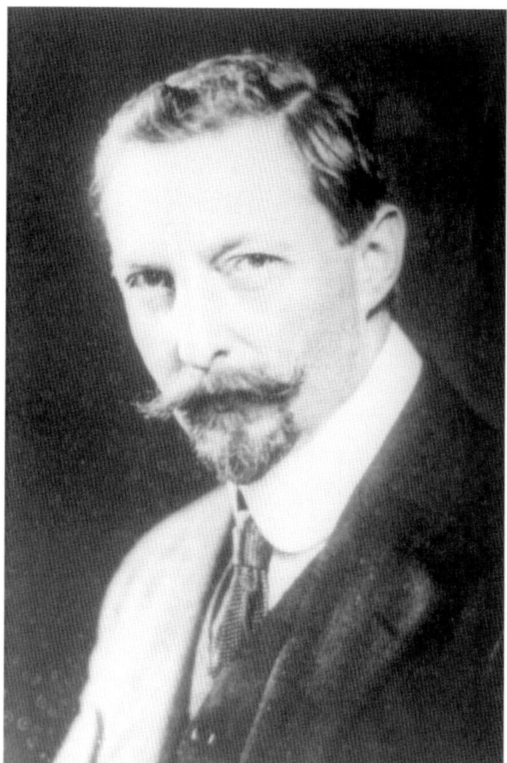

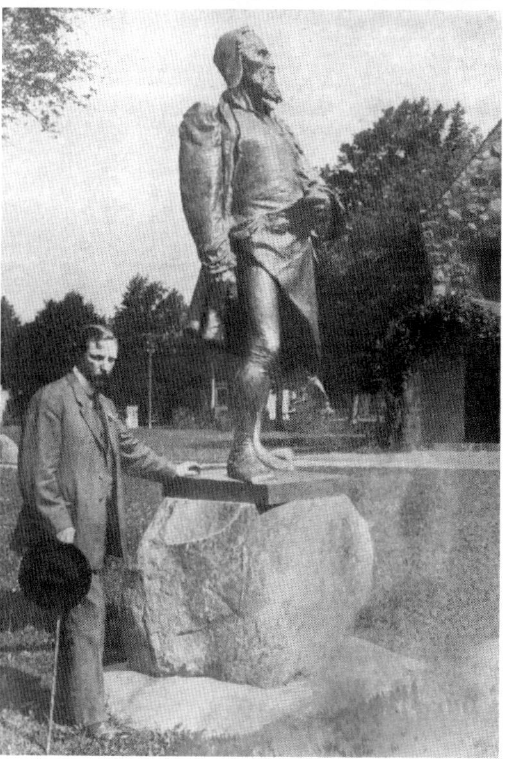

Do Not Rush Him
Elbert Hubbard commissioned American artist Paul Wayland Bartlett to sculpt Michelangelo for the Roycroft campus. It was a replica of one Bartlett created for the Library of Congress in Washington, DC. When Hubbard complained that Bartlett was taking too long, the sculptor sent back a small bronze turtle with a note stating, "Good art takes time." The sculpture was finally dedicated in 1908. The turtle was placed at the base of the statue. The Michelangelo sculpture and the Jerome Connor sculpture of Elbert Hubbard were moved across the street to the grounds of the school following the Roycroft bankruptcy in 1938. (Top, courtesy of the National Archives and Records Administration.)

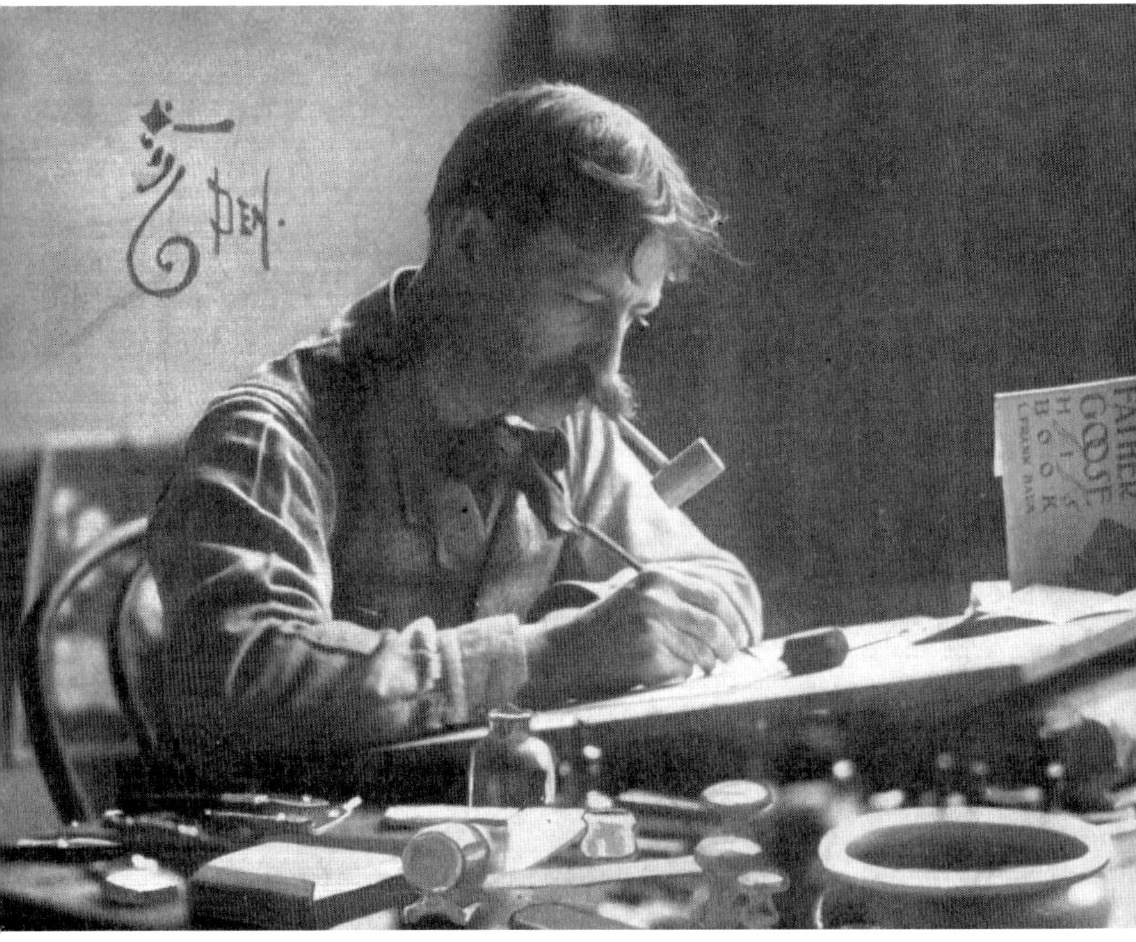

King of Denslow Island

Before he gained international fame as illustrator of *The Wonderful Wizard of Oz*, W.W. Denslow was invited to the Roycroft campus as the first professional artist hired by Elbert Hubbard for his books and magazines. Denslow's trademark seahorse signature became so popular that it was reproduced into doorknockers, fireplace andirons, and other items. After leaving the Roycroft in 1899, he moved to New York City. Denslow, an eccentric man known for his walrus mustache and "foghorn for a voice," used some of the royalties from *The Wonderful Wizard Oz* to buy himself an island off the coast of Bermuda and proclaimed himself "King Denslow I of Denslow Island." Married and divorced three times, Denslow struggled with a drinking problem and unemployment after his fame diminished. When *Life* magazine purchased one of Denslow's illustrations for a full-color cover in the spring of 1915, the artist got drunk while celebrating, caught pneumonia, and died.

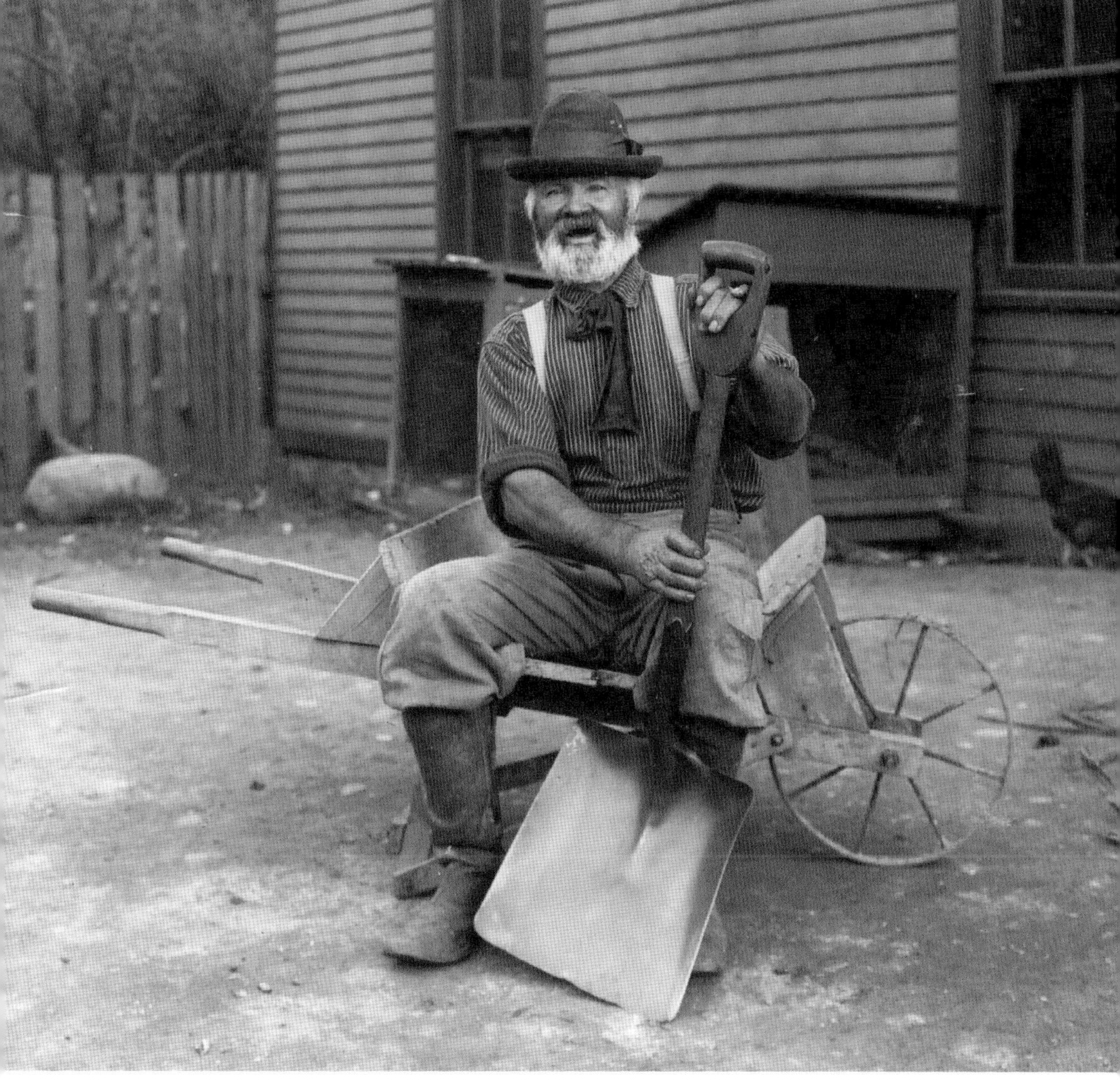

Roycroft's Witty Handyman

Anson Blackman—known as Ali Baba—was Elbert Hubbard's handyman, but he became world famous when the Roycroft founder shared stories about him in his magazines. Many of the stories were manufactured by Hubbard, who used Blackman as his alter ego. However, the stories were good enough to be believable. Visitors to the Roycroft often asked to see the famous handyman. One visitor noted, "Until I saw Ali Baba I never believed for a moment that he really said the things that have been credited to him in the *Philistine*." Blackman's likeness appeared on a number of Roycroft postcards. His legend lived on years later when a bar in the basement of the Roycroft Inn was named for him. Blackman is said to have earned his nickname after he was caught filling his pipe from the tobacco pouch of W.W. Denslow's, who joked that Blackman must be related to the Ali Baba of the Forty Thieves story. Blackman and his wife, Abbie, remained close to the Hubbards, often serving as the family's babysitters. In 1903, he related, "I've been here 20 years and I've seen every one of those Hubbard children grow up from babyhood. They have always minded me as much as their parents and sometimes more." (Courtesy of the Elbert Hubbard Roycroft Museum.)

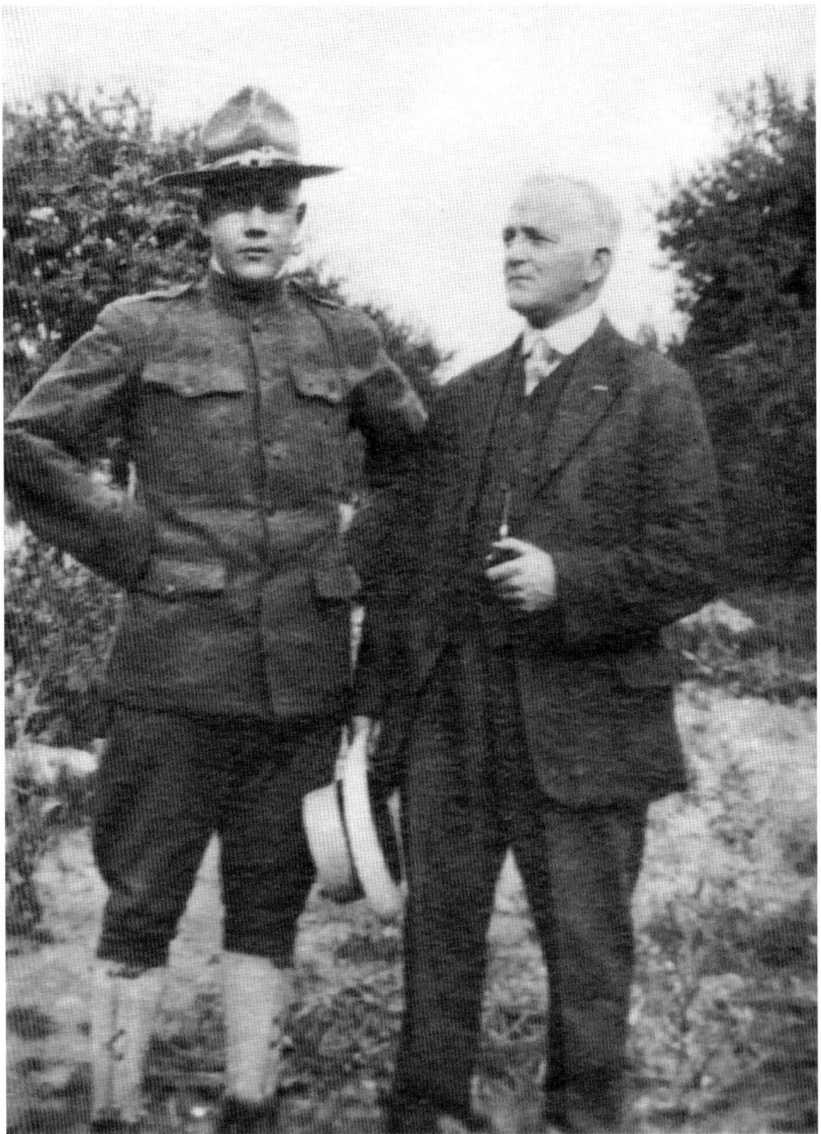

Roycroft's Wordsmith

Frederick W. "Freddie" Bann, pictured on the right with his son Eric, had only $60 and two tin trunks when he came from England with his wife and two children in 1909. A friend in East Aurora helped him secure a job at the Roycroft. "He had been a butcher back in England—and claimed no more talent," his boss Elbert Hubbard II later wrote. "A butcher was not needed at Roycroft just then, but a janitor was. So Freddie took the job." When not sweeping the floors, Bann studied advertising, which, along with "a sheer force of desire," led to a new career, which was writing for Roycroft publications. "There was a new janitor on the job downstairs," his boss noted. Bann's quest for the American dream took a tragic turn when his son, who had been among the first drafted into World War I, was killed in action in France. "Freddie knows the pang and pain of adversity, and yet faces his problems with a calm philosophy," Hubbard II wrote. "His example has been an inspiration and help to many of us when things were bad." In his later years, Bann started the Kiwanis Club's Senior Citizens Christmas Party, a longtime community tradition.

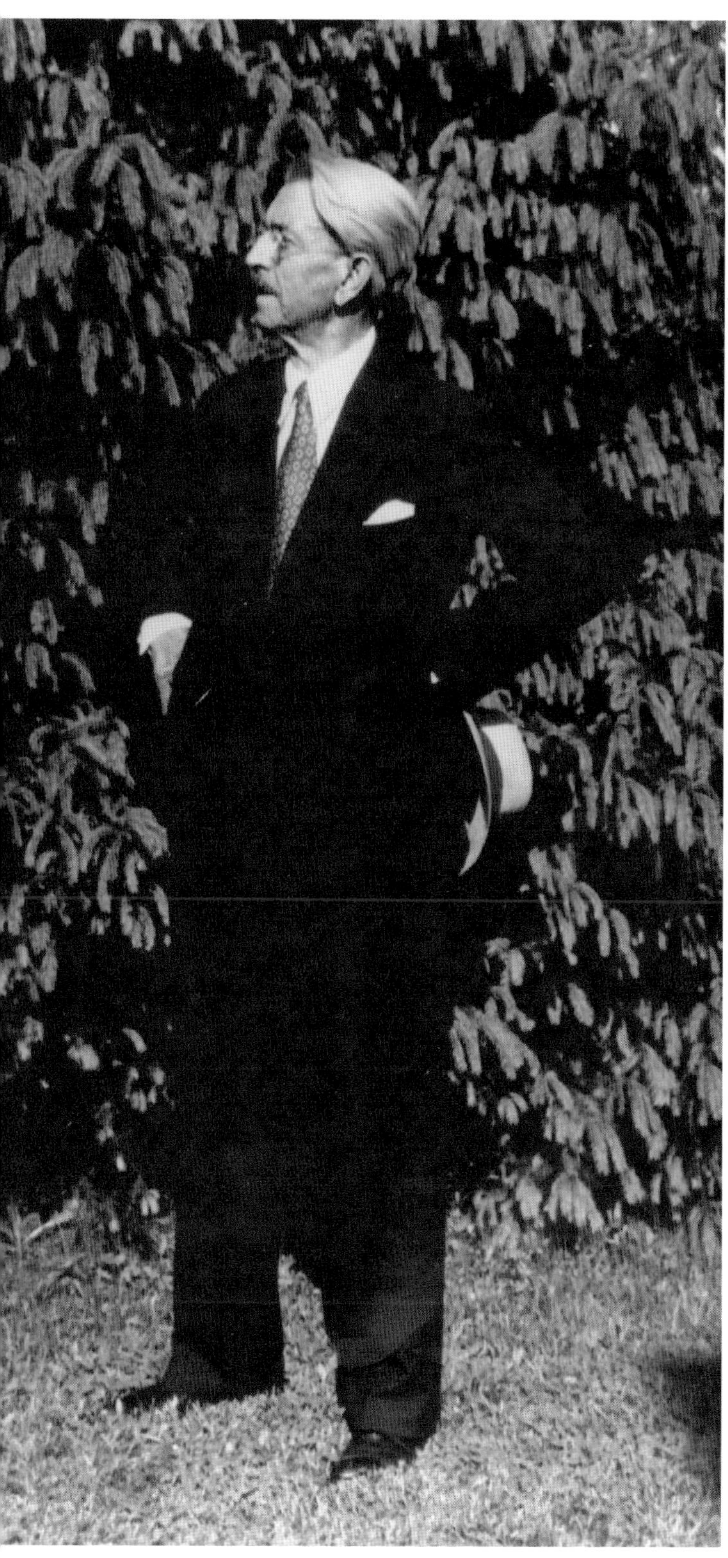

East Aurora's Barbizon
Alexis Jean Fournier was 16 when he started painting signs for $2.50 per day. With money earned from sketching and painting images of houses in the Southwest United States, he traveled to Paris to study with some of the greatest artists of his time. He was a disciple of the Barbizon School, a group of mid-18th-century artists who gathered around the home of master painter Theodore Rousseau in the village of Barbizon near Paris. While in Chicago in 1903, Fournier crossed paths with Elbert Hubbard, who invited the artist to the Roycroft. "Come see me," Hubbard reportedly told Fournier. "June 1, at sun-up." Fournier kept the appointment, and Hubbard convinced him to stay in East Aurora, where he built a home on Walnut Street and painted stunning images of East Aurora's Cazenovia Creek valley that solidified his international reputation. "I love that valley as much, if not more, than I did Normandy," Fournier said. "It possesses all the brightness of Normandy, and it is so near home." Today, Fournier's work is on exhibit at the Roycroft Inn, the Elbert Hubbard Roycroft Museum, Aurora Public Library, and in many private collections. Fournier died in January 1948, four days after he slipped on the ice during his daily trip with his wife to the mailbox at the corner of Walnut Street and Oakwood Avenue.

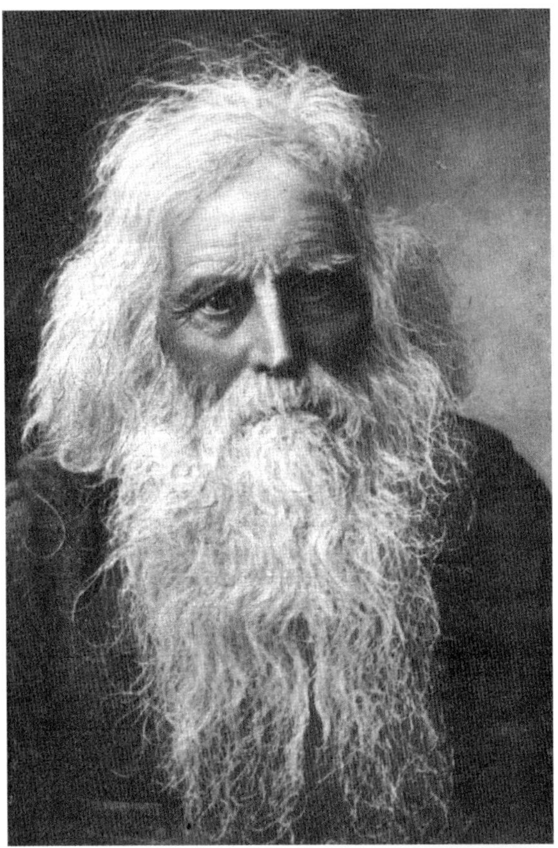

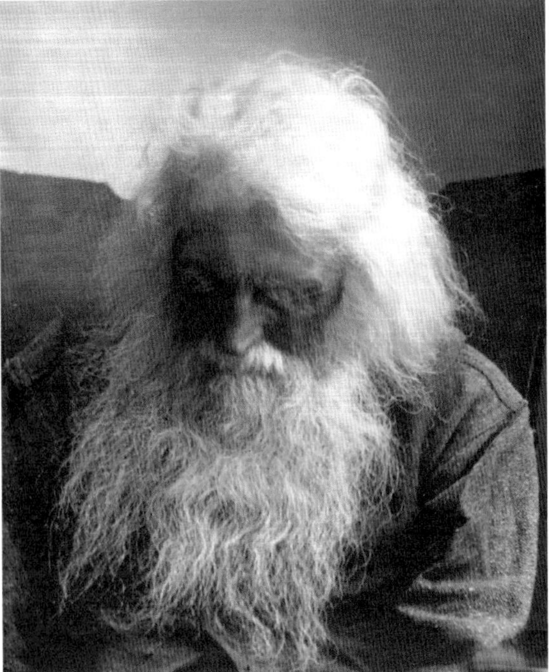

Old Uncle John
John Foster was a woodworker and horse trainer on the Roycroft campus. He was also one of the characters often seen around the village and highlighted by Elbert Hubbard on Roycroft postcards and in publications. Few people even knew his last name, as he was most often referred to simply as "Uncle John" or "Old John." Little is known about his life, but he was one of a number of unique subjects from the Roycroft captured by photographer Paul Fournier.

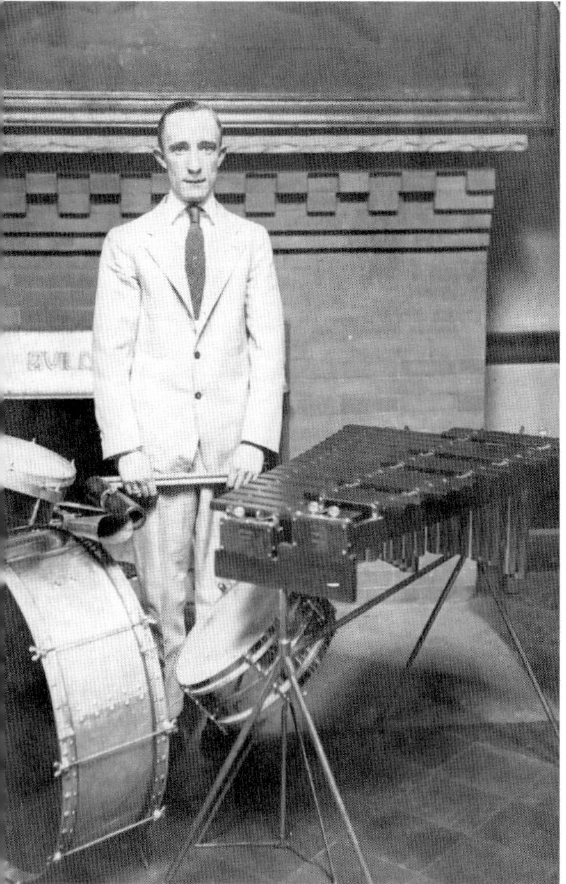

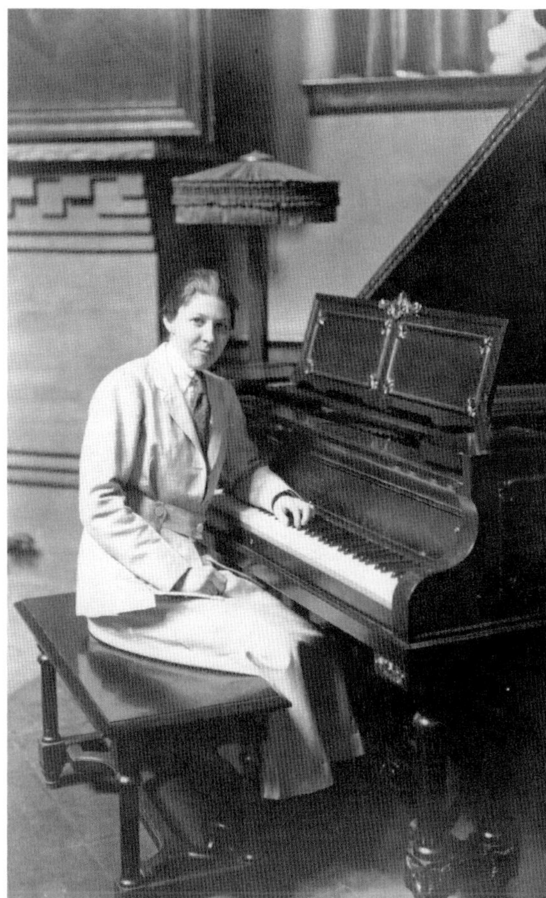

The Band Leaders

Clayton F. Fattey Sr. and his wife, Eleanor, both pictured in the Roycroft Inn, launched their own dance band, Clayton Fattey and His Roycroft Orchestra, in 1914. Clayton Fattey was the drummer; Eleanor Fattey played the piano. The band toured around Western New York and Pennsylvania and appeared on the earliest Buffalo radio programs. Eleanor Fattey also played the organ for the First Presbyterian Church. Both she and her husband were cashiers at the Roycroft. Their son, Clayton Jr., followed in their footsteps with a successful musical career of his own. His orchestra played at the Erie County Fair's Slade Park for many years.

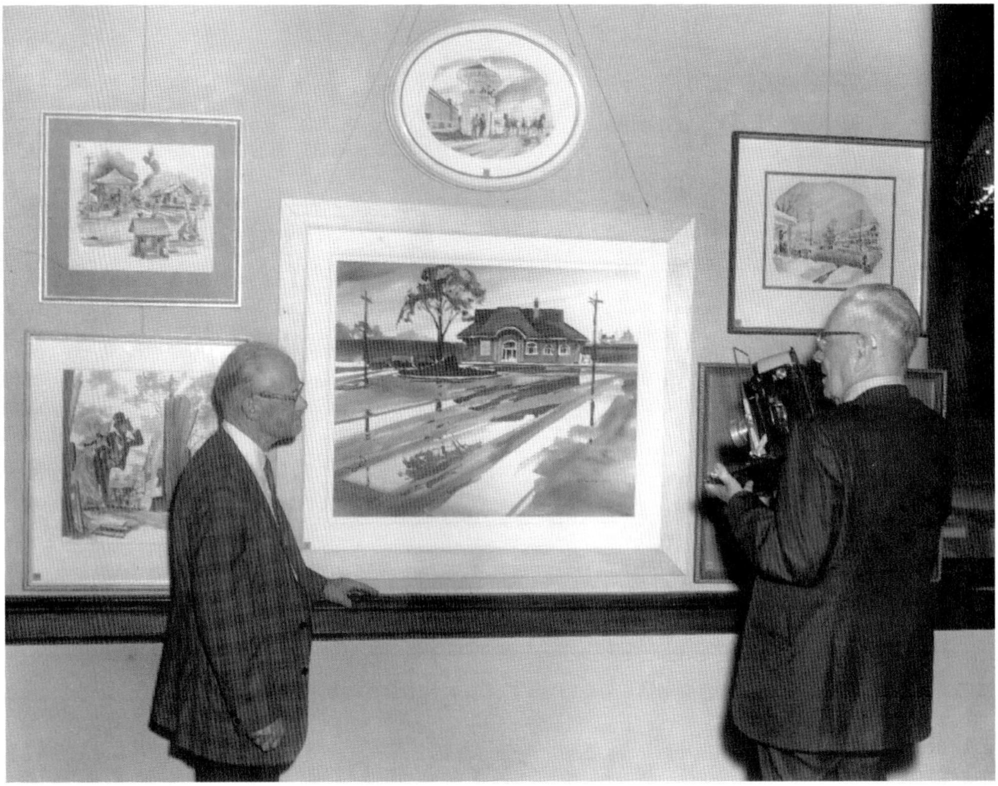

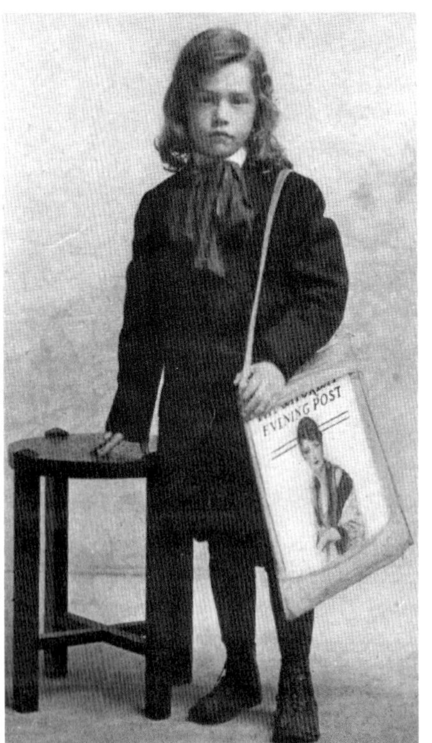

Lifelong Roycrofter

Rixford Jennings grew up on the Roycroft campus, where his father, Walter Jennings, was a skilled coppersmith. After several years of study at art schools, he took classes at the Walt Disney animation school in California and worked on the 1946 movie *Fantasia*. He moved back to Western New York in the 1950s and became one of East Aurora's most prolific artists. In addition to his renowned watercolor landscapes, Jennings, shown above being photographed by Rile Prosser, designed numerous logos and sketched hundreds of historical East Aurora scenes. In the 1970s, he created murals highlighting more than two centuries of East Aurora's history. They are on display in the Southside Municipal Center on Gleed Avenue. As a boy (left), Jennings emulated Roycroft founder Elbert Hubbard with his long hair, which was featured in an advertisement in a Roycroft magazine.

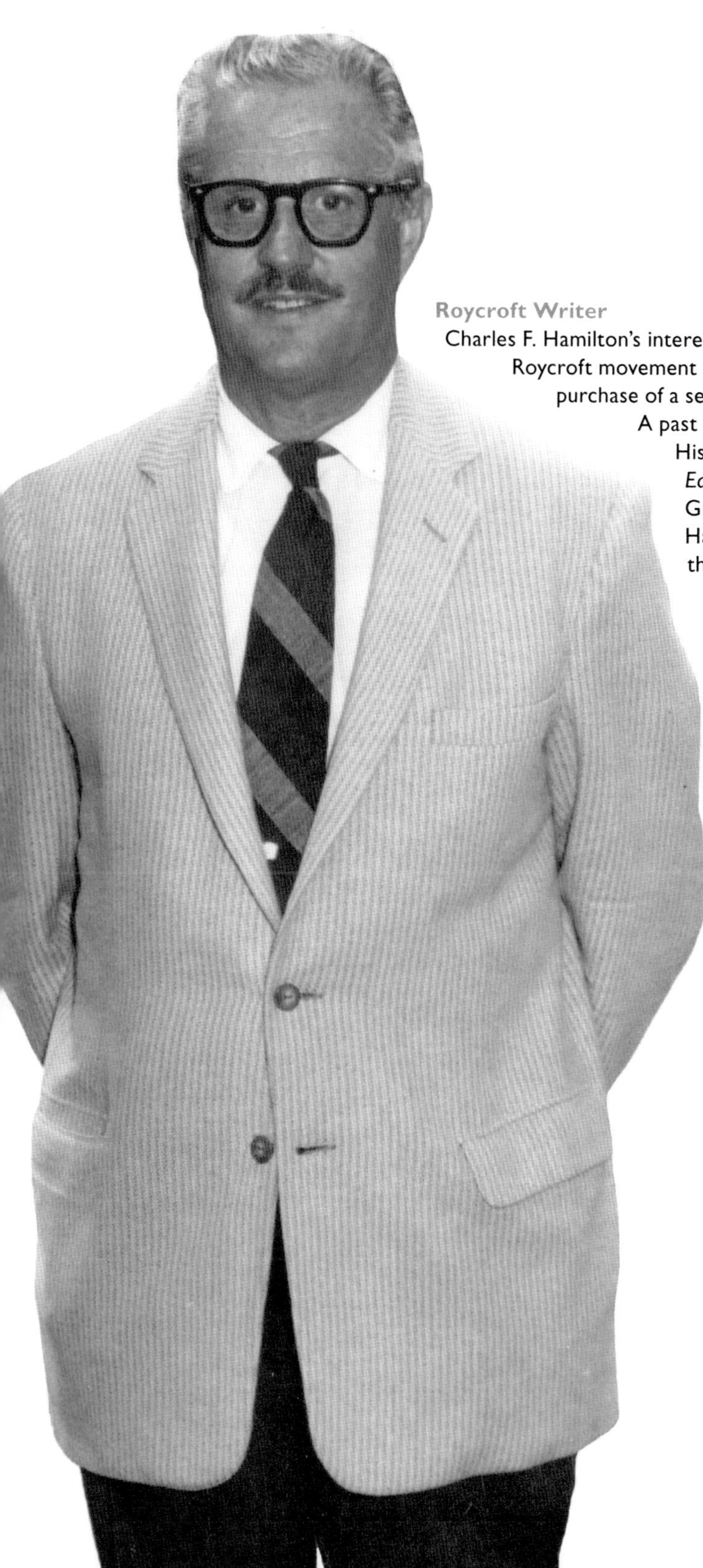

Roycroft Writer

Charles F. Hamilton's interest in Elbert Hubbard and the Roycroft movement began in the 1950s with the purchase of a second-hand Roycroft book. A past president of the Aurora Historical Society and father of *East Aurora Advertiser* publisher Grant M. Hamilton, Charles Hamilton became an expert on the Roycroft while conducting research for several books and magazine articles. He was the first author to have access to the private letters of Elbert Hubbard and his second wife, Alice, which became the basis of Hamilton's book *As Bees in Honey Drown*. Hamilton died at the age of 87 in 2002.

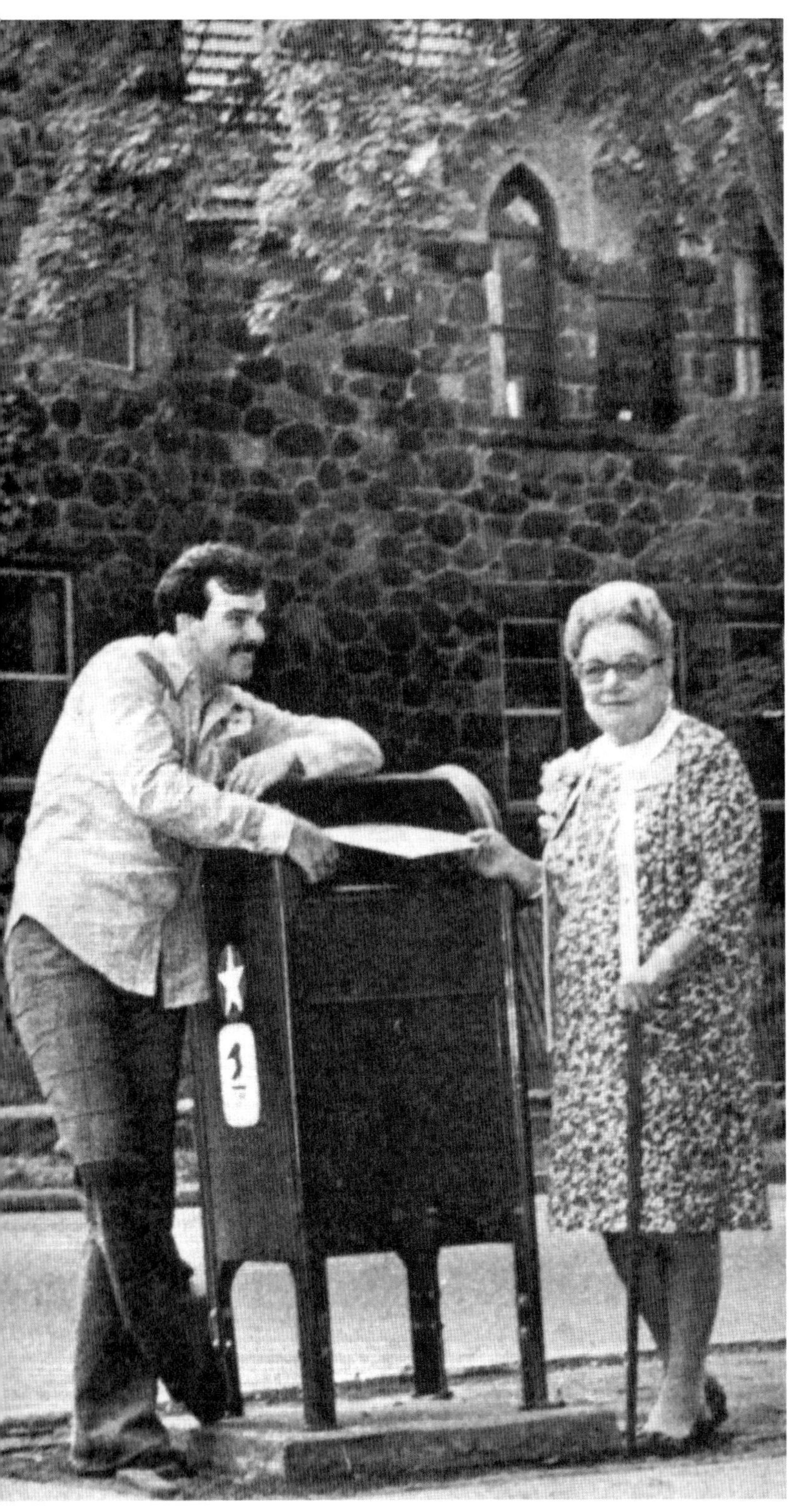

Preserving Grandfather's Legacy
Nancy Hubbard Brady was born a year before her famous grandfather went down on the RMS *Lusitania*. The daughter of Elbert Hubbard II, Brady grew up on the Roycroft campus and spent much of her life studying and furthering the philosophy of her grandfather. About three decades after the Roycroft went bankrupt in the late 1930s, Brady was a major force behind a renaissance of the Roycroft movement. After a career in teaching, she joined her father in republishing several of Hubbard's works, including the famous *A Message to Garcia*, under the "House of Hubbard" label. One of the last hand-illuminator artists of the original Roycroft era, Brady led efforts in 1976 to form the Roycrofters-at-Large Association, which continues today to promote excellence among artists much like Elbert Hubbard did. Also in the 1970s, Brady led efforts to garner National Register and National Historic Landmark statuses for the Roycroft campus. She is pictured with Michael Starks mailing an application to the federal government. (Courtesy of the *East Aurora Advertiser.*)

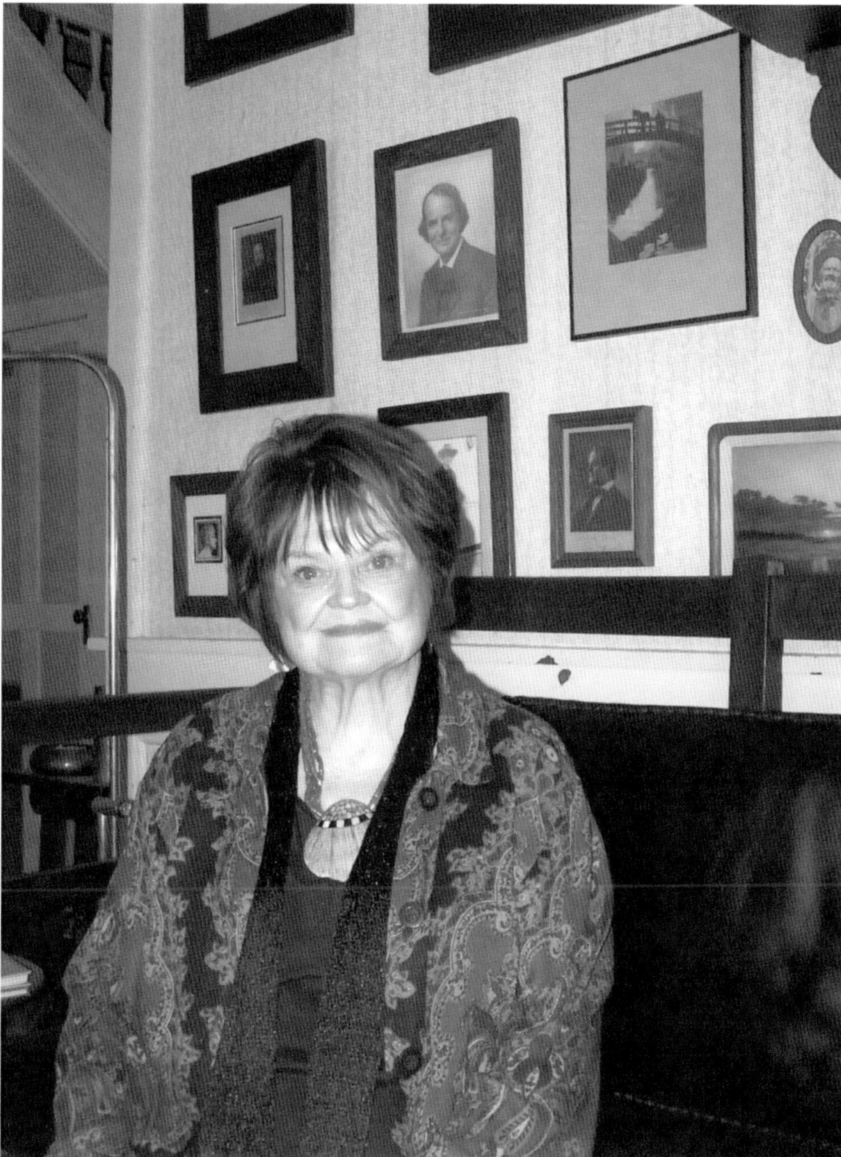

Renaissance Woman

Edythe "Kitty" Turgeon knew nothing about the Roycroft when her then husband, restaurateur Frank Turgeon, came home one day in the early 1970s and announced that they had bought the Roycroft Inn. Forty years later, Turgeon is one of the most outspoken champions of the study of the Roycroft movement and of the philosophy of its founder, Elbert Hubbard. She no longer owns the Roycroft real estate she once did, admitting that maintaining historic structures was a hefty task. Today, she prefers to concentrate her efforts on educating the younger generation about the original Roycroft movement and its renaissance. She lives in the home once occupied by Roycroft painter Alexis Fournier. Turgeon says one of her fondest memories is the day in 1986 when, in Washington, DC, she listened as officials announced that the Roycroft campus had been declared a National Historic Landmark. "They went in alphabetical order; they started with Alcatraz and ended with Roycroft," Turgeon said. (Photograph by the author.)

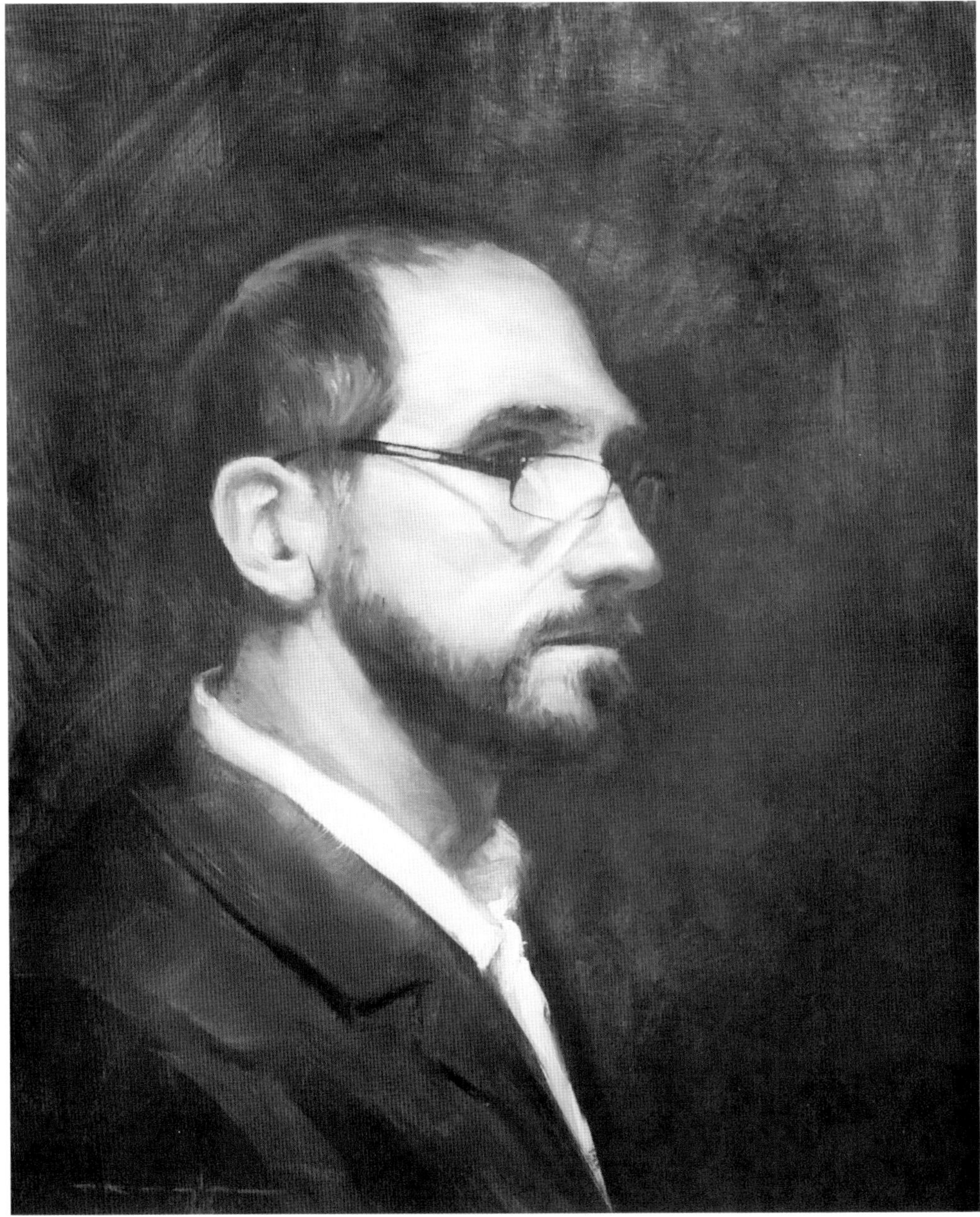

Modern Roycroft Artist

A century after Elbert Hubbard went down with the *Lusitania*, artists are still working in the Roycroft tradition in East Aurora. Thomas Kegler, a teacher at East Aurora High School, is a Roycrofters-at-Large master artisan, a distinction earned by only a few artists after an extensive peer review. The Roycrofters-at-Large Association promotes artists working in a variety of media and sponsors two annual festivals to celebrate the renaissance of the Roycroft Arts and Crafts movement. (Self-portrait courtesy of Thomas Kegler.)

CHAPTER FIVE

Women of Distinction

One woman carried her newborn baby on horseback all the way from Massachusetts so her family could build a better life in East Aurora. Another helped launch one of the world's most successful toy companies. Yet another spearheaded an effort to build an outdoor pool so local children would have a safe place to swim.

Women have always played a significant role in the growth and success of East Aurora. Sadly, their contributions were not always recognized. Available historical records often omit the women who helped build East Aurora. Early property records nearly always failed to include the names of the women who settled here with their husbands. Until just a few decades ago, local newspapers maintained the more traditional style of referring to a woman by her husband's name.

Their stories are harder to track down, but the women of East Aurora have proven to be just as fascinating, and just as significant, as their male counterparts. During World War I, women stepped forward in droves to join the American Red Cross and nurse injured soldiers back to health and send care packages overseas. During World War II, they contradicted long-held stereotypes by learning auto mechanics at local repair shops to fill in for the men, while also continuing their more traditional work at home.

In politics, East Aurora for many years remained in the center of the women's suffrage movement. Susan B. Anthony stopped at the Roycroft campus, where the idea of extending voting rights to women was already popular. Local women also pushed for political reform as members of the local Temperance Union. It took some time, but the glass ceiling was finally broken at Aurora Town Hall in 1975, with the election of the first town councilwoman, and again in 2009, with the election of the first female town supervisor.

Alice Moore Hubbard, suffragist and wife of Roycroft founder Elbert Hubbard, once said, "It is every woman's obligation to make her life a denial of this tradition that clings to her, that she is weaker than man."

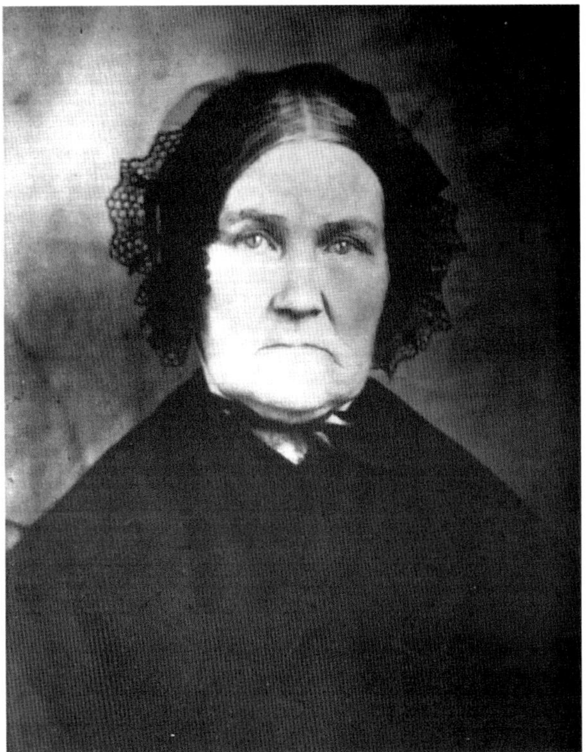

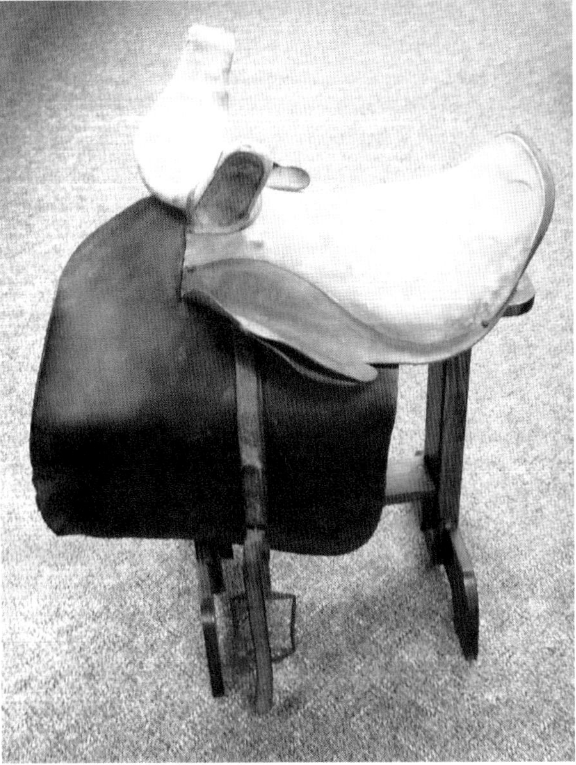

Pioneer Mother
Martha Richardson Adams rode horseback on this sidesaddle while carrying her infant daughter, Relief, on the long journey from Braintree, Massachusetts, to the town of Aurora in 1805. After settling on Olean Road as one of the area's earliest pioneers, she and her husband, Enos, went on to raise a total of eight sons and four daughters. The family donated the sidesaddle to the Aurora History Museum, where it is on exhibit. (Bottom, photograph by the author.)

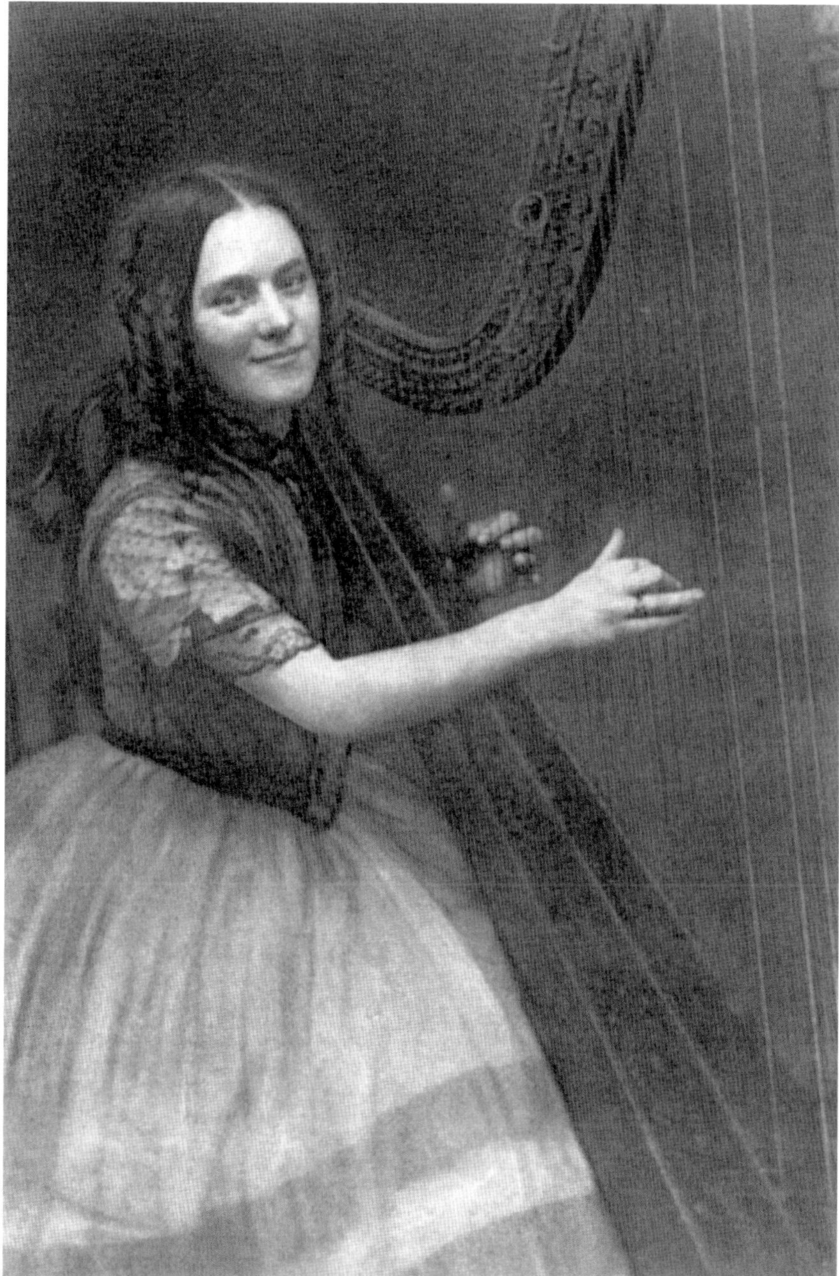

White House Hostess

Mary Abigail "Abby" Fillmore, the only daughter of Pres. Millard Fillmore, served as hostess many times during her father's presidency because her mother could not stand for long periods of time due to a broken ankle that had never healed properly. Mary Abigail played several instruments, including the harp and piano; was an accomplished painter; and spoke five languages. Her life, however, was cut short. On July 26, 1854, while visiting her grandparents in East Aurora, she died of cholera at the age of 22. Her death came just 16 months after the death of her mother. (Courtesy of the Millard Fillmore Presidential Site.)

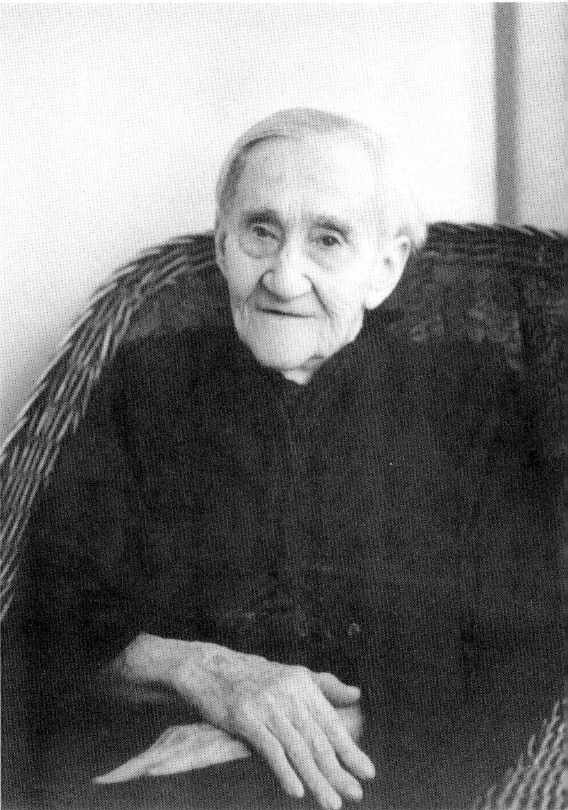

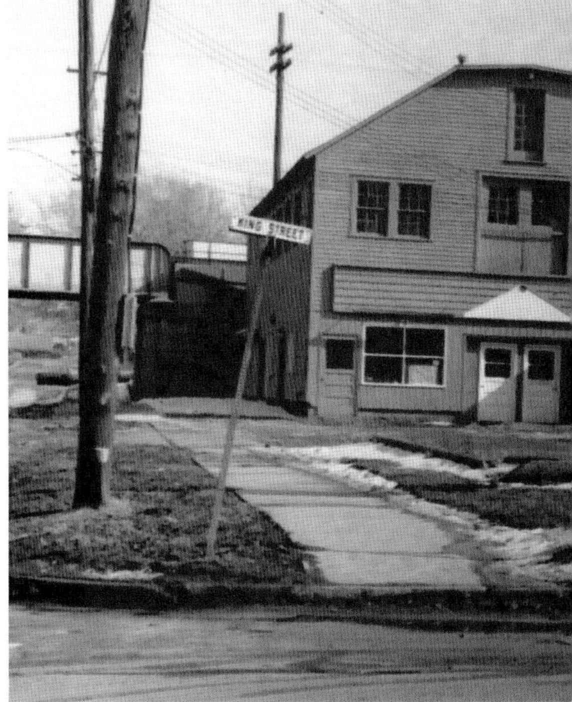

Last War of 1812 Widow

When Lydia Ann Graham of West Virginia died in April 1936, Caroline King of East Aurora became the last surviving War of 1812 widow. Born in Germany in 1849, Caroline King came to Buffalo with her family at the age of four. When she was 20 years old, she married 72-year-old War of 1812 widower Darius King. "We loved each other very much," Caroline King later said. "I never noticed the great difference in our ages." They lived on their farm in Colden for 18 years until he died. "After his death, I had to sell the place," King said. "I am alone, for my son died when he was only 24." Caroline King died at the age of 89. Mechanic Street, where she lived for many years, was later renamed King Street in her honor. She said the secret to a long life was avoiding alcohol and tobacco. "Drinking and smoking are bad," she once told a newspaper reporter. "Many a time Darius wanted me to sit by his side and smoke a pipe like the other ladies of those days did. But I couldn't. I couldn't stand the thought of it."

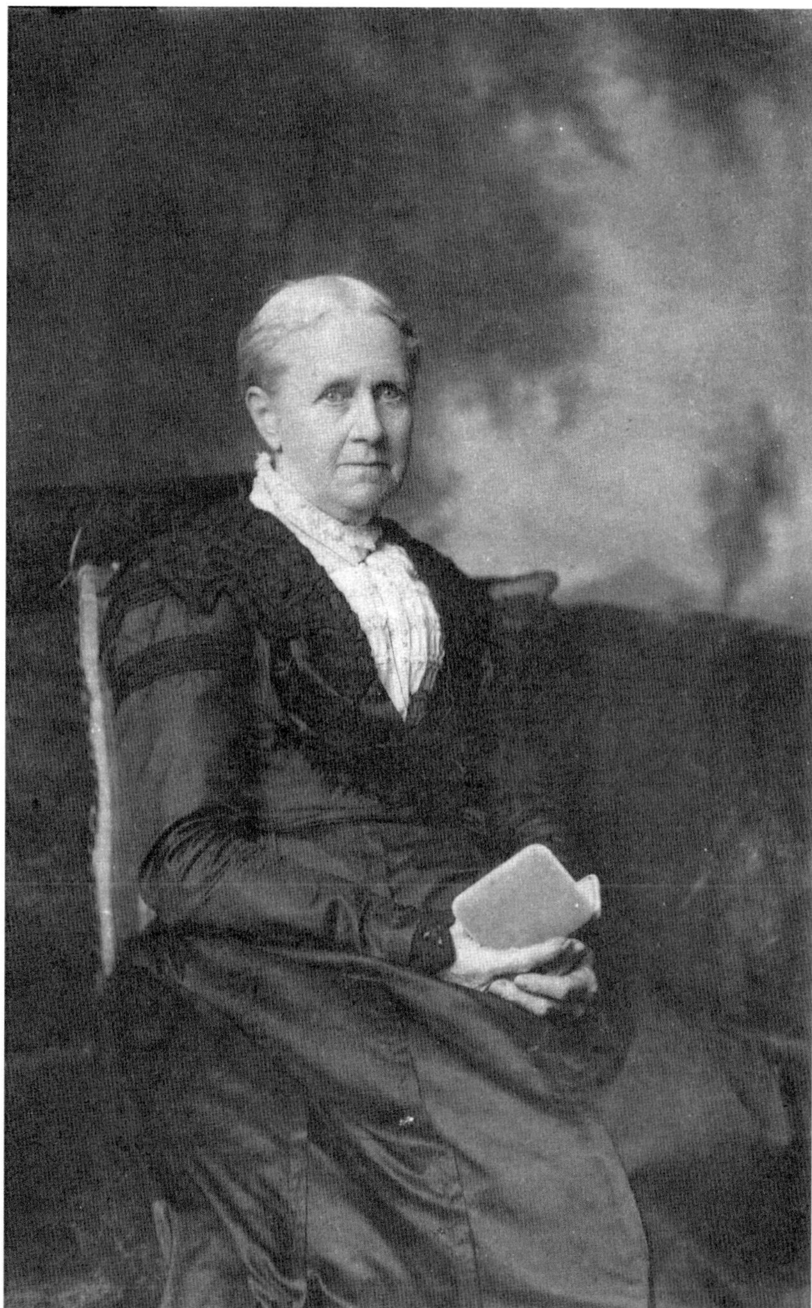

Proud Presbyterian

Mary Persons, wife of prominent East Aurora banker and merchant, was 85 years old when she died on March 26, 1907. She lived in nearby Orchard Park until she married her husband in 1848. She joined the Presbyterian Church early in life, was a Sunday school teacher for more than 40 years, and was an active organizer of church social events. She and her husband were one of the largest contributors toward the construction of a church building at Main and Paine Streets in 1892. That building was destroyed by fire in 1902 and rebuilt.

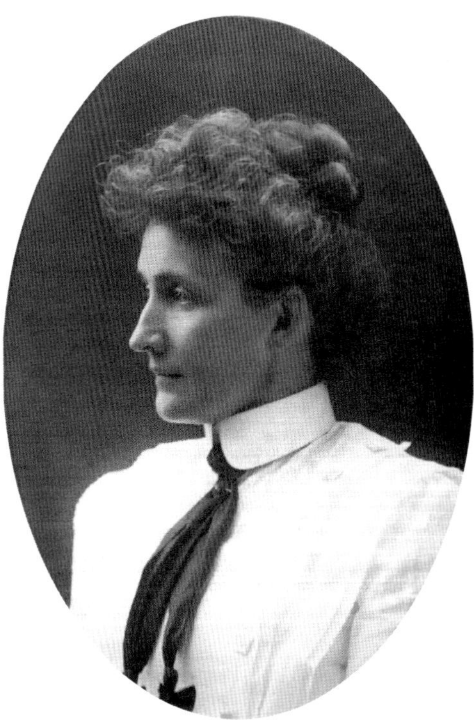

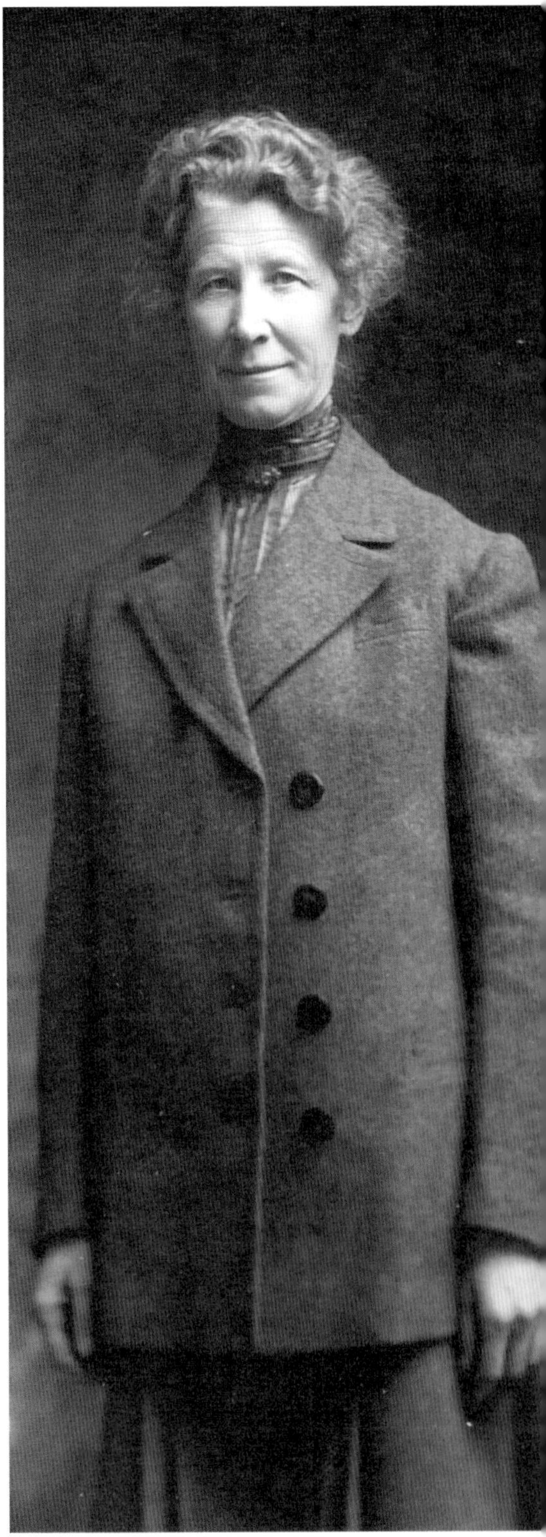

Women behind the Roycroft
The talents of Elbert Hubbard's two wives, Bertha Crawford Hubbard (above) and Alice Moore Hubbard (right), contributed greatly to the success of the Roycroft. Bertha greatly influenced the development of the campus in East Aurora and was a collaborator on the early publications that made her husband famous. Bertha, however, left the scene after news of her husband's affair with local schoolteacher Alice Moore became public in 1904. Bertha filed for divorce, and Hubbard subsequently married Alice, who became an integral part of the operations of the Royroft as well as an influence on her husband's writings. Considered an early feminist, she was also active in the fight for women's suffrage. Alice perished on the *Lusitania* with her husband off the coast of Ireland in May 1915. Bertha died in 1946. (Both, courtesy of the Elbert Hubbard Roycroft Museum.)

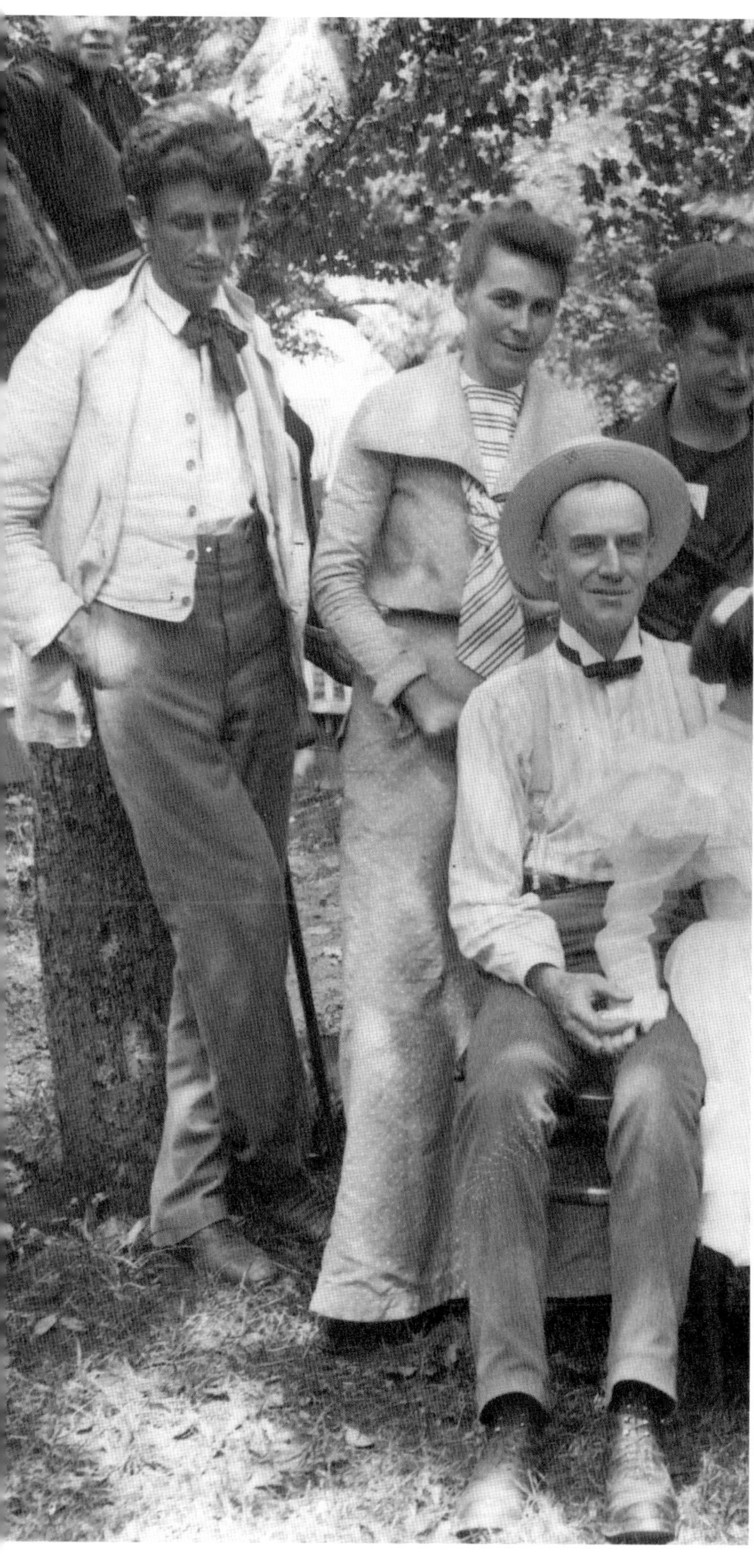

The Rugged Individualist
Eleanor Douglas, shown standing next to fellow artist Carl Ahrens (leaning against the tree), was described as a "rugged individualist." Born in Canada, she moved to East Aurora, where she set up her studio in the former schoolhouse on Hamburg Street. Douglas was known for her paintings of woodland scenes throughout East Aurora. She died in her early 40s while at her mother's home in Chicago in 1914. The village later named the street next to her studio Douglas Lane. The studio is now home to the West End Gallery.

First Postwoman

Frances Reed became one of the first five female letter carriers in the nation when she joined the US Post Office Department in 1918. To address a shortage of letter carriers during World War I, a special act of Congress allowed women to become rural letter carriers. Reed left her job as a teacher at the end of the school year in June 1918 and began delivering the mail the next day. She took over her brother's route so he could return to the farm on behalf of the war effort. "Many can remember how she drove a Model T in good weather and a horse and cutter in the winters to serve 200 postal patrons during the years outside," a newspaper article about her in 1972 noted. "One day, the tug broke on my harness," Reed, who died in 1982, recalled in an interview, "and I walked waist deep in snow alongside my horse holding that strap in one hand and delivering the mail with the other."

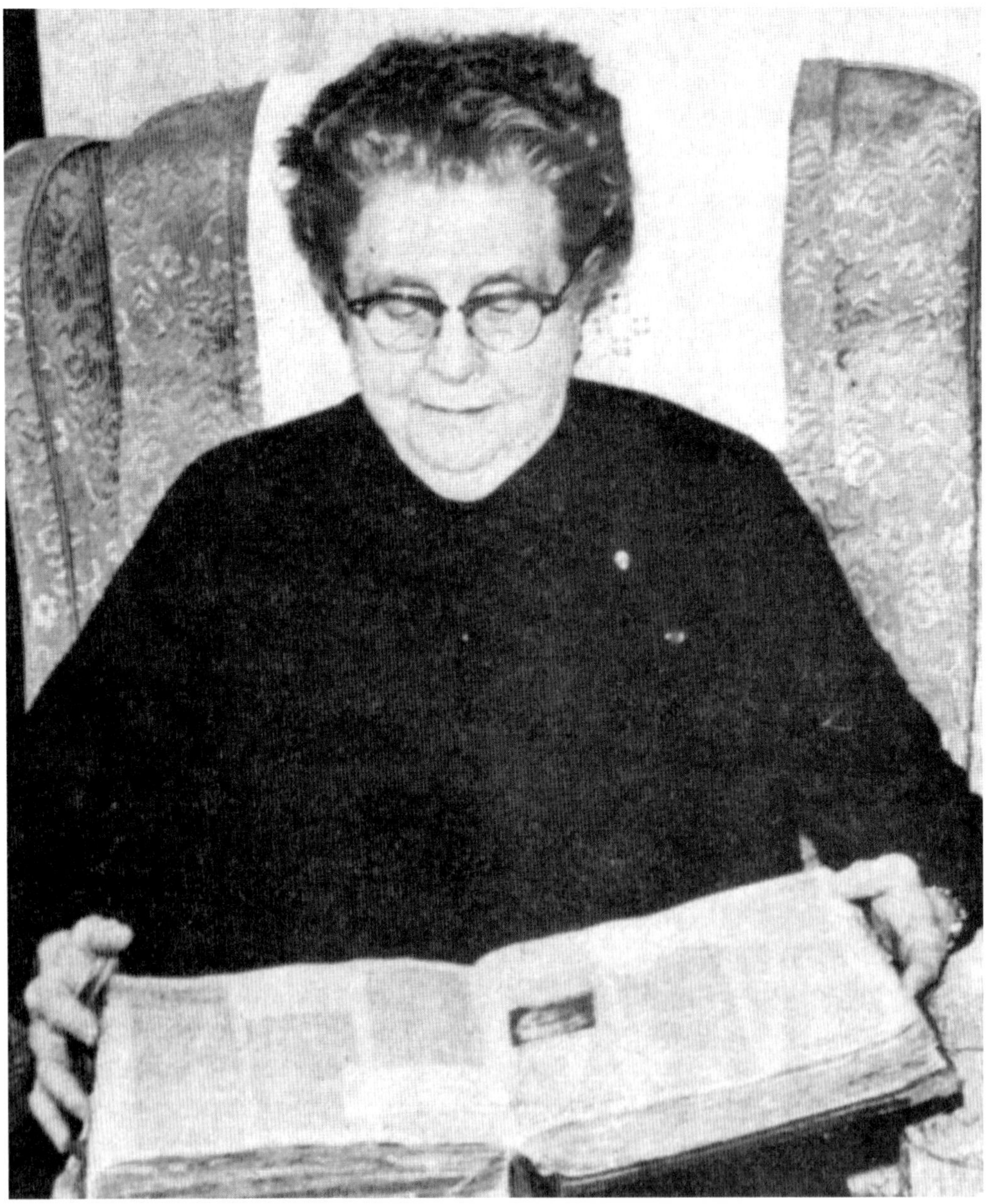

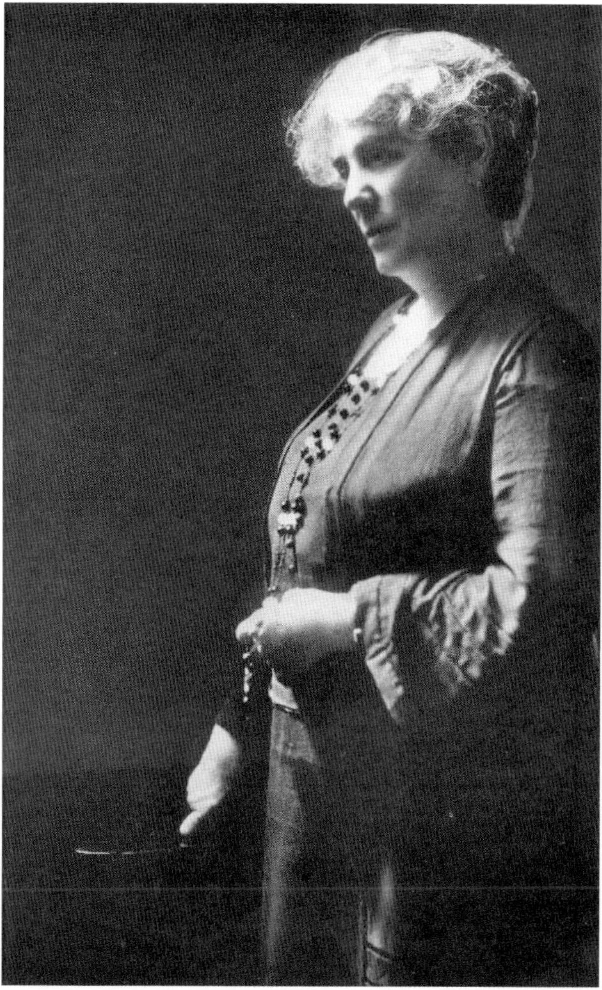

She Fled the Russian Revolution
Emma Cochran Ponafidine, wife of Russian diplomat Pierre Ponafidine, successfully escaped the country after the Bolshevik Revolution broke out during World War I. She was born in Persia (now Iran) while her American parents were on a Presbyterian mission in 1863. After graduating from nursing school in Buffalo, she returned to Persia in 1885 to assist her brother Dr. Joseph Cochran at a hospital. After marrying her husband in London, they lived in Turkey, Armenia, and Iran during Pierre's various diplomatic assignments. After his retirement, they were living on his family's centuries-old estate in Russia when the revolution began. The Soviet government seized the family's home and possessions, even though the former diplomat was blind and was so sick he could not be moved. After her husband's death, Emma Ponafidine and two of her sons, Alexander and Joseph, escaped Russia with the help of family and friends in Buffalo and East Aurora. Her oldest son, George, remained behind and was killed fighting the revolutionists in 1920. In the early 1920s, Emma and Alexander moved to Knox Road in East Aurora, where she remained until her death in 1956. In 1925, she was able to help her son George's widow and their daughter escape from Russia. Ponafidine became known around the world for her articles on various aspects of the Russian situation. She wrote two books, *Russia—My Home* and *My Life in the Moslem East*. "She was an implacable foe of the Communist regime in Russia," one obituary noted. "Hers was almost the first authoritative voice that emerged from what is now called the Iron Curtain," said another.

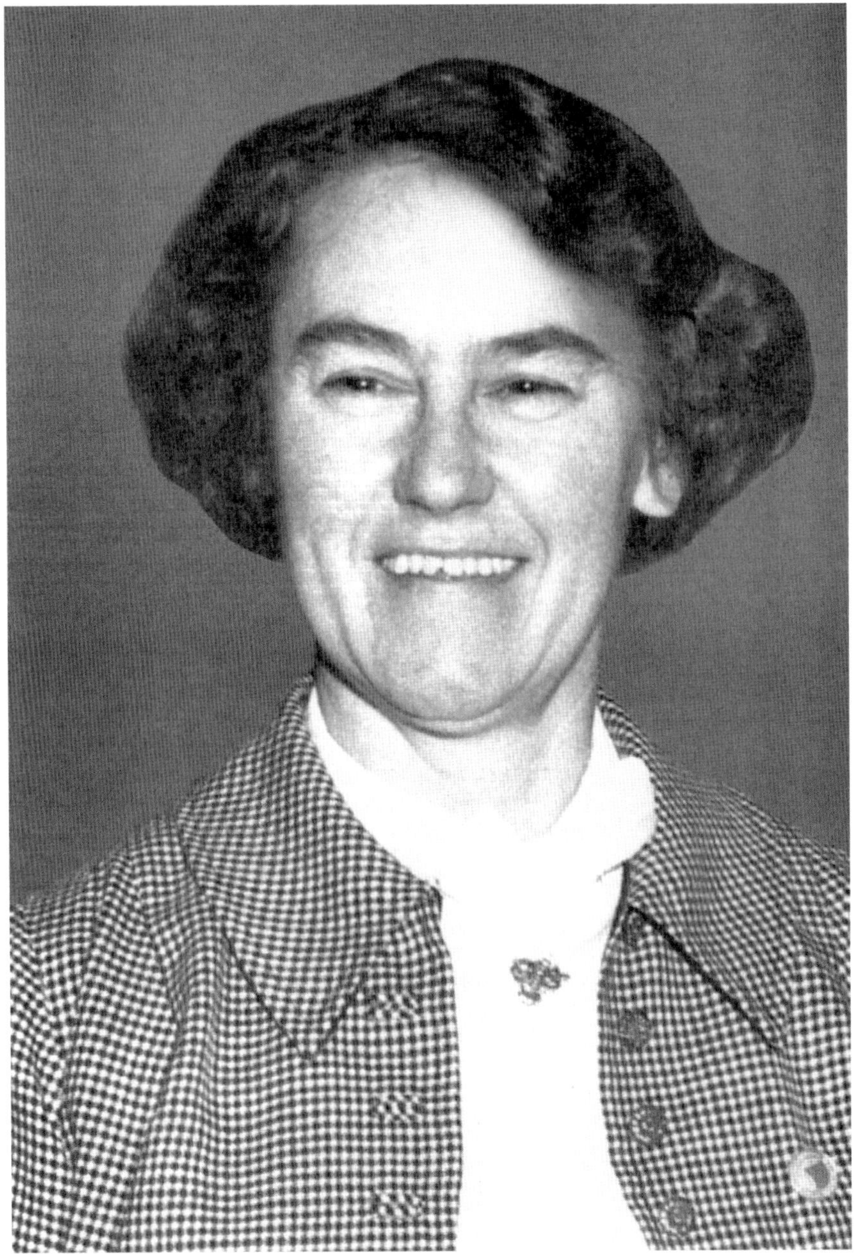

Forgotten Founder
Helen M. Schelle is often overlooked as one of the three founders of Fisher-Price in East Aurora for one simple reason—her name is not part of the company name. Herman Fisher once said that he and Irving Price would not have succeeded in launching the East Aurora toy company if it was not for Schelle. She owned the Penny Walker Toy Store in Binghamton, New York, before coming to East Aurora to help launch Fisher-Price in 1930. She and Margaret Evans Price collaborated on the design of the earliest Fisher-Price toys. A private person, Schelle often kept herself out of the limelight even though she was secretary and treasurer of Fisher-Price. Never married, she loved spending time with her horses. She retired to Piqua, Ohio, where she died April 12, 1984, at the age of 91.

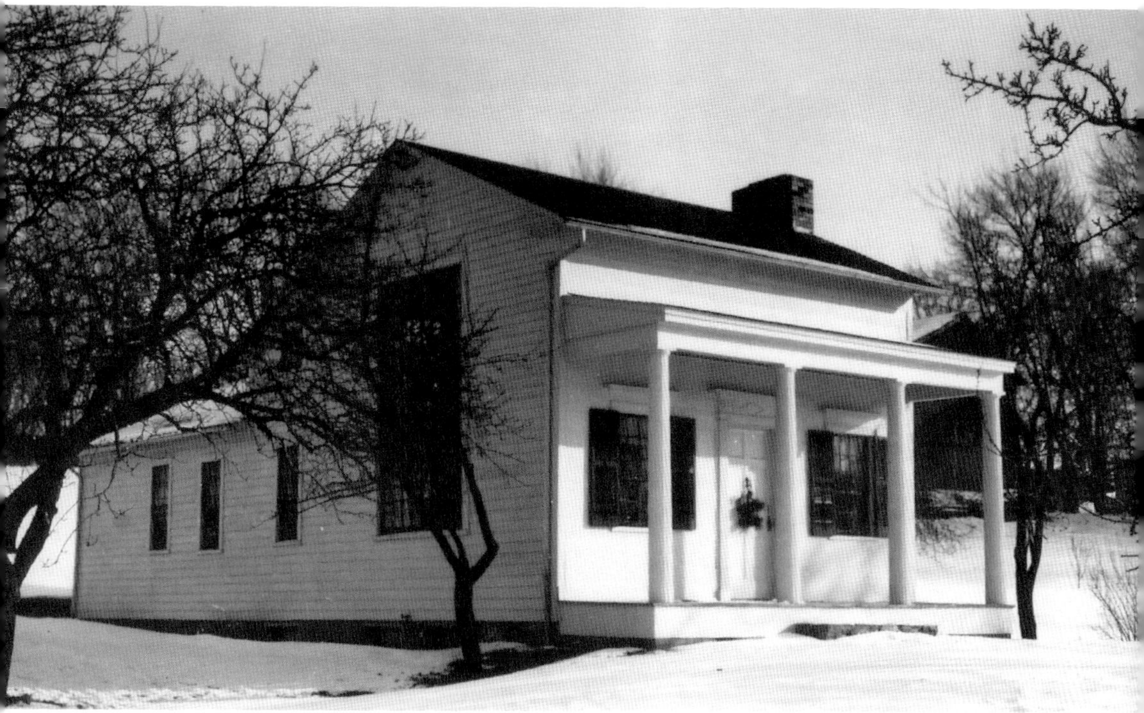

An Artist at Work

Margaret Evans Price, wife of Fisher-Price founder and one-time East Aurora mayor Irving Price, took her artwork so seriously that it is said she would spend days at a time in her studio with instructions not to be disturbed. Price used Pres. Millard Fillmore's house, which she purchased and moved to Shearer Avenue in 1930, as her artistic getaway, and is credited with saving the home. Price was renowned for her illustrations of children's books and portraits. She installed a large window on the north side of the Millard Fillmore House, pictured above, to take advantage of the natural light while painting. The window was removed when the Aurora Historical Society restored the house as a museum in the 1970s.

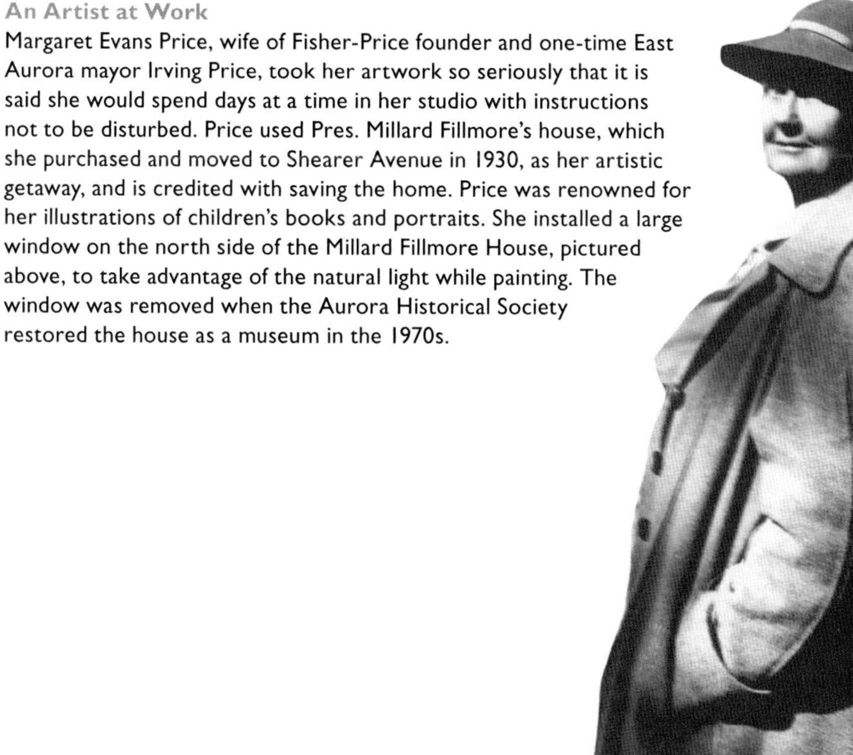

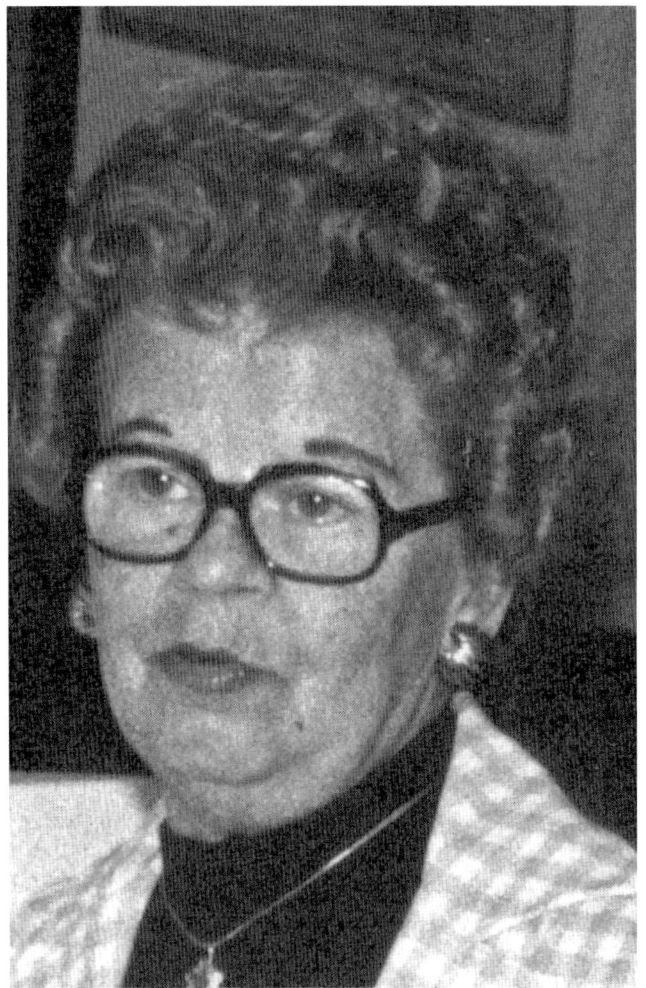

A Mighty Pen

For nearly three decades, Signe Spooner offered her personal spin on events around town in her weekly "Smatterings by Sig" column in the *East Aurora Advertiser*. Spooner, wife of the publisher and the newspaper's society editor, used her popular column to highlight local heroes and civic groups, but she also irritated local government officials when she took them to task. "Smatterings by Sig" carried a lot of weight in the community. It is said Spooner's opinion led to the success or failure of the annual school budget vote. Spooner continued her "smatterings" until shortly before her death in 1988.

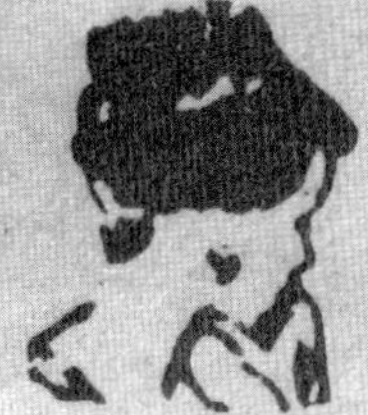

Smatterings By Sig

Main St. 200 Years Ago

Some people are annoyed with the present detouring on Main St. due to the collapse of the road a few weeks ago. We better all

It rained and it snowed, h related, and the mud was so dee at times that the horses had rest every little ways. A 'recor

Making a Splash

It took nearly 15 years, but Janet Vosseller's persistence paid off. Troubled that the community's children had no safe place to swim during the hot summer months, Vosseller launched a campaign to build an outdoor swimming pool. Her first effort failed in November 1956, when voters rejected an outdoor pool after the school district moved ahead an indoor pool at the Main Street building. Things stood still until 1963, when members of the Kiwanis Club joined forces with Vosseller to resurrect the plans. A door-to-door fund drive was launched in 1965, and the pool opened in August 1966. Vosseller's legacy lives on each summer as families enjoy the community pool at the corner of Olean Road and South Street. (Both, courtesy of the *East Aurora Advertiser*.)

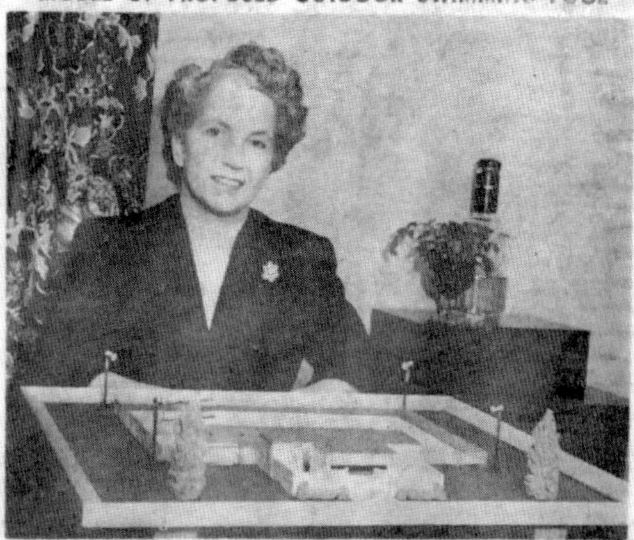

MODEL OF PROPOSED OUTDOOR SWIMMING POOL

Mrs. Vernon A. Vosseller, active as a member of the Steering Committee for the proposed outdoor swimming pool, explains a model made by William R. Trautman, consulting engineer. A referendum will be voted on at the Nov. 3 election by eligible voters, owners of property in the Town of Aurora. Site of the proposed pool is in South street just west of Olean street. The pool, 42 by 80 feet, will have a 20-foot apron. The bathhouse, 39 by 50, includes space for toilets, showers, storage, office, first aid, check and dressing rooms and pool equipment. There will be a fence around the pool and fences to the west, east and north sides of the property, also parking facilities for 100 cars and bicycle racks. Sufficient space will be available for additional parking when needed.

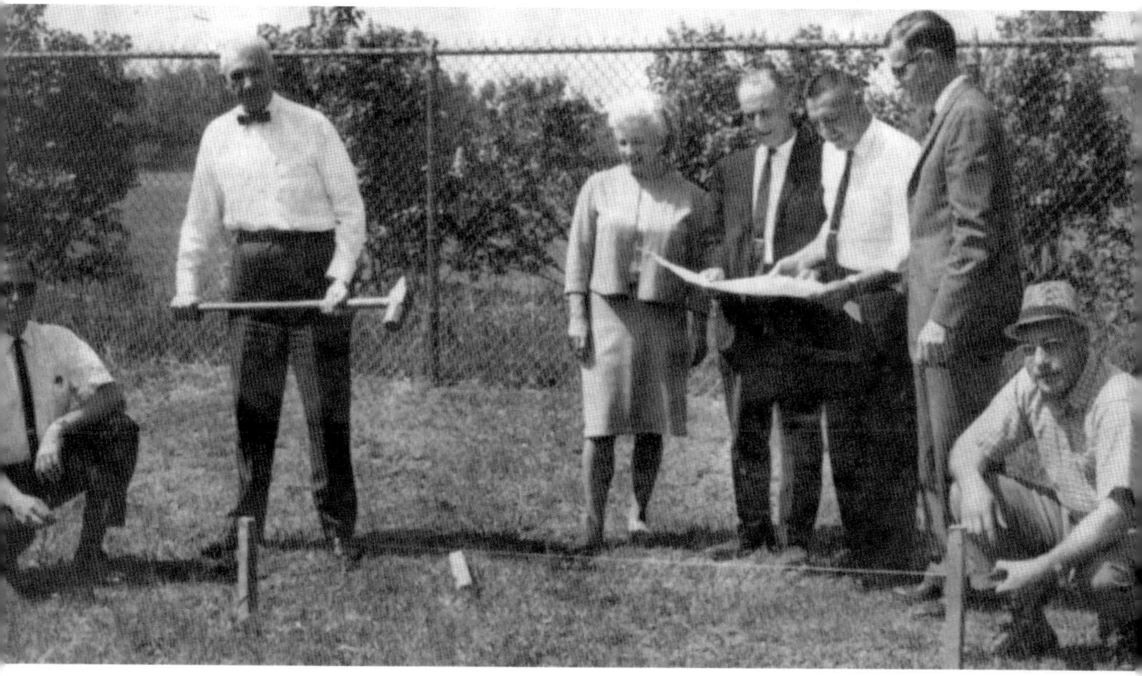

She Gave Her Home

Instead of opening gifts on her 100th birthday in 1985, Gladys ScheideMantel gave the community one. Gladys and George ScheideMantel met at the Roycroft, where Gladys's mother was a cook. George later became head of the leather department. Their Craftsman-style home was built at 363 Oakwood Avenue in 1910. For more than two decades it has been the Elbert Hubbard Roycroft Museum, owned and operated by the Aurora Historical Society. Gladys ScheideMantel was 105 when she died in 1991.

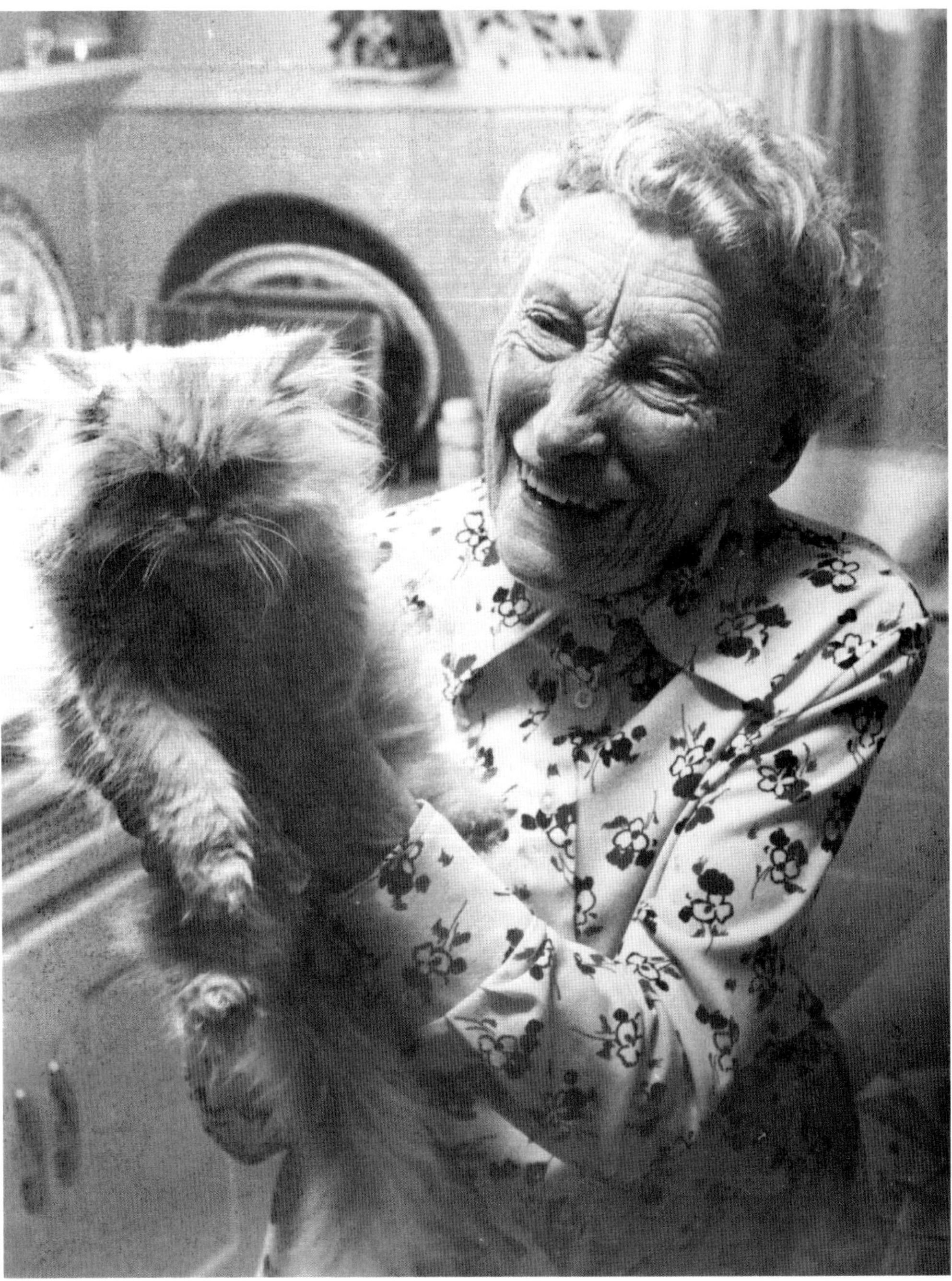

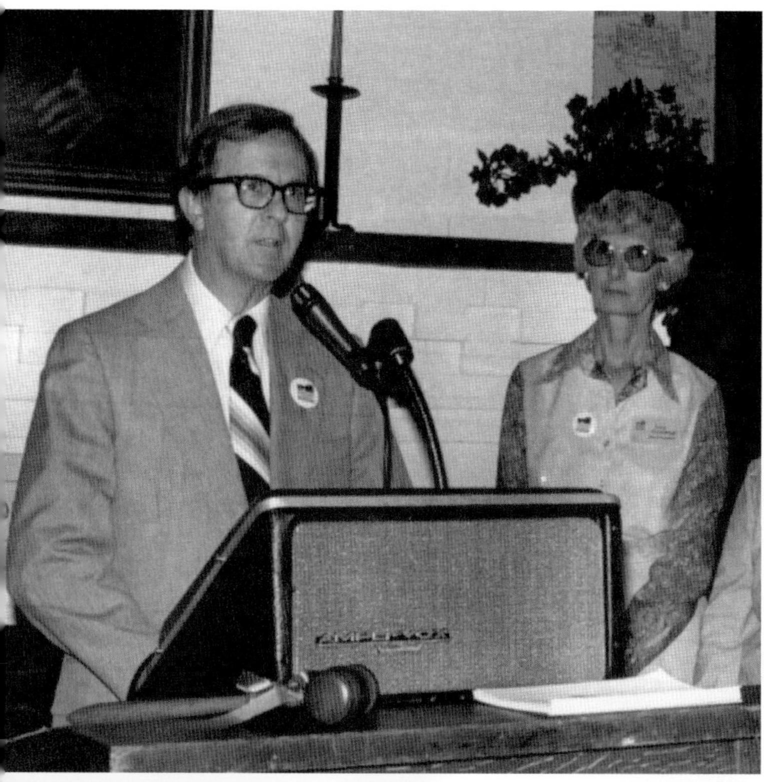

First Councilwoman
June M. Greenwood rode into Aurora's history books in 1975, when she was elected the first woman member of the Aurora Town Board. She and her Republican running mate, Charles F. Hamilton, conducted their door-to-door campaign on a bicycle built for two. They won the Republican primary before capturing the general election victory two months later. Greenwood served two four-year terms. She is pictured at left with Aurora town supervisor Abbott Henshaw.

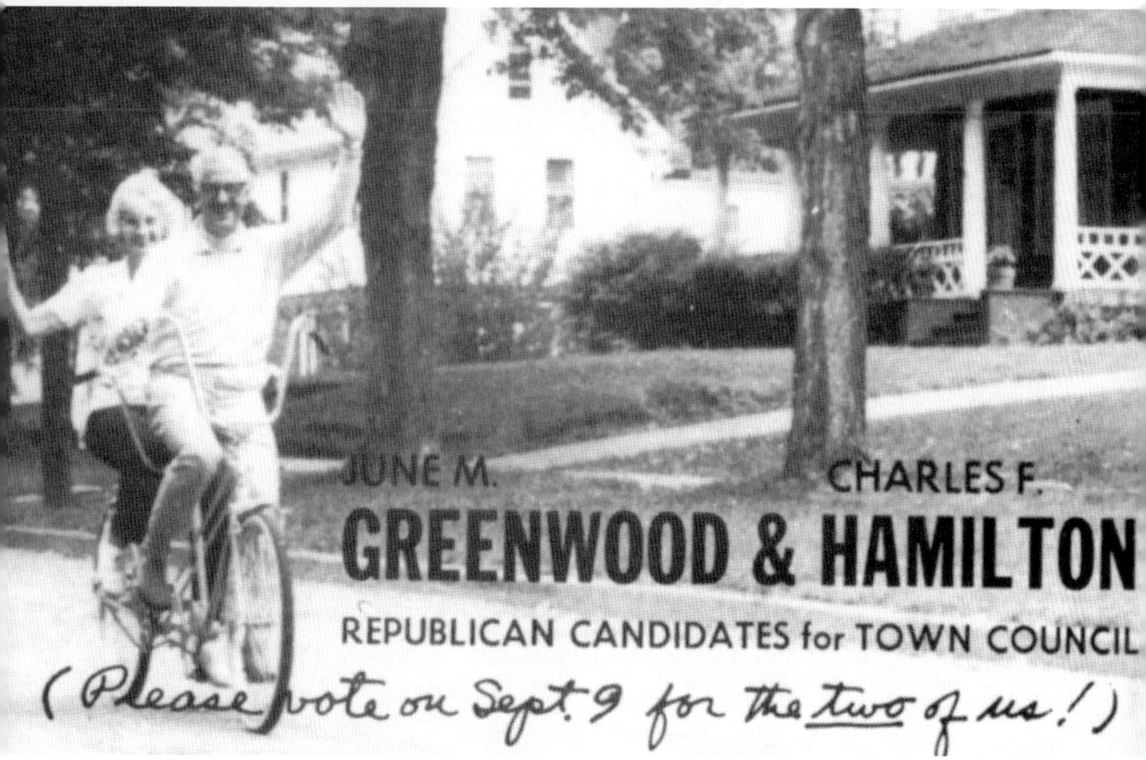

JUNE M. CHARLES F.
GREENWOOD & HAMILTON
REPUBLICAN CANDIDATES for TOWN COUNCIL
(Please vote on Sept. 9 for the two of us!)

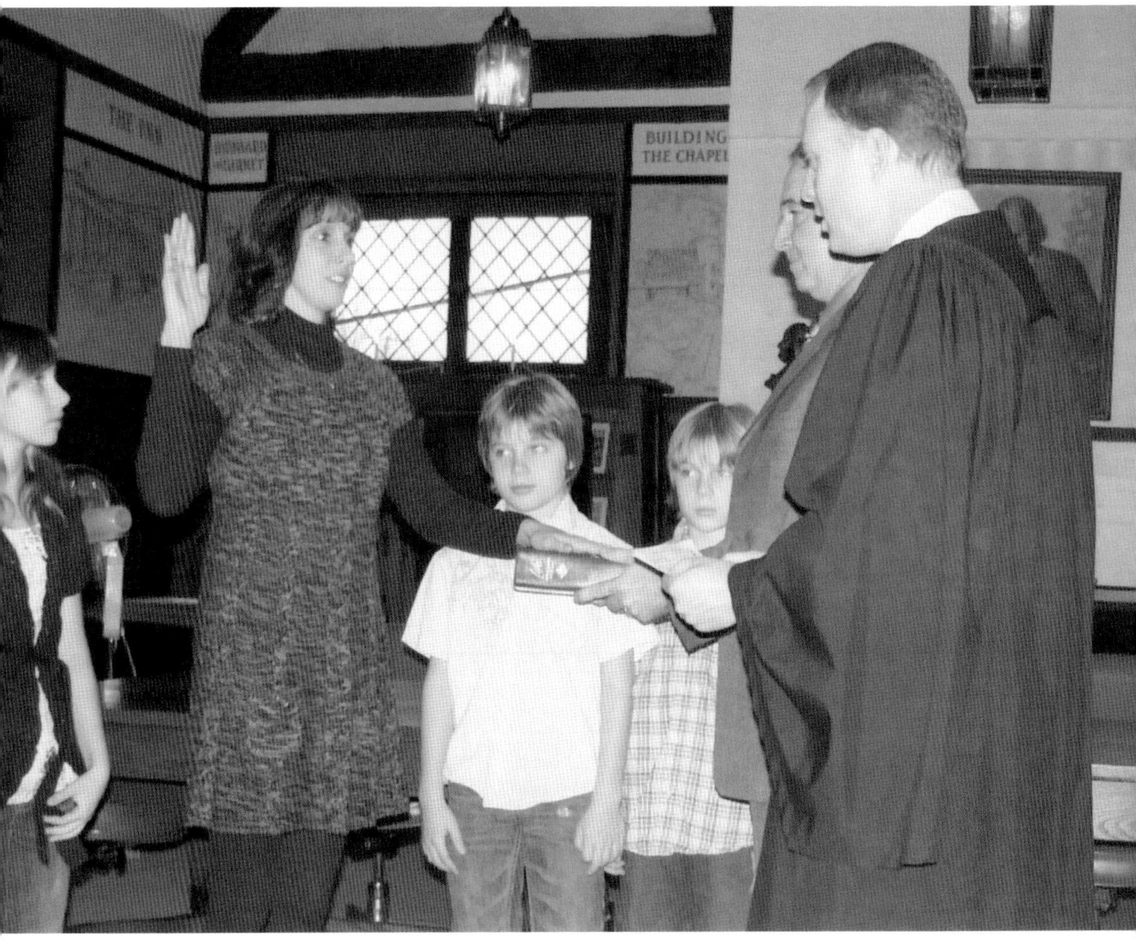

Madam Supervisor

Jolene M. Jeffe made history in 2009 when she defeated an incumbent to become the first woman elected Aurora town supervisor. The mother of three and former human resources supervisor, Jeffe (pictured taking the oath of office on January 1, 2010) served in the town's top post for four years before stepping down in 2013 to run for town councilwoman. While Jeffe broke the glass ceiling in the supervisor's office, as of 2014, no woman has been elected mayor of the village of East Aurora. (Courtesy of Jolene M. Jeffe.)

CHAPTER SIX

They Answered Their Country's Call

East Aurorans have answered the call each time there has been a war. The American Revolution had been over for 20 years when East Aurora was first settled, but several of the pioneers were veterans of the war for independence. The first settler, Jabez Warren, and the first pioneer to spend a winter in Aurora, Joel Adams, both served in the war before migrating to East Aurora. In all, 21 Revolutionary War veterans are buried in Aurora's cemeteries, including 11 in the Pioneer Cemetery behind the Aurora Theatre and two in the Oakwood Cemetery on the west end of the village.

Seventeen local men served in the War of 1812. With major battles just a few miles away in Buffalo and Niagara Falls, it is likely that even more of East Aurora's residents participated in the war effort in an unofficial capacity.

East Aurora's population had grown significantly by the time the Civil War broke out, and more than 150 local men fought for the Union. 207 town of Aurora residents served in World War I. Many of their stories are outlined in two large scrapbooks put together by American Red Cross volunteers, which are currently preserved in the town archives. The call for service members was even greater in World War II, and more than 750 Aurorans served.

Each Memorial Day, the sacrifices of war veterans are honored at two memorial monuments in Oakwood Cemetery—one for the Civil War and the other for World War I and all the conflicts that followed. More recently, a monument to honor the veterans of the Korean War was erected on the grounds of the American Legion on Center Street. Aurorans also answered the call in Vietnam, the Persian Gulf War, Iraq, and Afghanistan.

Beyond the statistics are hundreds of interesting stories of East Aurora war veterans. Some are fascinating. Sadly, others are heart wrenching. Several legendary veterans have been featured in previous historical accounts. One of them was Lawrence Ernst, the first East Aurora soldier to die in service overseas in World War I. Ernst Place, the little road in front of McDonald's at the Circle, was named in his honor.

Every military veteran's story is worth telling. Unfortunately, there is not enough room to fit them all. This chapter features just a small representation of the hundreds of military veterans who qualify as legendary.

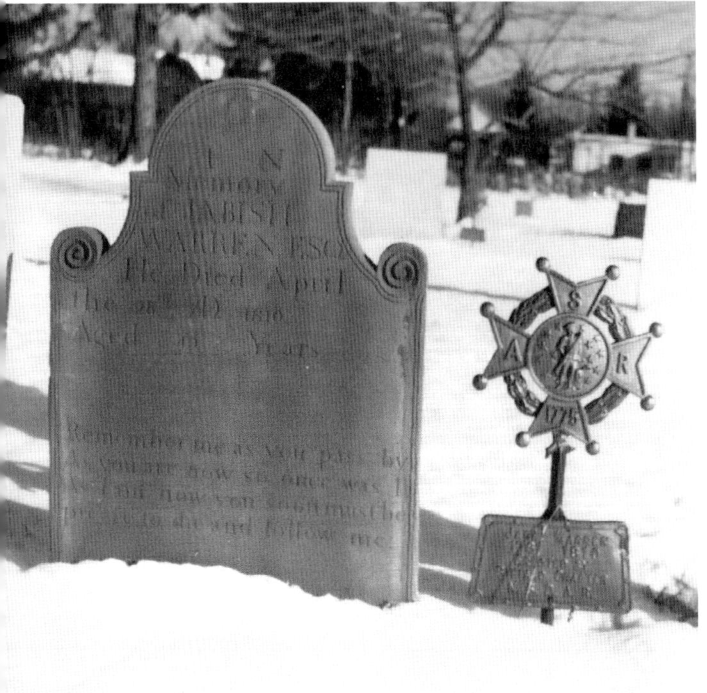

Aurora's First Settler

Revolutionary War veteran Jabez (Jabish) Warren was the first settler in what is today the town of Aurora. He first saw the area, on the banks of Cazenovia Creek, while helping Joseph Ellicott lay out the Middle Road (today's Route 20A) for the Holland Land Company. That effort, in 1803, is highlighted on a historical marker erected in 1976. It is currently located outside the nursing home on Main Street (pictured below). Warren's gravestone (at left) is one of the most interesting in Pioneer Cemetery, on account of the verse, which was common on gravestones of the period: "Remember me as you pass by. / As you are now so once was I / As I am now you soon must be, / prepare to die and follow me."

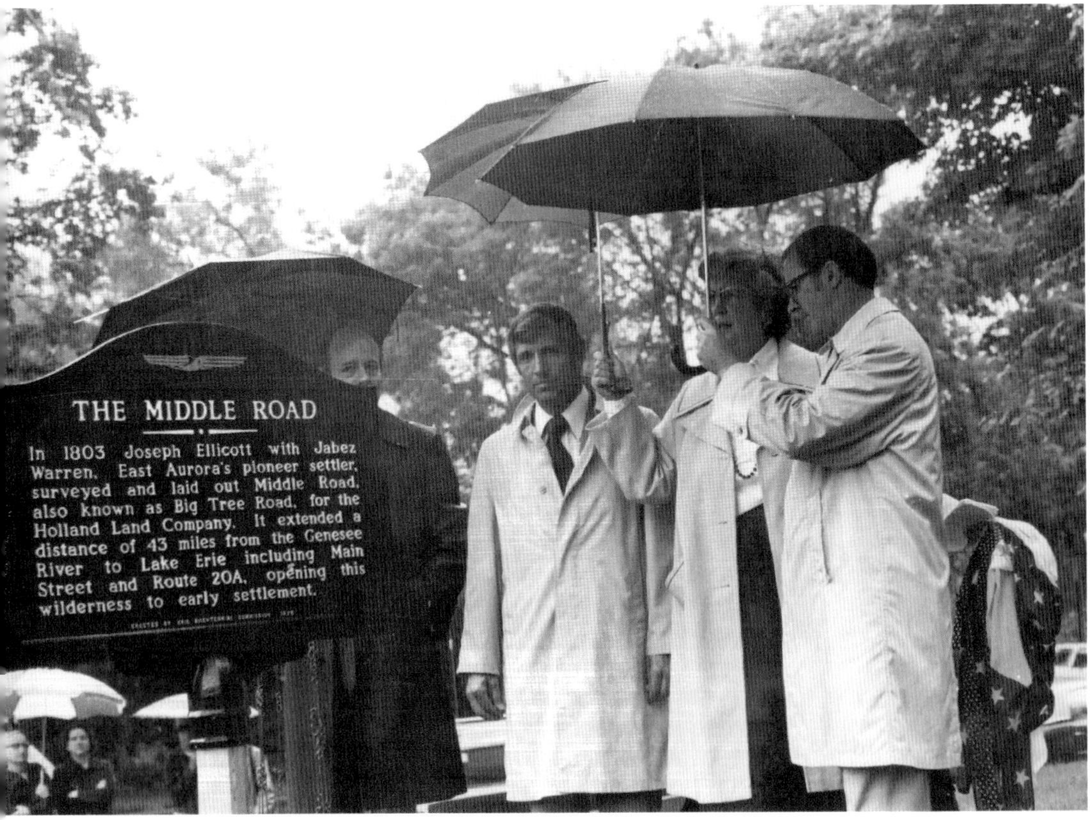

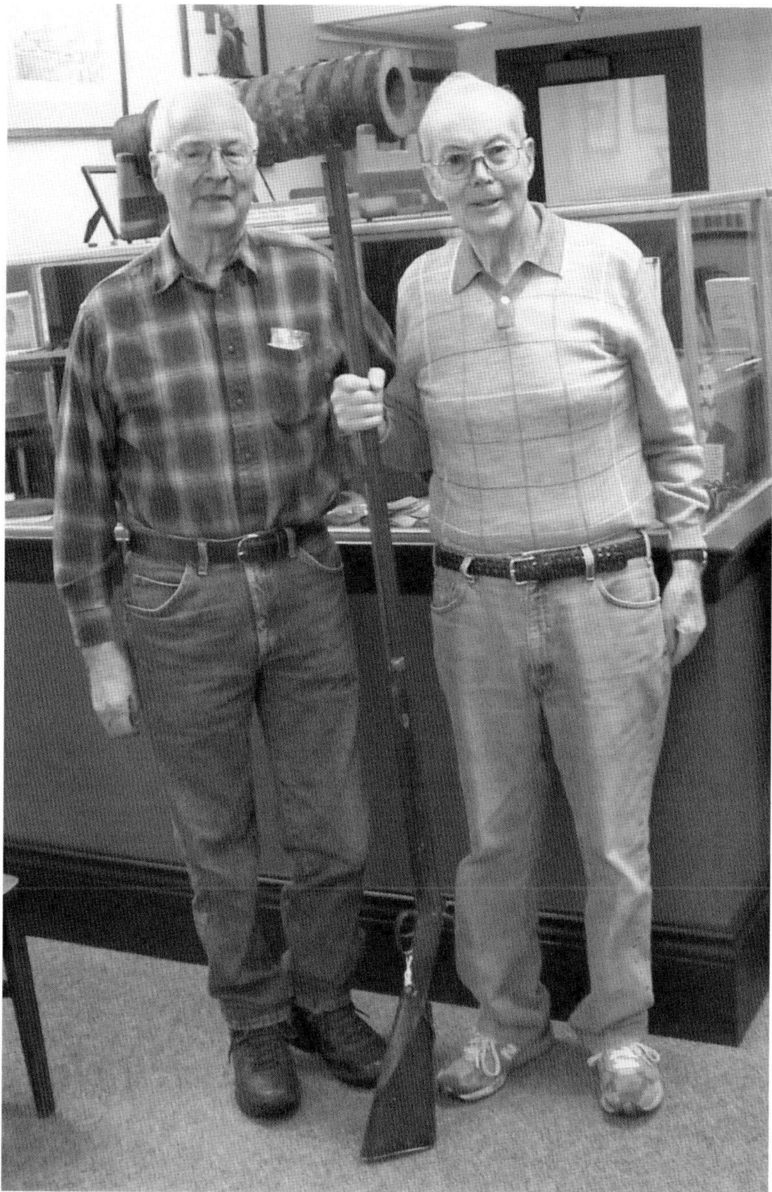

The Revolutionary Joel Adams
Brothers Ed and Bill Adams, members of the sixth generation of their family to live in the town of Aurora, display the musket that belonged to their ancestor Joel Adams. After serving in the Revolutionary War, Joel Adams and his sons settled in the town of Aurora. They were among a handful of men to purchase land in 1804. Before winter arrived, most of the men returned to New England and brought their families back with them the following spring. Joel and his sons, however, stayed in Aurora before traveling back to New England to get their families. That gives them the distinction of being the first settlers to spend a winter in Aurora. The Adams Pioneer Farm on Olean Road has remained in the family for more than 200 years. Joel and Lydia Adams, as well as other early members of the clan, are buried in Pioneer Cemetery, south of the Aurora Theatre. Joel Adams's musket is on exhibit in the Aurora History Museum. (Photograph by the author.)

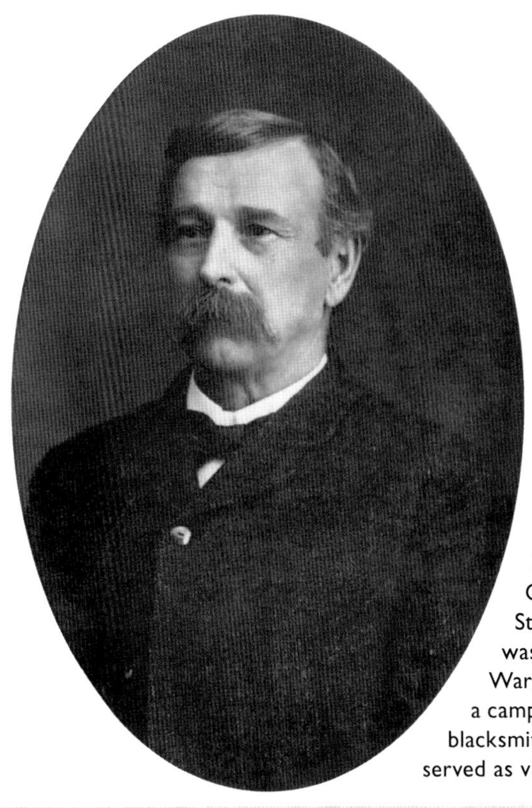

The Last Man

George A. Edwards was accustomed to being last. He was East Aurora's last surviving Civil War veteran when he died just days before Memorial Day in May 1942. He was also the last postmaster of the Willink Post Office (pictured below) at the west end of Main Street before it consolidated with the East Aurora Post Office on the east end in 1913. Born on Hamburg Street in East Aurora on April 12, 1844, Edwards was only a teenager when he enlisted in the Civil War; he was assigned to oversee prisoners of war at a camp near Elmira, New York. Though he trained as a blacksmith, he opened a mercantile after the war. He also served as village mayor for three years, from 1904 to 1907.

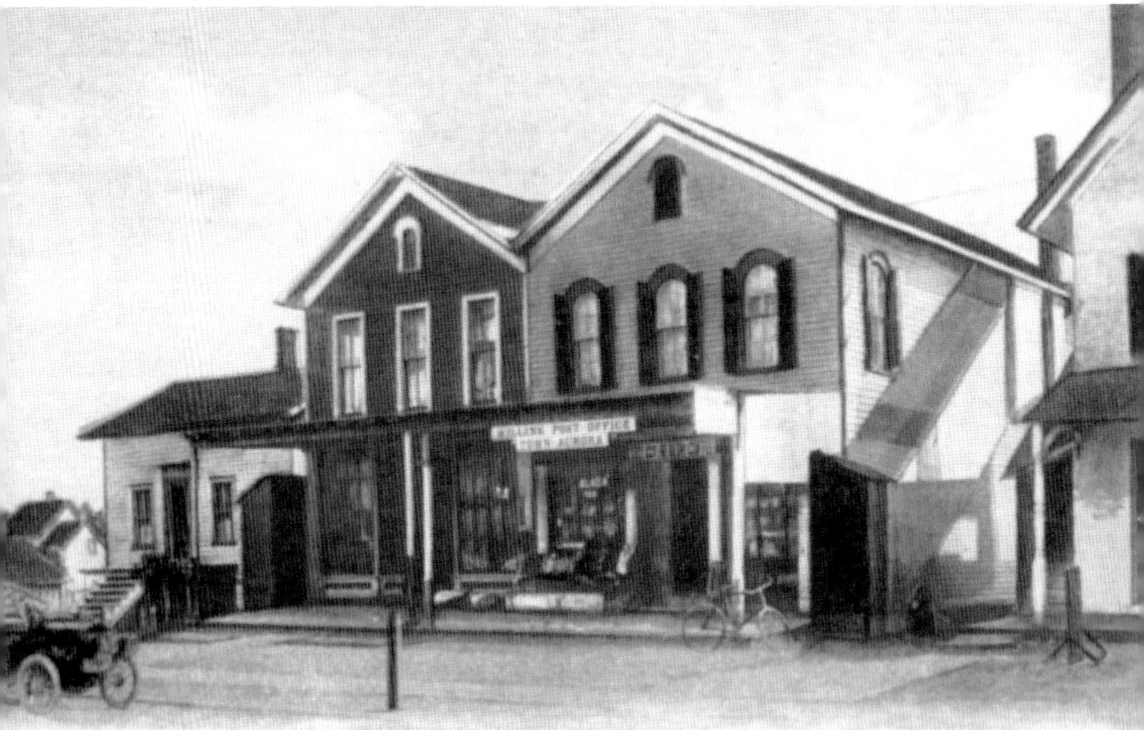

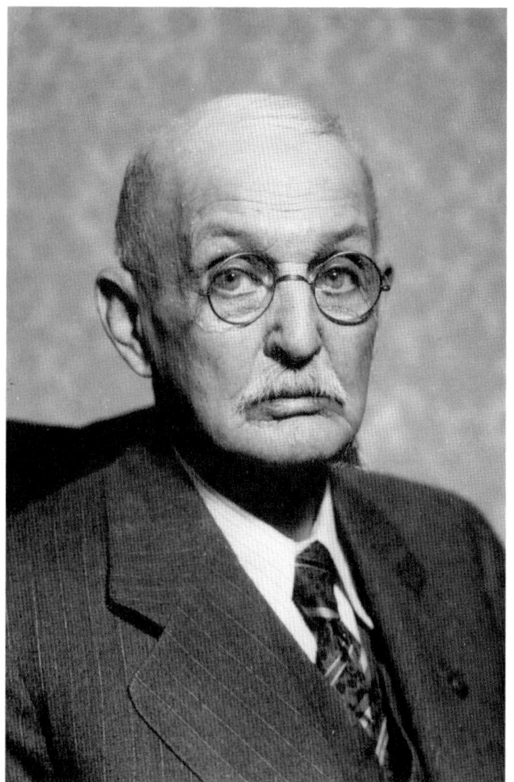

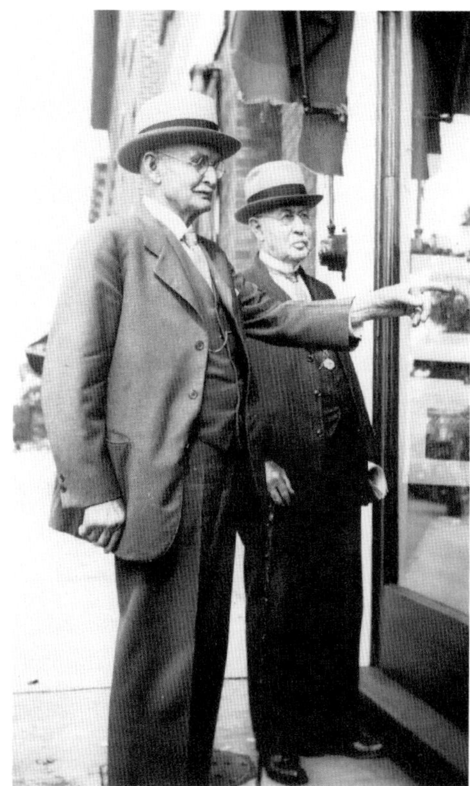

Lincoln's Messenger

In the early days of the Civil War, 16-year-old Joseph C. Kent left home in the middle of the night and trudged to Buffalo to enlist. He was soon transferred to Washington, where he met President Lincoln, who came to the barracks to find a dispatch carrier. The job entailed several trips each week over 80 miles of countryside to the battlefront. Kent later related to a newspaper reporter: "It was in my early days as dispatch rider that we—'Jim,' my horse, and I— discovered Confederates all about us. We made a dive for a gulch where the thicket was dense. For nearly a week, we remained hidden. At night we made our way to a brook for water. Our food was exhausted. It seemed as though the end was near for us two, when the enemy moved." Known later in life as "Uncle Joe," Kent, pictured on the right (pointing) on Main Street with fellow Civil War veteran John Buffum, died in December 1937 at his home on North Grove Street.

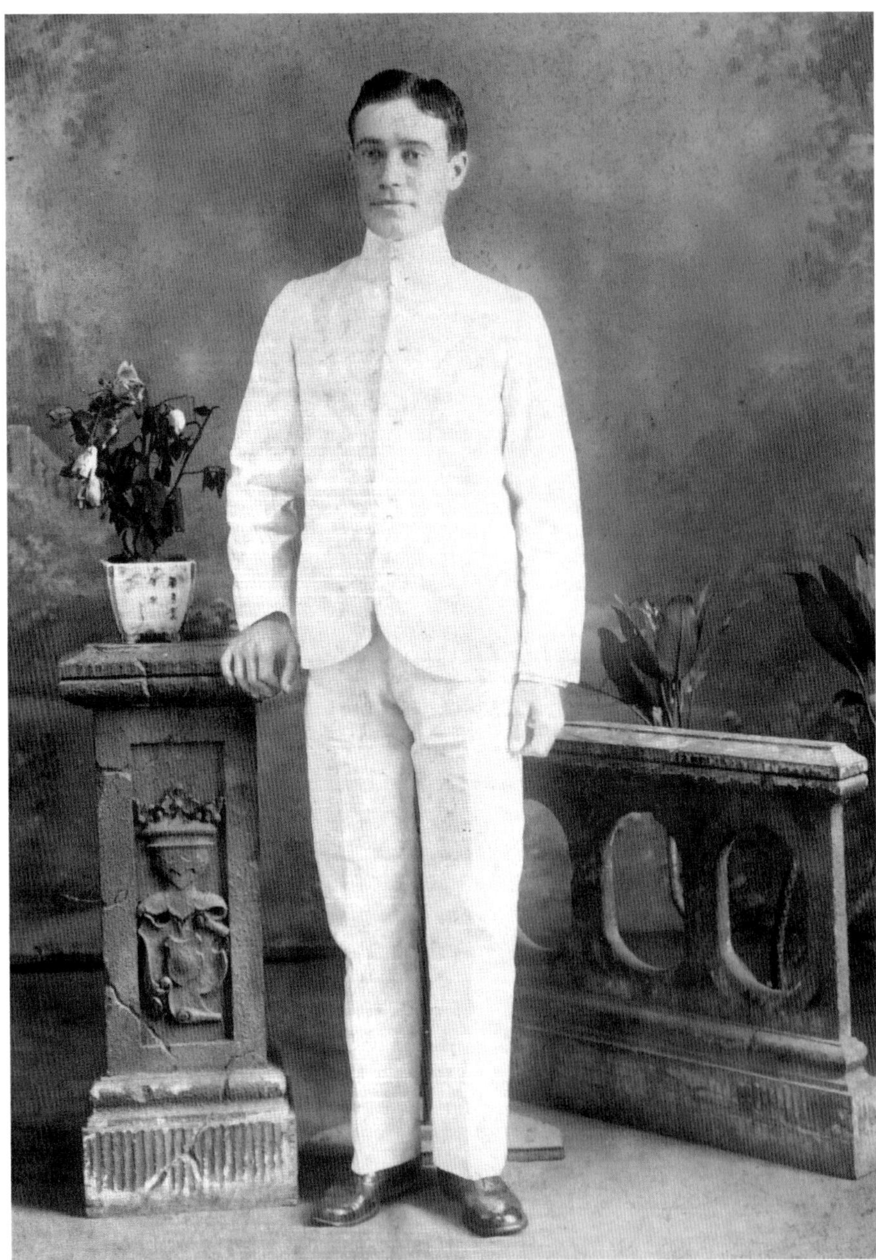

Dutiful Letter Writer

Alonzo Parker, pictured in about 1901, dutifully wrote letters home to his aunt and uncle while serving in the Philippines and China during the Spanish-American War. Parker's mother died shortly after he was born in East Aurora on January 20, 1878. After his father moved to Nebraska, he and his brother were adopted by his aunt and uncle, Augusta and Edward Pratt of East Aurora. Parker enlisted in the Army on December 7, 1898. His letters home, which were kept by his adoptive parents and passed down through the family, were later compiled into a book by family member Carolyn H. Weber. Parker stayed in the Philippines, where he married and raised his family. He never returned to the United States and died in 1936.

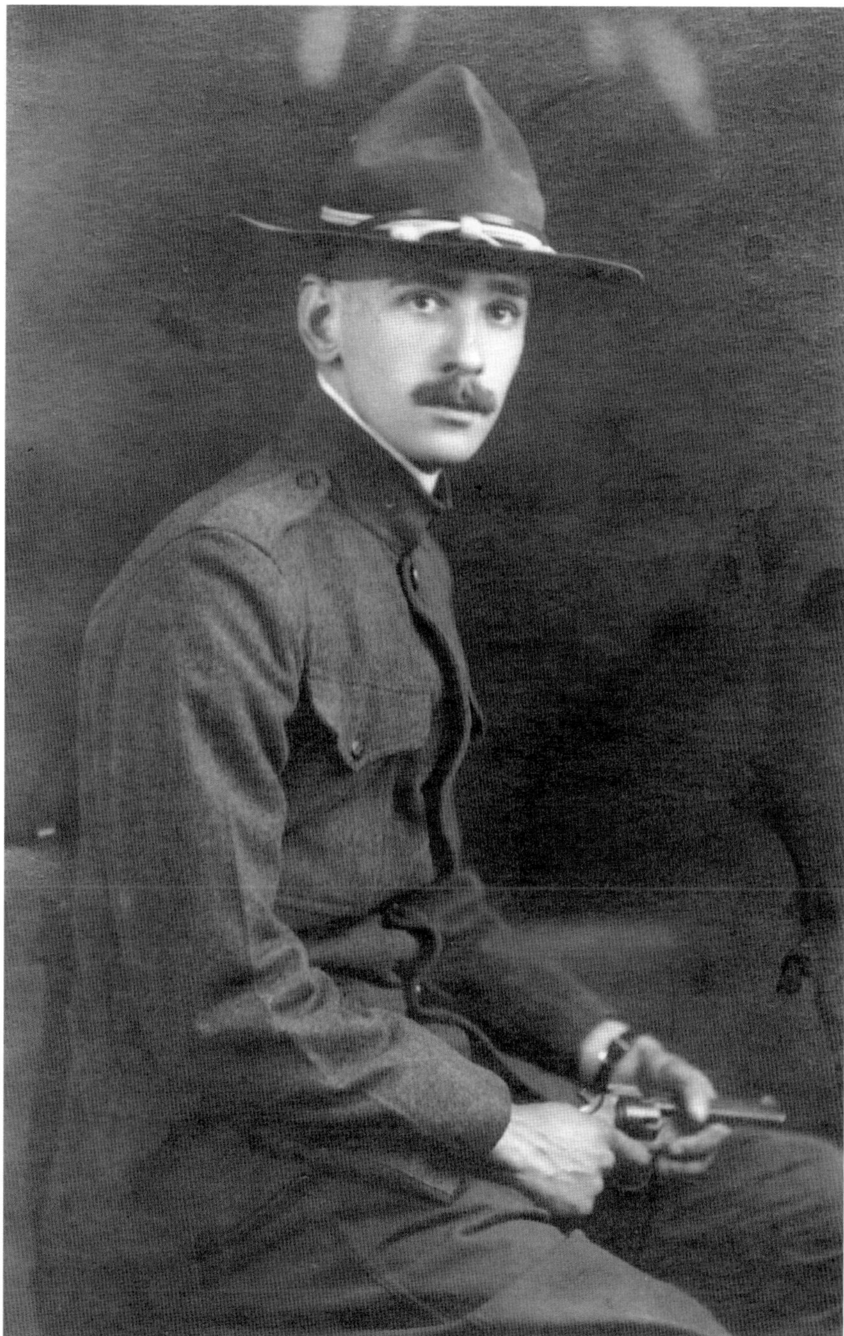

World War I Mechanic

Sanford C. Peek was a sergeant first class in the Motor Transport Corps during World War I. He was responsible for keeping vehicles running at Fort Riley, Kansas, throughout the war. He returned to East Aurora, where skills he learned during the war no doubt helped him when he and his brothers took over operations of the family business, S.H. Peek and Sons lumber mill at King Street and Oakwood Avenue. Sanford Peek kept it running until 1958. He died in 1984 at the age of 92.

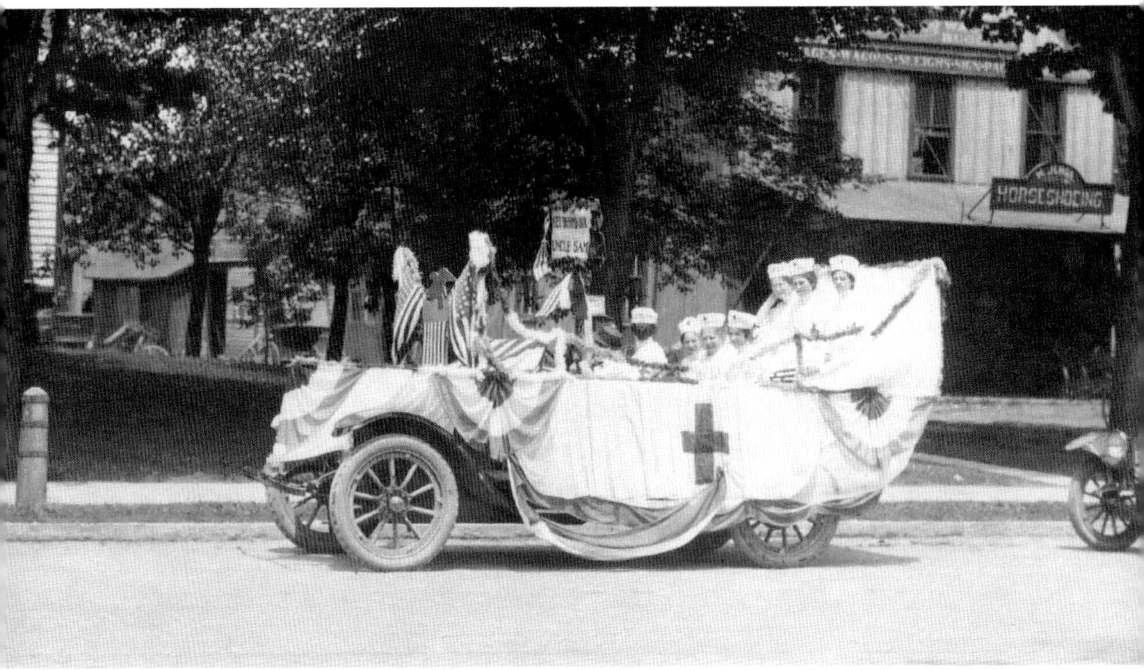

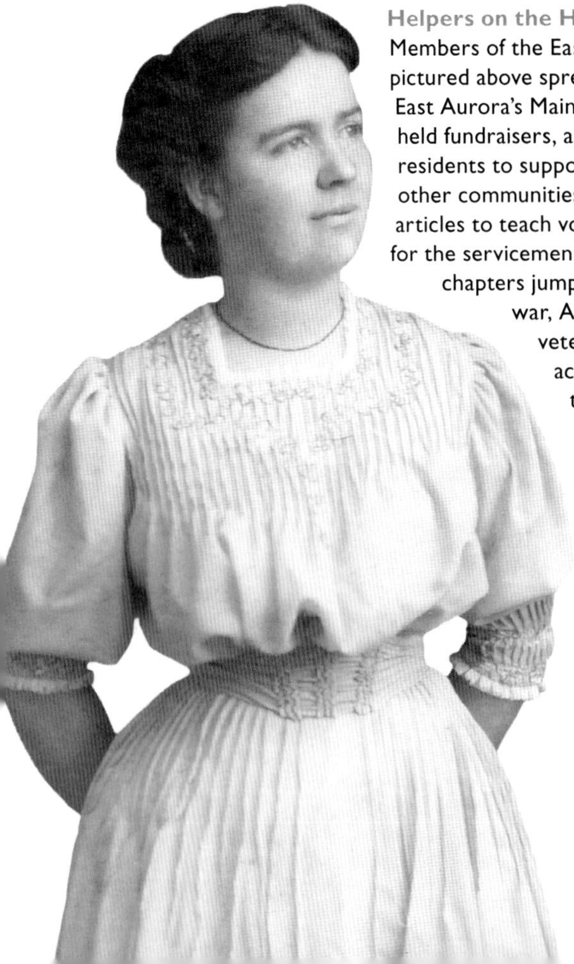

Helpers on the Home Front

Members of the East Aurora chapter of the American Red Cross, pictured above spreading their message during a parade down East Aurora's Main Street, recruited nurses to staff hospitals, held fundraisers, aided returning soldiers, and encouraged local residents to support the World War I effort. In East Aurora and other communities, they held special classes and wrote newspaper articles to teach volunteers how to knit sweaters, socks, and scarves for the servicemen. Nationwide, the number of local Red Cross chapters jumped from 107 in 1914 to 3,864 in 1918. After the war, American Red Cross volunteers continued to help veterans, and focused their efforts on safety training, accident prevention, and nutrition education. Some of the volunteers became victims of the war. Frances A. Little (pictured at left) died from complications of the Spanish influenza epidemic that spread to East Aurora and other area towns in the fall of 1918.

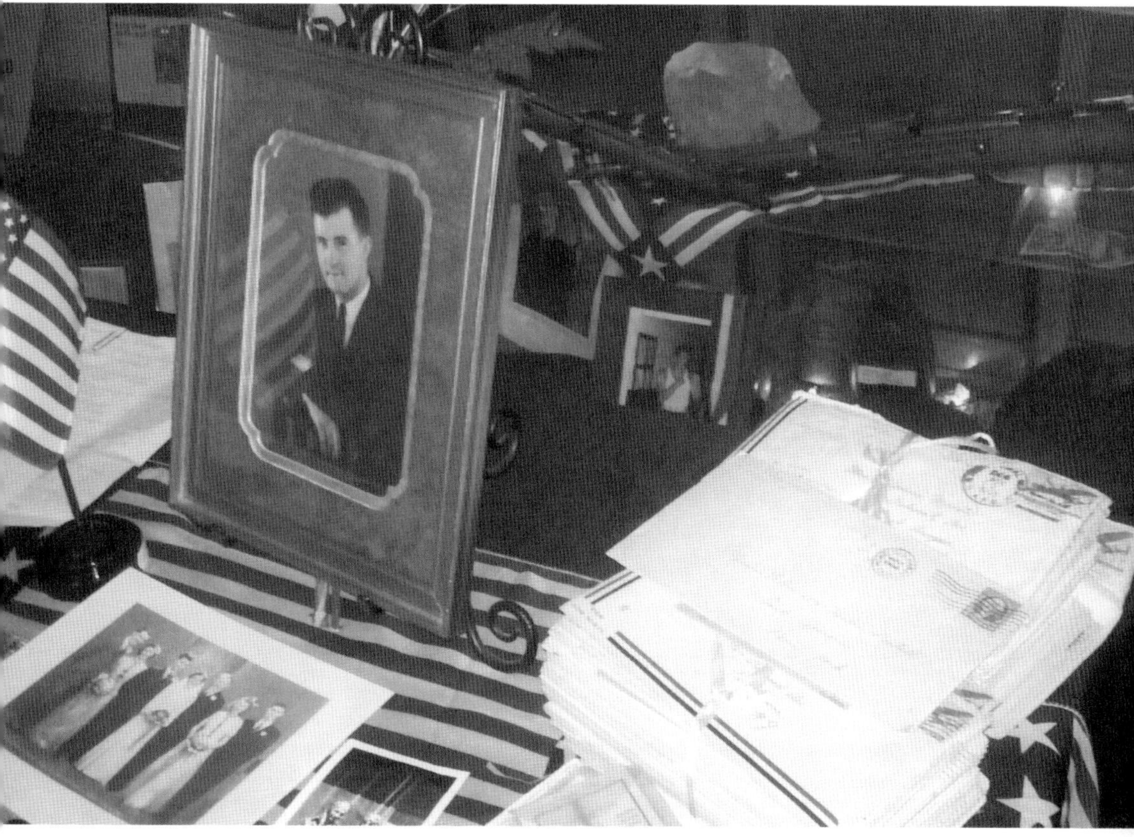

Purple Heart Hero

A stack of letters addressed to his wife and a photograph from his wedding day were among items returned to the family of Army staff sergeant Kendall L. Morrow during a ceremony on Monday, December 2, 2013, almost exactly 70 years after he was killed in action in Germany during World War II. Most of the letters were addressed to the home of his in-laws, Mr. and Mrs. Frank Nestell, at 764 Oakwood Avenue. Morrow's wife, Florence, was living with her parents while he was serving overseas. Thanks to the efforts of the Patriot Guard Riders motorcycle club, Morrow's Purple Heart, which was also found among the items in a box in a Rochester apartment complex, was also returned. Born in Canada in 1915, Morrow became a US citizen before enlisting in the Army on November 21, 1942. According to a front-page article in the *East Aurora Advertiser* on January 6, 1944, the US War Department had sent Florence Morrow a telegram just two days after Christmas informing her that her husband, a waist gunner on a Flying Fortress, had been considered Missing in Action ever since his plane went down over the ocean near Germany during a bombing raid on December 11. "Mrs. Morrow said that the telegram said that she would be notified when more information was known about her husband," the *Advertiser* reported. Morrow's body was never found, and he never had the chance to see his daughter, who was born after he went to war. (Photograph by the author.)

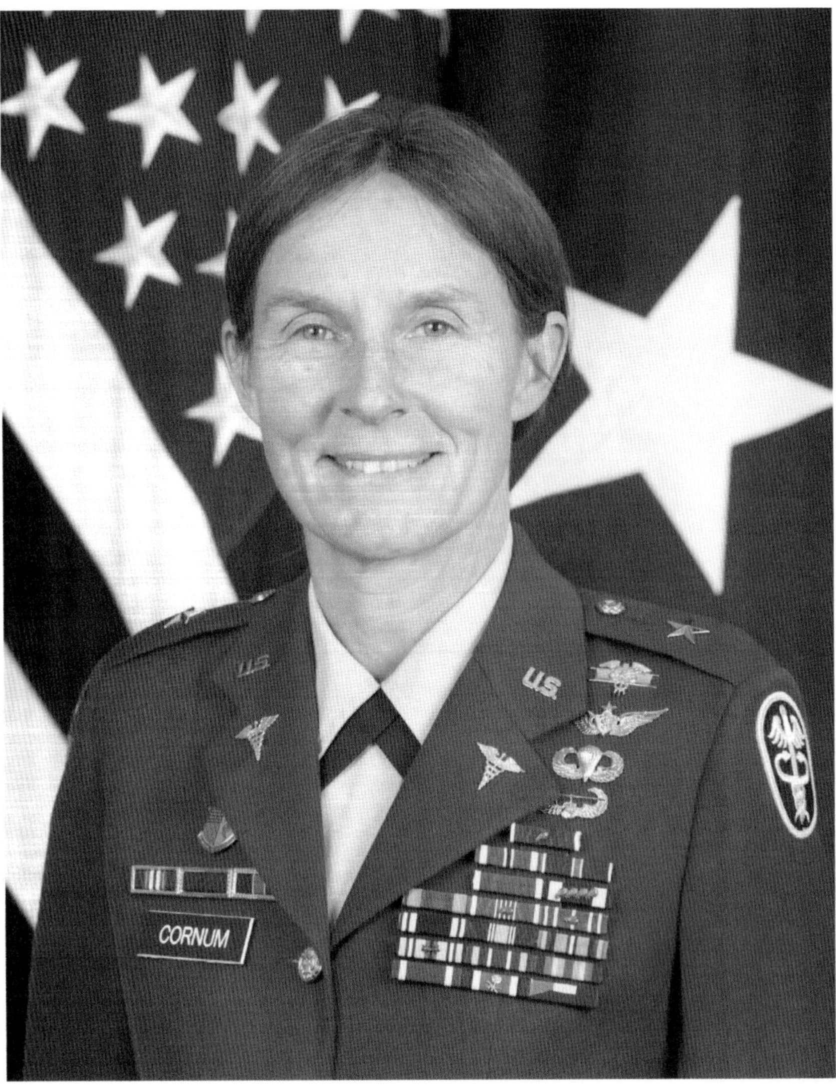

Shot Down Over Iraq

Army flight surgeon Rhonda Scott Cornum, a 1971 East Aurora High School graduate, was one of only three survivors of the eight-member Black Hawk helicopter crew that was shot down during the Persian Gulf War while attempting to recover an Air Force pilot on the morning of February 27, 1991. "We got within a kilometer of him when we were shot down by the same people that shot him down," Cornum recalled in April 1993 while speaking to students during a return visit to East Aurora High School. With two broken arms, a severely injured leg, and a gunshot wound in one of her shoulders, Cornum managed to crawl out of the wreckage only to find five Iraqi guns pointed at her. "I figured being a POW was better than being dead," she said. Cornum gained heightened attention after a photograph of her walking off a plane with both arms in casts appeared on newspaper front pages across the country following her release after eight days in captivity. She later cowrote a book about her experiences, *She Went to War: The Rhonda Cornum Story*. Cornum's experiences and later testimony during hearings led to expanded combat roles for women. After a 35-year military career, which included leading a program to help veterans deal with the effects of traumatic situations, Cornum retired in 2012 as a brigadier general. (Courtesy of the US Army.)

CHAPTER SEVEN

Mascots

This group of legendary locals cannot even talk. Horses, dogs, and even a collection of toys have become famous ambassadors for East Aurora. Traditionally, mascots are associated with sports teams, but in East Aurora they have come in many forms.

Throughout East Aurora's history, animals have added to the village's quality of life. Some have even put East Aurora on the map. Thousands came to the village in the late 1800s to see "the handsomest horse in the world" at Cicero Hamlin's Village Farm. A dog named Rex served as the mascot—and more importantly, the companion—of service members stationed on Prospect Avenue during World War I. Another canine companion drew daily attention for helping the US Post Office Department.

Even East Aurora High School's mascot is legendary. The Blue Devil has been a part of the community's culture since the 1930s. It has endured a few controversies along the way, but has survived each time and remains more popular than ever.

Each year for more than two decades, a different toy was crowned the symbol of the annual ToyFest celebration in the village. Even after the last ToyFest in 2007, the commemorative toys unveiled each year still continued to draw interest from collectors and local residents alike.

One human is part of this group. She did not attain her status as a local legend until long after her death. Vera Wood, the young daughter of a former *East Aurora Advertiser* publisher, became a mascot for the newspaper nearly a century after she was photographed as a toddler inviting East Aurorans to "read all about it."

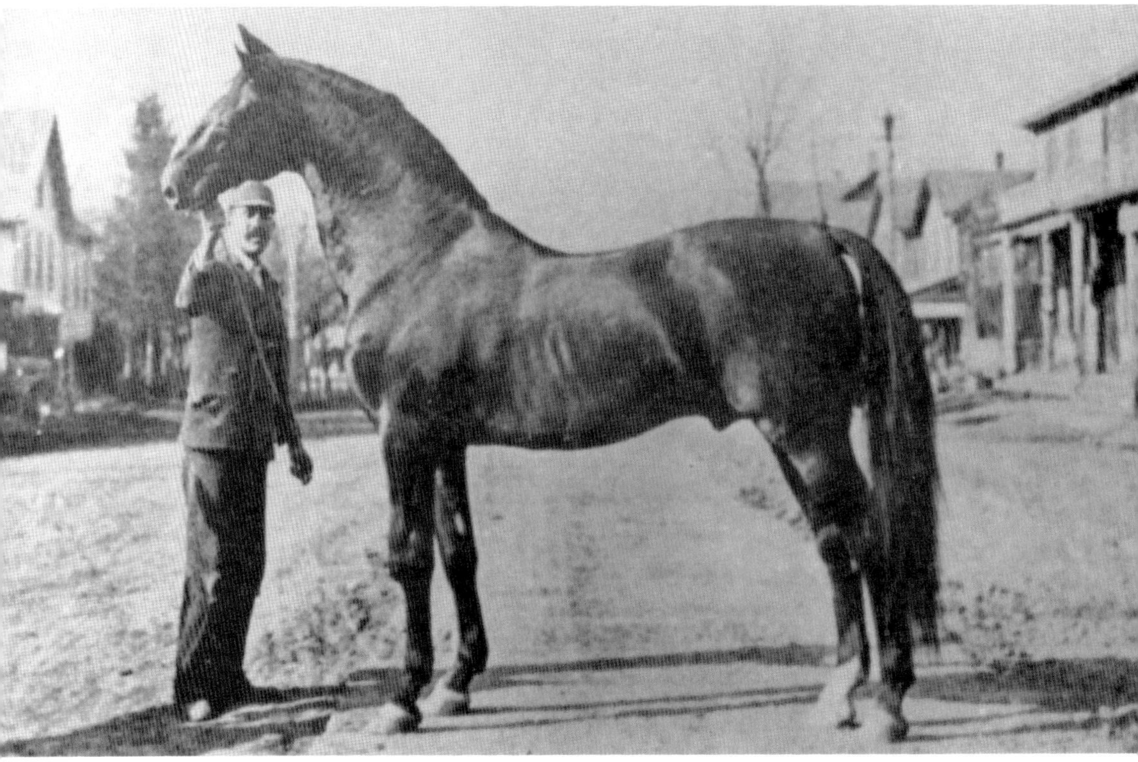

Handsomest Horse

Mambrino King was judged to be "the most handsome horse in the world" and sired many record-setting racehorses. Cicero J. Hamlin, who owned and operated the Village Farm on the north side of Main Street near the Circle, purchased Mambrino King in 1882 for $17,000. Tens of thousands of people came to East Aurora from around the world to admire the famous horse. On December 5, 1899, Hamlin ordered the 27-year-old dark chestnut horse euthanized. Mambrino King's grave is now located in a front yard at the corner of North Willow Street and Parkdale Avenue, where the Aurora Historical Society placed a marker in 1985.

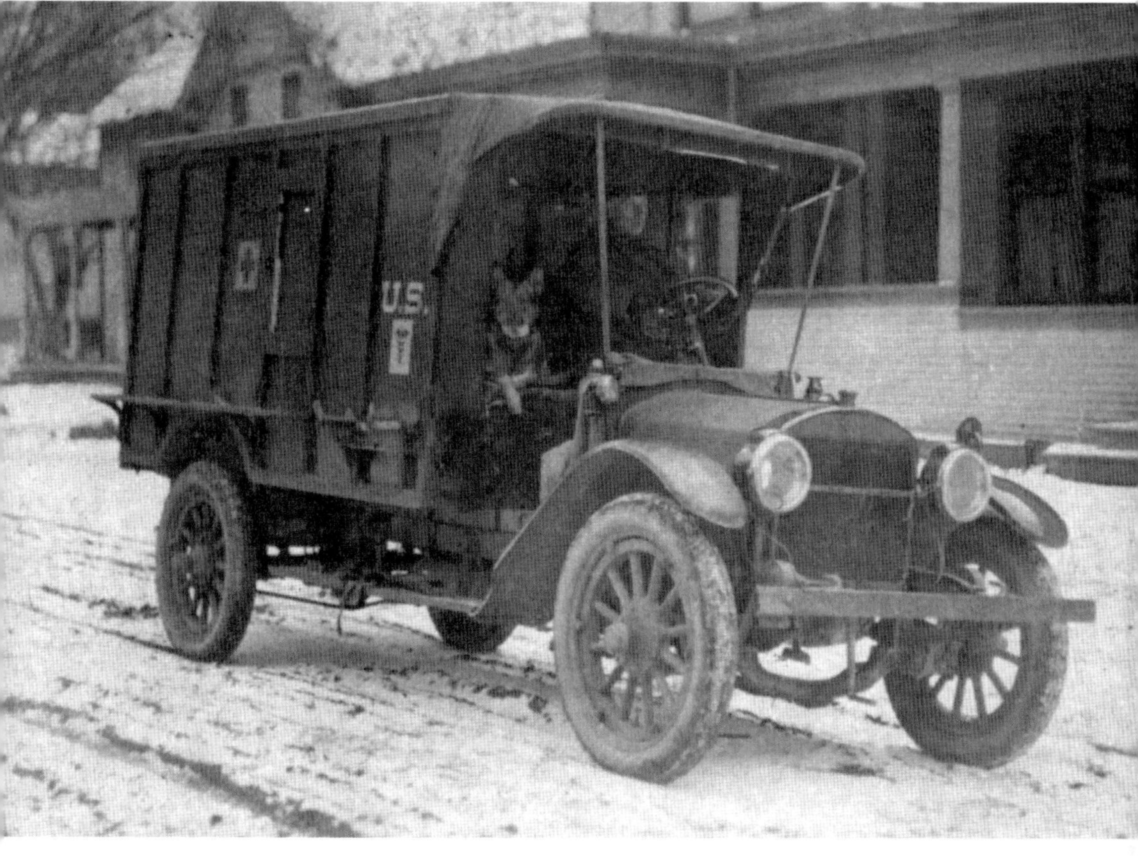

Canine Comrade

Rex, shown riding along with soldier Charles E. Simmons, was born overseas in a trench on the front lines of World War I. His mother was a Red Cross service dog in the war. He was brought to Emerson Hall on Prospect Avenue, which is now an apartment building but was used as headquarters for a local company of the home guard during the war. He kept the soldiers company during the day and spent his nights with a local family. When he first arrived in East Aurora, Rex only knew French commands, but he quickly learned English. He was afraid of thunder, fireworks, and rifles, most likely a result of his time on the front lines.

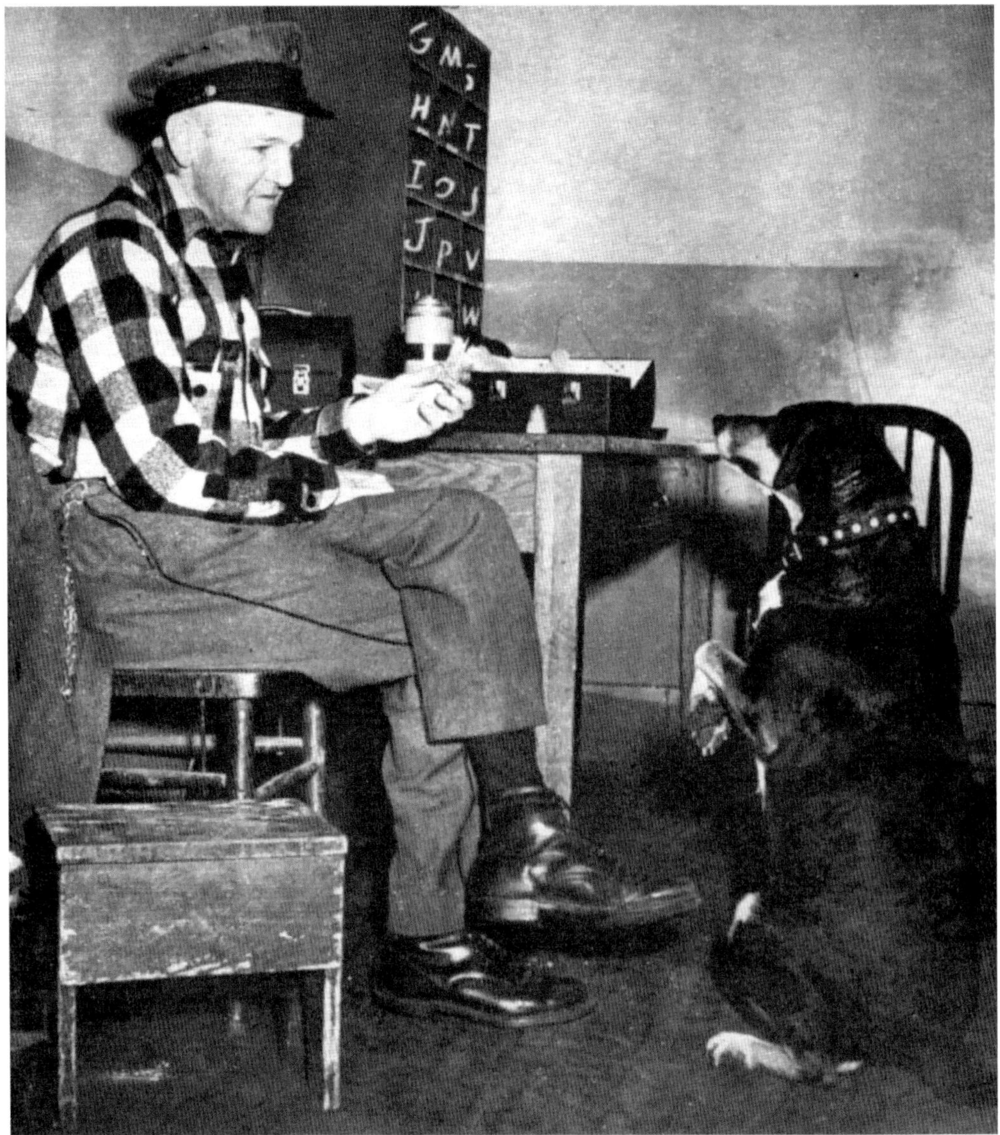

Postman's Pal

Each day for several years in the 1950s, Tipper Bell, a member of the Bennett family of Pine Street, walked with the children on their way to school. However, the beagle-shepherd always stopped at Main and Church Streets, to keep a careful eye on the post office door across the street. As soon as her favorite letter carrier, Harry Armading, pictured, appeared through the door, she enthusiastically ran across the street to begin accompanying him on his entire route. Tipper Bell never missed a day, and she never accompanied any other letter carrier. On Armading's days off, she would wait for him until after noon before giving up and walking back home.

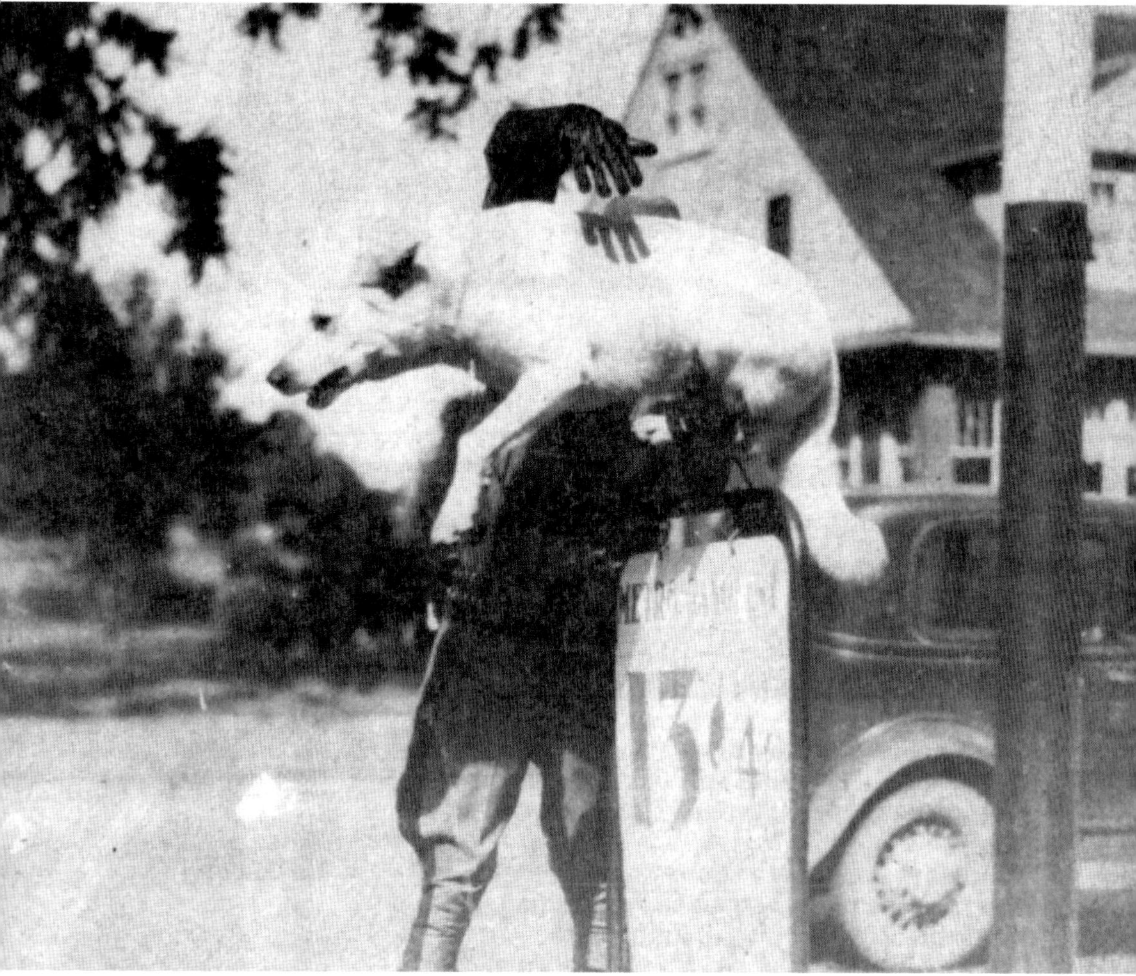

Valuable Dog

Another dog named Rex was the mascot of Russell Cotton's gas station, which was located at the corner of Knox Road and Seneca Street. According to local legend, Cotton loved his dog so much that he turned down a $400 offer to buy him. Rex, pictured demonstrating his proficiency in jumping in June 1931, could cross the Circle and bring back lunch for Cotton.

Extra, Extra!

Vera Ella Wood became the face of the *East Aurora Advertiser* when she posed with the latest edition of her father's newspaper around 1897. Walter Wood published the newspaper from 1878 to 1901. More than a century after the photograph was taken, the publishers of the modern *Advertiser* used the image in a popular promotional campaign. Subscribers were invited to put a picture of Vera in their windows for a chance to win prizes as part of the *Advertiser*'s 130th anniversary in 2002. Despite efforts by current *Advertiser* staff members to track her down, it is unknown where life took Vera after her father sold the *Advertiser* and moved from East Aurora. (Courtesy of the *East Aurora Advertiser*.)

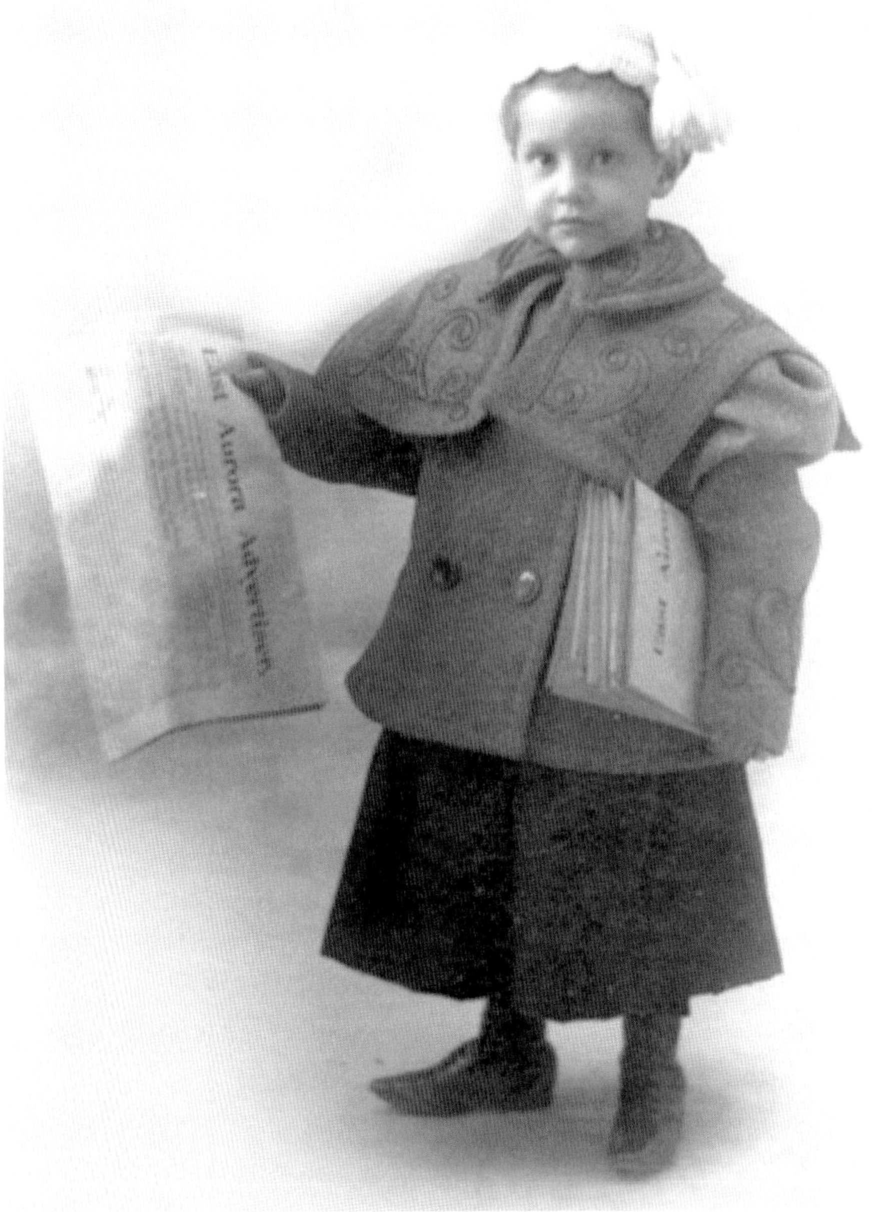

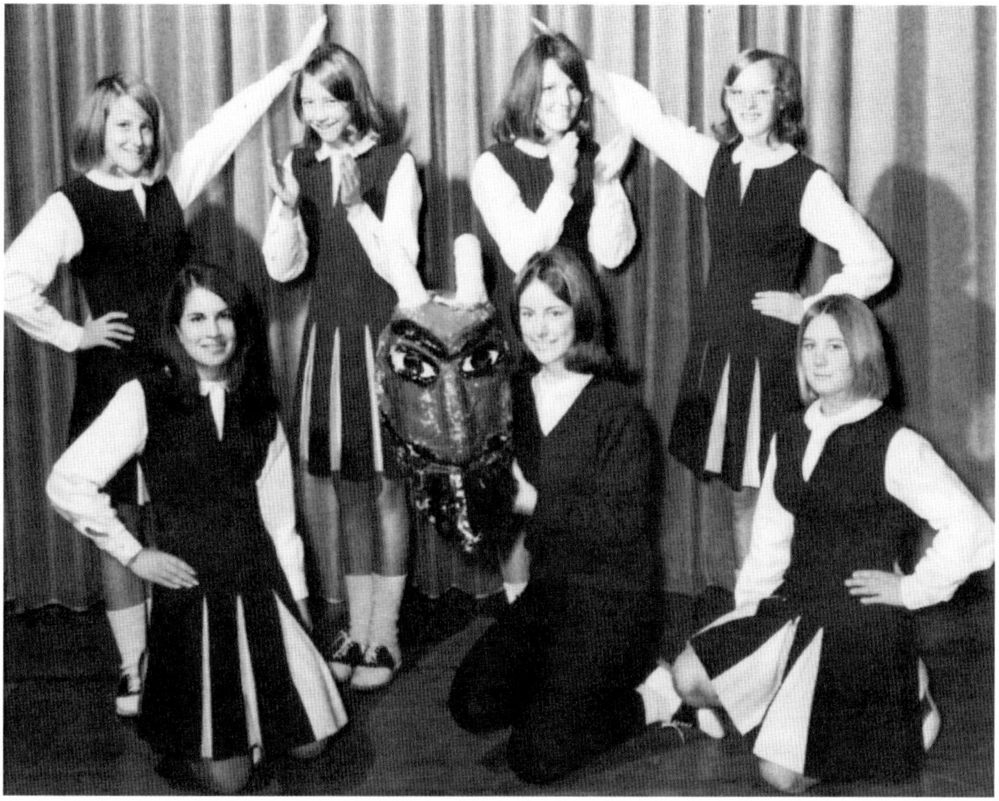

The Blue Devil

East Aurora High School's mascot, the Blue Devil, made its debut in December 1934, when the members of the boys' basketball team ran out on the court with, according to the *East Aurora Advertiser*, "a devil's head sewn onto each sweatshirt and the words 'The Blue Devils' sewn onto the jerseys." The Blue Devil has been the official mascot ever since. Above, posing with the Blue Devil for the 1968 yearbook are, from left to right, (first row) Debby Seeber, Diane Gressman, and Ann Thayer; (second row) Kyle Power, Laurie Elder, Tina Bailey, and Kim Sand. The mascot has not been without controversy, however. At one point, a local minister led a small movement to retire the mascot, but it was determined that the Blue Devil is not based on any religious context. Like Duke University's mascot, East Aurora's Blue Devil likely traces its roots to a mentally and physically strong French military unit during World War I. Known as the Blue Devils, they were distinguished by their royal blue uniforms, flowing capes, and berets. (Below, photograph by the author.)

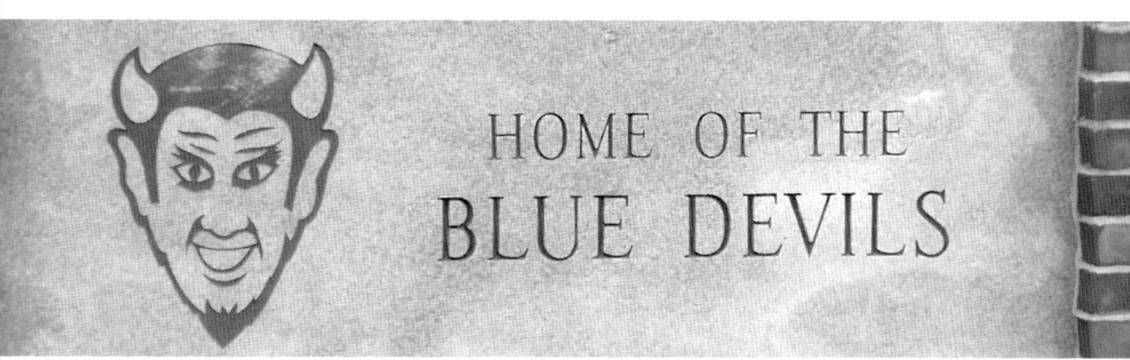

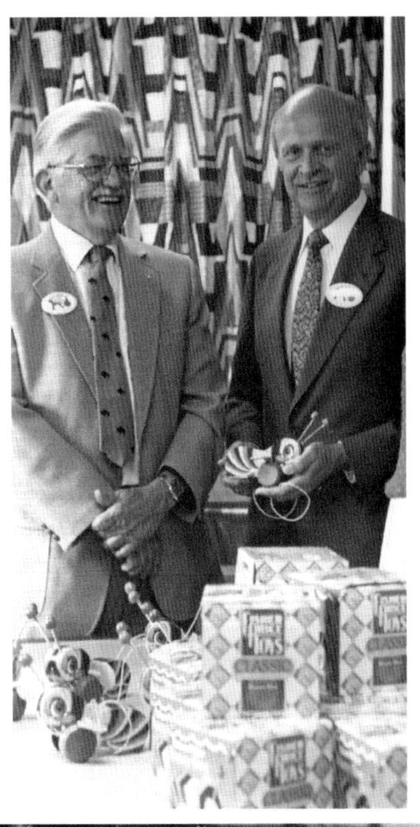

The ToyFest Toys

These local legends include a handful of dogs, two trains, two bears, and two cows. A frog and an elephant are in the group, too. For more than 20 years, from 1987 to 2009, the ToyTown Foundation released a commemorative toy that also served as the mascot for the annual ToyFest, a festival that drew thousands to East Aurora during the last weekend of August. Most of the toys were recreations of earlier Fisher-Price toys, but there were a few exceptions. Even after ToyFest was called off, commemorative toys were issued in 2008 and 2009. Facing challenges, the ToyTown Foundation, which operated the Toy Town Museum on the Fisher-Price campus, dissolved in 2010. Pictured at left unveiling the first ToyFest toy, Buzzy Bee, in 1987 are then chamber of commerce president Jack Waterhouse (left) and Bruce Inglis, Fisher-Price plant manager. Below, Fisher-Price employees put the final touches on Buzzy Bees.

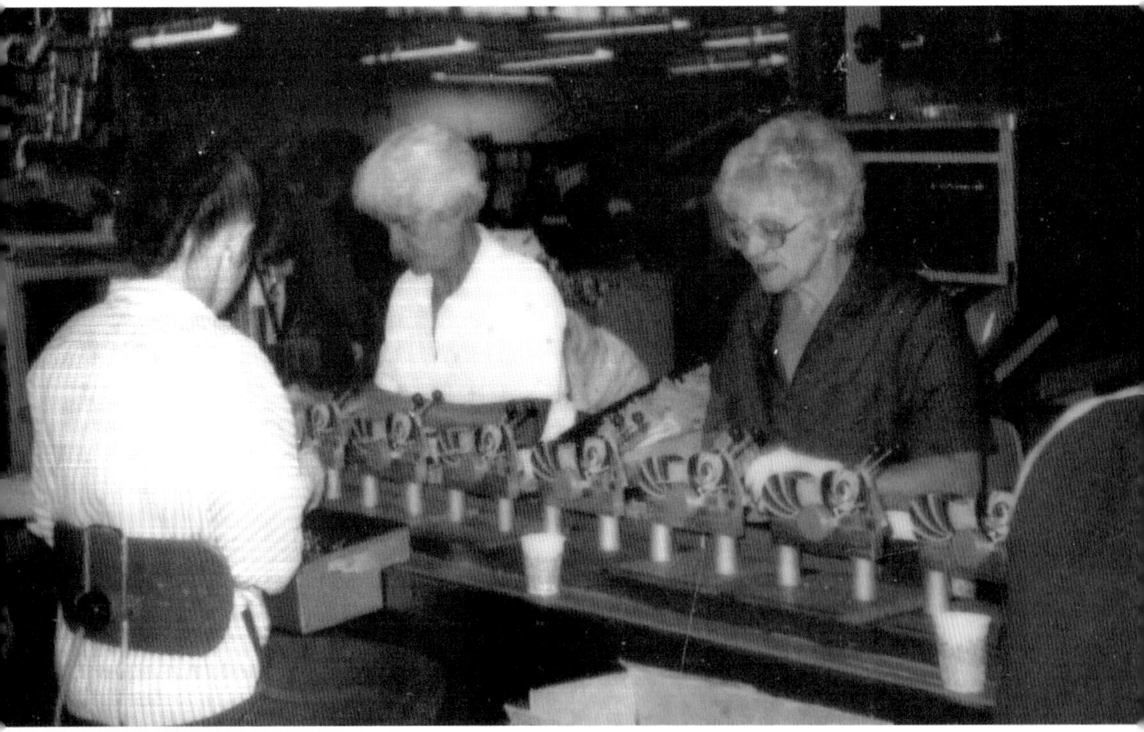

CHAPTER EIGHT

The People in the Neighborhood

East Aurora is home to many people who never set out to be legendary, but through a unique talent, vocation, or hobby have become an integral patch in the community quilt. These folks most likely will never be featured in the more traditional history books. After all, they are not business owners or government officials. They are, however, just as important—if not more important—to the community's story.

Throughout history, the people in the neighborhood have often been the pulse of the village. Due to their unique vantage points, they have often been the best ones to turn to when it is time to find out what is going on. They have been out and about and have been the eyes and ears of the village.

In an age when hundreds commuted by train to Buffalo, the ticket clerk at the East Aurora railroad depot probably knew more people—and more news—than anyone else in town. At one point or another, everyone must have seen Arthur Dorshide, who cleared the sidewalks of the village with his unique horse-drawn plow in the 1950s.

Today, anyone who has ever walked down Main Street would recognize Nelson Welch, who has spent years shoveling the sidewalks, and Daniel Wurzer, who has changed the letters on the marquee at the Aurora Theatre for nearly three decades. Nearly every resident was familiar with Peter Andersen, who spent hours walking around the village, but many did not know that his walks led to well-researched and detailed surveys of the community's architecture.

The people in the neighborhood are among the countless locals who have given East Aurora its hometown energy. Perhaps that is also why they are the most difficult to place into categories. They are legendary for simply being themselves and sharing their unique talents with the community.

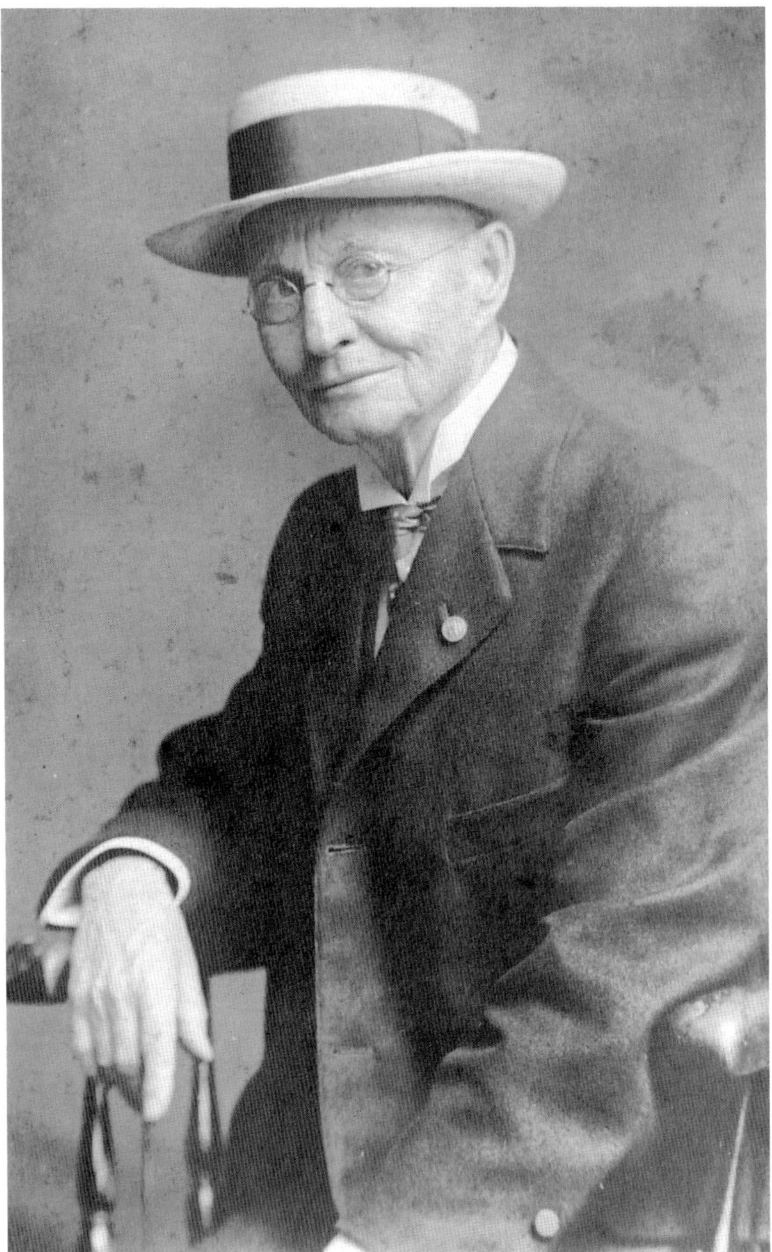

The Colonel

Arthur Avery, or "Colonel" as he was known by locals, was born in Rome, New York, in 1841, and served in the Civil War before entering the railroad business in 1879. He had worked his way up through the ranks of the Western New York & Pennsylvania Railroad and eventually became the chief clerk to the railroad's purchasing agent. When the rail line was taken over by the Pennsylvania Railroad in 1900, the main office—and Avery's job—were transferred to Philadelphia. Instead of moving, he finished his career as the railroad ticket clerk in East Aurora, where he was also active with veterans groups, the board of trade, and the Masonic temple. In 1909, he became the oldest employee named to the Pennsylvania Railroad's Roll of Honor.

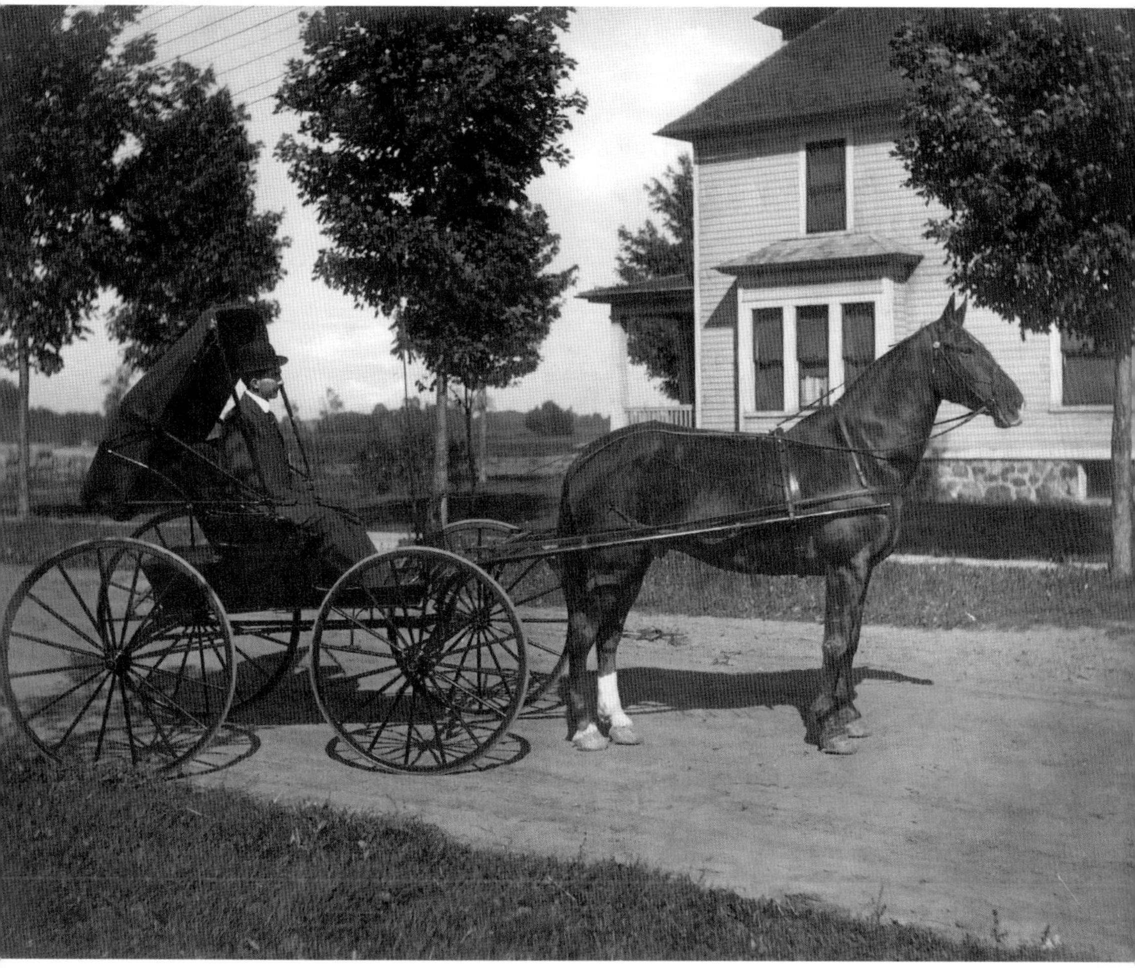

The Country Doctor
Dr. Floyd Richardson made house calls throughout the East Aurora area with his horse named Cancer. A graduate of East Aurora High School and the University of Buffalo Medical School, Richardson practiced medicine in East Aurora for the half century between 1904 and 1954. He was born on his family homestead in South Wales in 1882 and died in 1954.

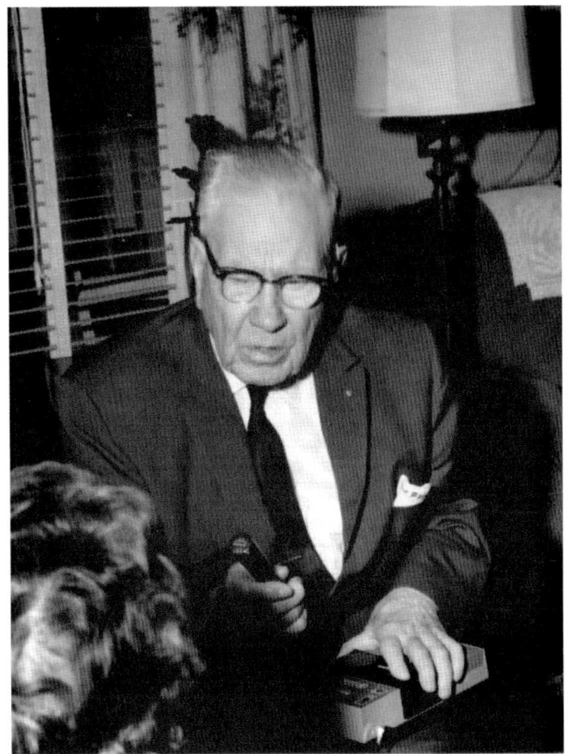

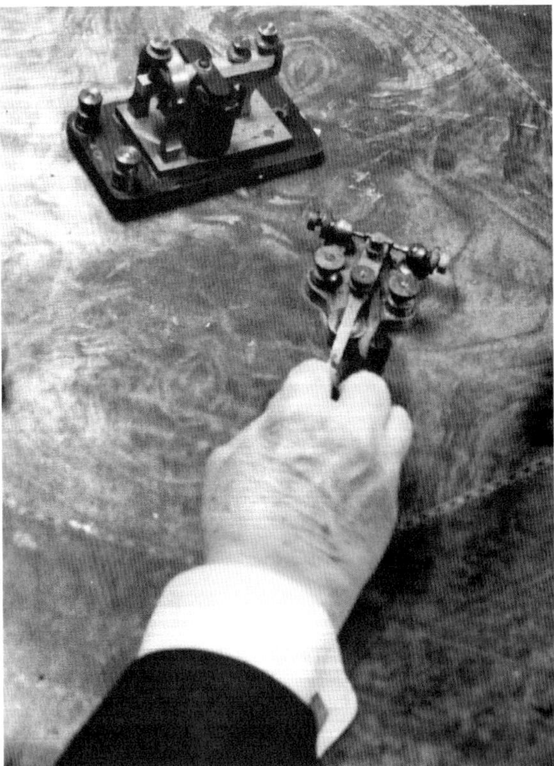

Two Careers, One Lifetime

For most of his life, Rile Prosser enjoyed two careers. He was a successful newspaper reporter/photographer and, after learning Morse code in his spare time as a teenager, he worked for the railroad as a telegrapher. The two careers worked hand-in-hand. When a big news story broke, he would telegraph his own dispatches to the major city newspapers from his headquarters in northern Pennsylvania. The railroad transferred Prosser to East Aurora in 1921, where he continued to work as a telegrapher and freelance journalist. He retired from the railroad on his 60th birthday in 1945, but took over as the full-time editor of the *East Aurora Advertiser* the very next day. Even after he officially retired from the newspaper in the mid-1960s, he continued working as a freelance writer and photographer well into his 80s and maintained an interest in the telegraph as a hobby. "If you're not active, you're done," Prosser said. He died in 1979 at the age of 94.

Winter Team

Before the advent of the village's motorized sidewalk plow, Arthur Dorshide and his horse-drawn plow kept the sidewalks of the community clear in the early 1950s. "He will be remembered for being out in all kinds of weather during the winters," Dorshide's obituary noted following his death January 10, 1957, from injuries he suffered when he was hit by a car while crossing Main Street on Christmas Eve. His wife, Laura, died Christmas Day in the same hospital after suffering a heart attack.

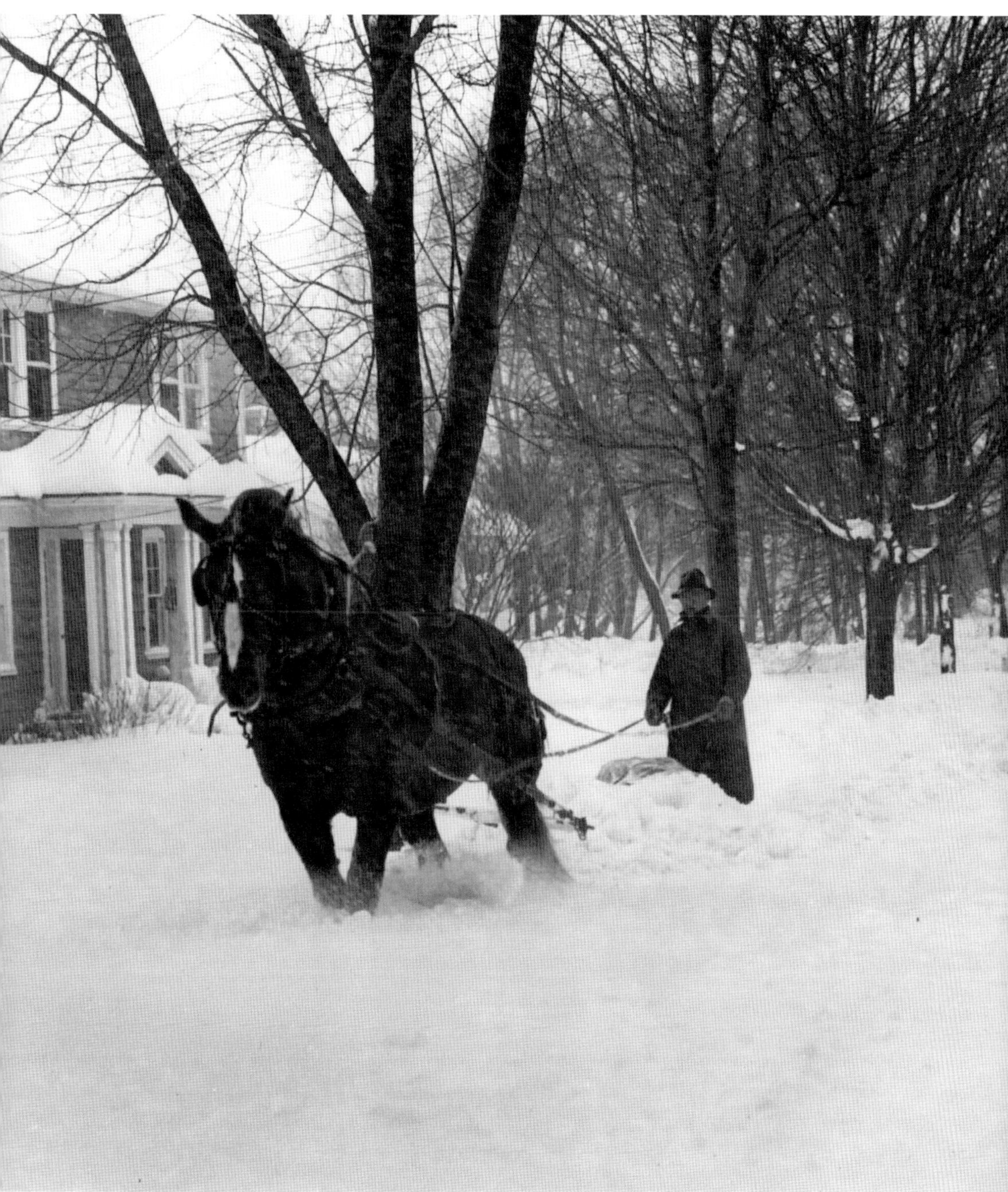

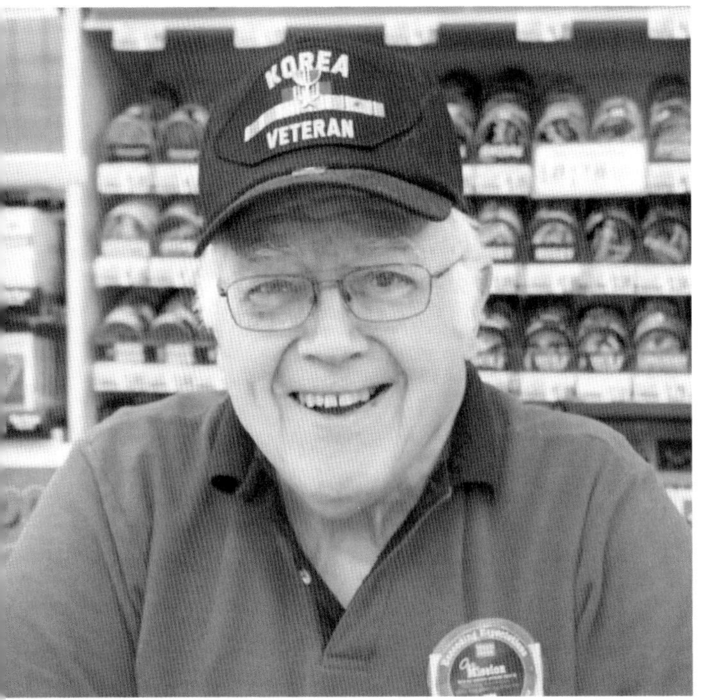

Christmas Caroler

Korean War veteran Billie Lucas volunteered many hours with civic causes, but he was probably best known around town for the one hour he spent each year leading more than 2,000 singers in Christmas carols in the middle of Main Street. Lucas, who was also a past president of Aurora Players and a member of American Legion Post No. 362, served as master of ceremonies of East Aurora's locally famous holiday tradition, Carolcade, for more than three decades before turning the job over to town historian Robert Lowell Goller in 2005. Lucas died on May 16, 2010, at the age of 81. (Left, courtesy of the *East Aurora Advertiser.*)

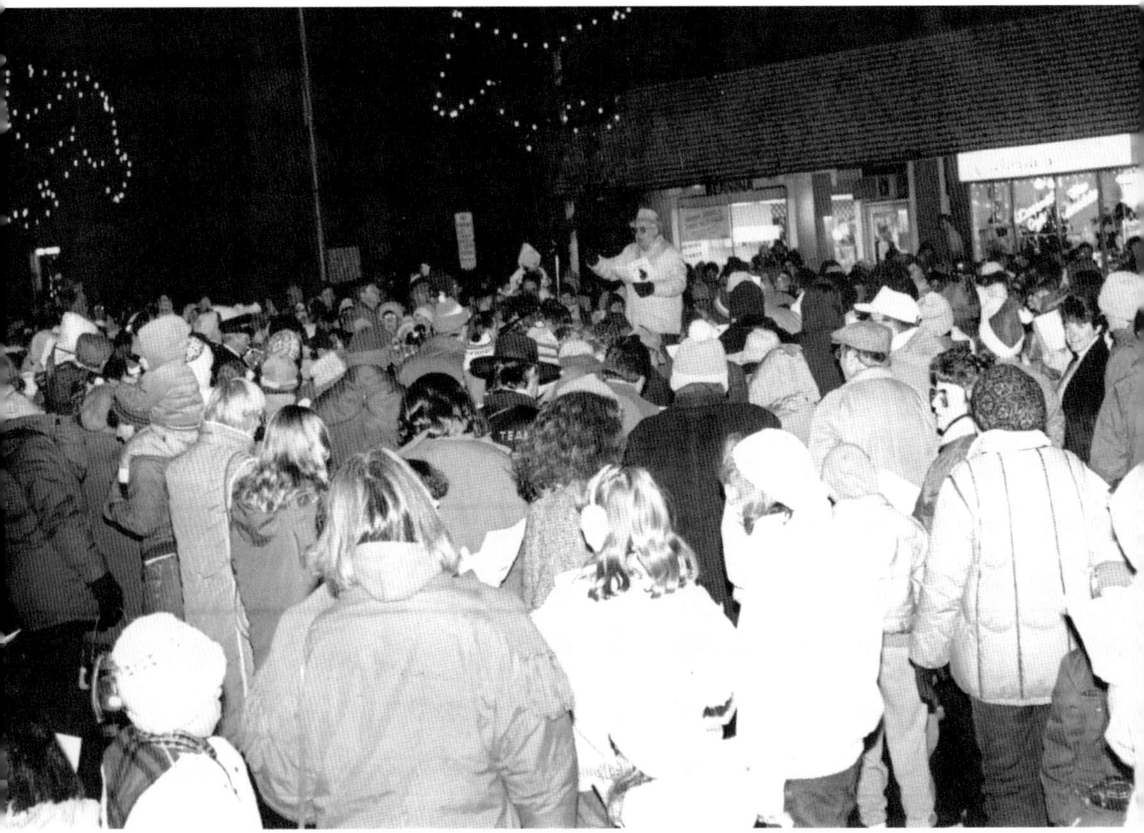

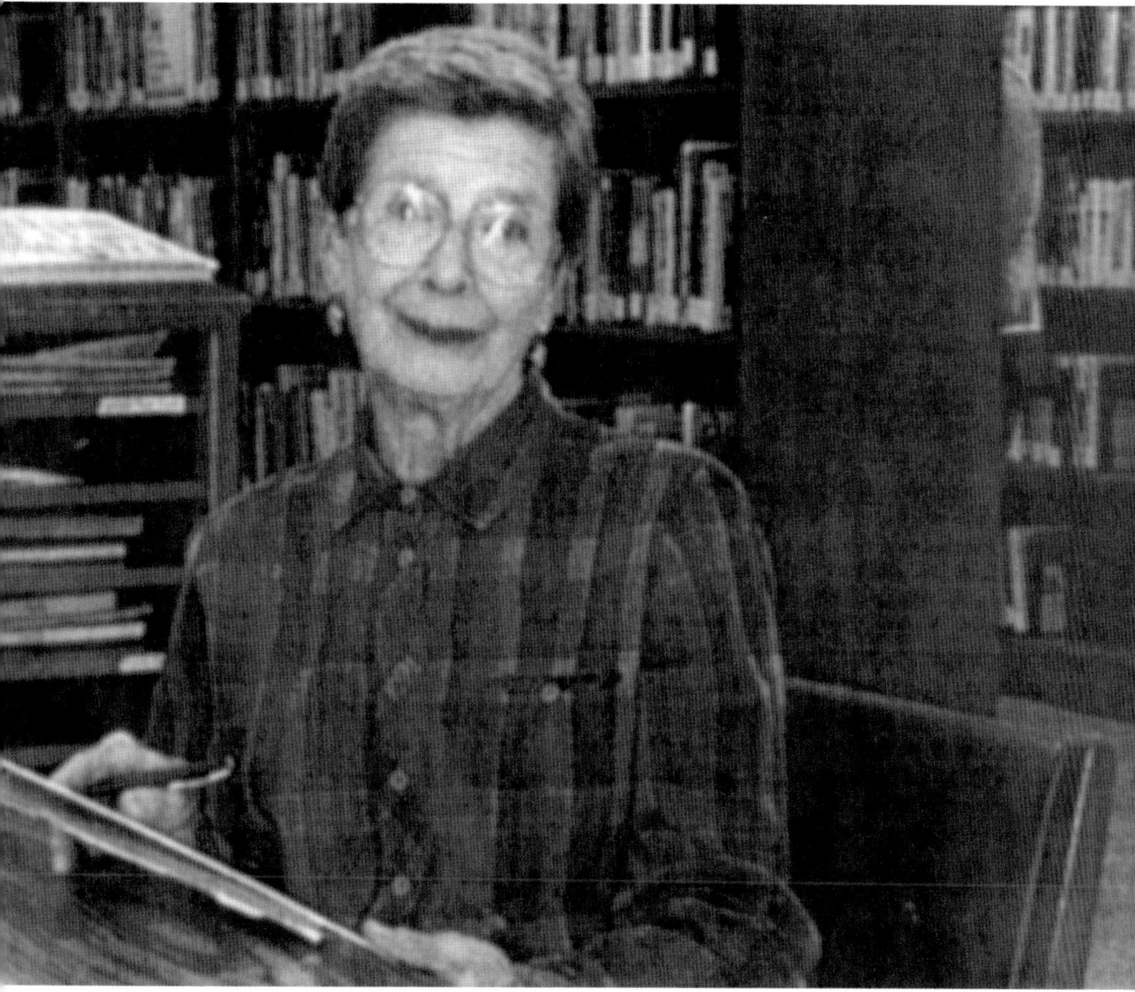

"May I Draw You?"
Beyond the sounds of turning pages, whispers, and the beeping of the computer checking out books at the Aurora Town Public Library was the sound of a 75-year-old woman's voice asking a simple question: "May I draw you?" For several years during the 1990s, Rose Sugnet made a habit of spending time at the library. While most people were looking for books, Sugnet was looking for models. She was seen a few times per week at the Main Street library harmlessly interrupting the concentration of strangers who were engrossed in their books. More often than not, the readers would go back to the words on the pages, and Sugnet would go to work sketching them. Sugnet's interest in creating portraits could be traced back to her years as a college student in Mississippi. Girls paid her $2.50 each to draw pinups to send to their boyfriends who were serving in the military or attending other colleges. Despite this, Sugnet never took an art class in college. She wanted to be a pianist. After college, she taught piano for one year but learned quickly that she did not like it. She joined the Navy, where she met her husband from Buffalo, and they eventually settled and raised their family in East Aurora. In retirement, Sugnet never accepted money for her work, and she often gave her sketches to the models once she was done. "I wouldn't enjoy it if I thought I had to be perfect," she said, "and when you're making money, there's pressure to be perfect." Sugnet said the best part of drawing portraits was meeting new people. Only a few people declined to be models. Of one woman who declined, Sugnet quipped, "I think she thought she was ugly." (Photograph by the author.)

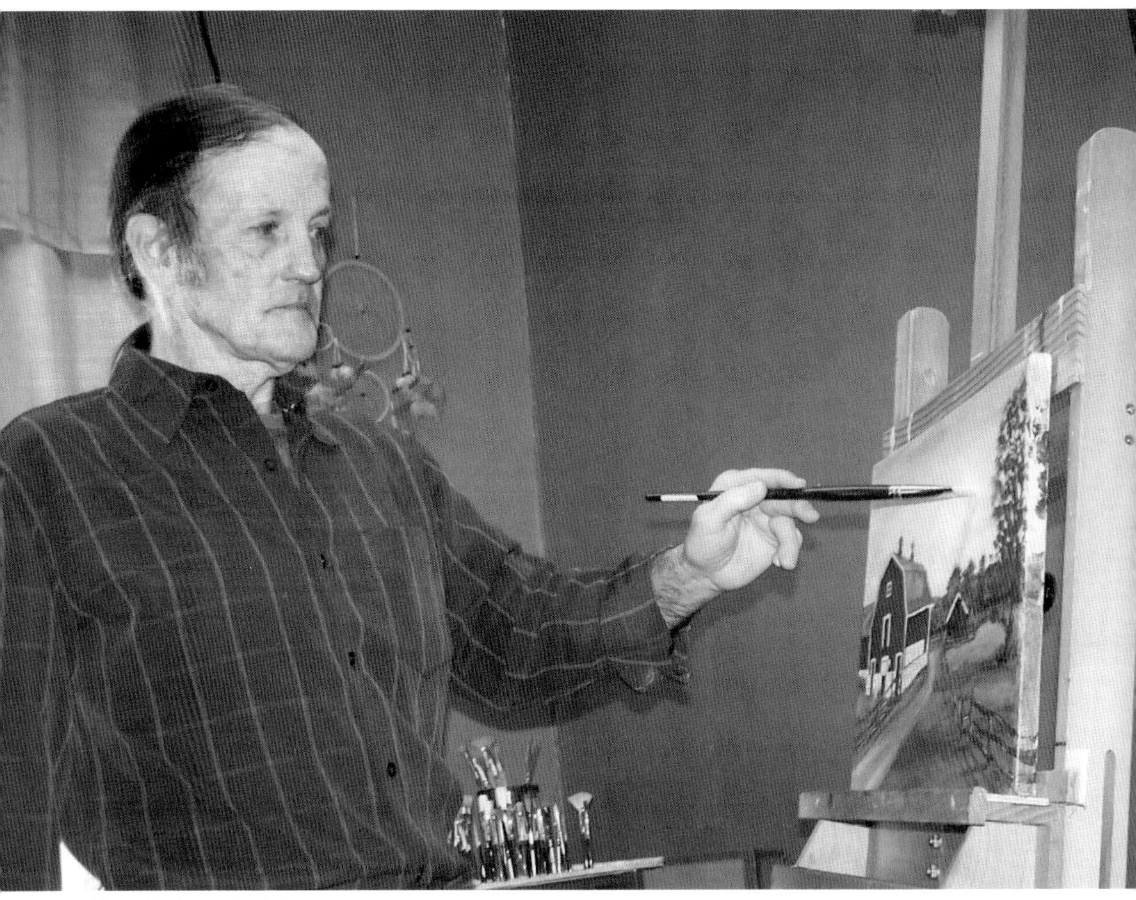

Don Paints the Town

Don King's paintings are on exhibit all around the village. His apartment overlooking Main Street doubles as his studio, where he creates images of East Aurora's signature buildings. Many of the images hang in their respective businesses around town. King began taking art classes about a decade ago and has been hooked ever since. In his paintings, King enjoys placing modern-day buildings in more bucolic settings. "The idea of taking a manmade structure and putting it with Mother Earth, and making it as one, that's what I like about painting," he says. King, an Army veteran of the Vietnam era who also served in the National Guard for 21 years, often finds inspiration for his paintings while walking around the village. King moved to East Aurora from South Buffalo in 1994 after his beloved wife died. "I needed to start over," he said, "so I came to East Aurora." (Photograph by the author.)

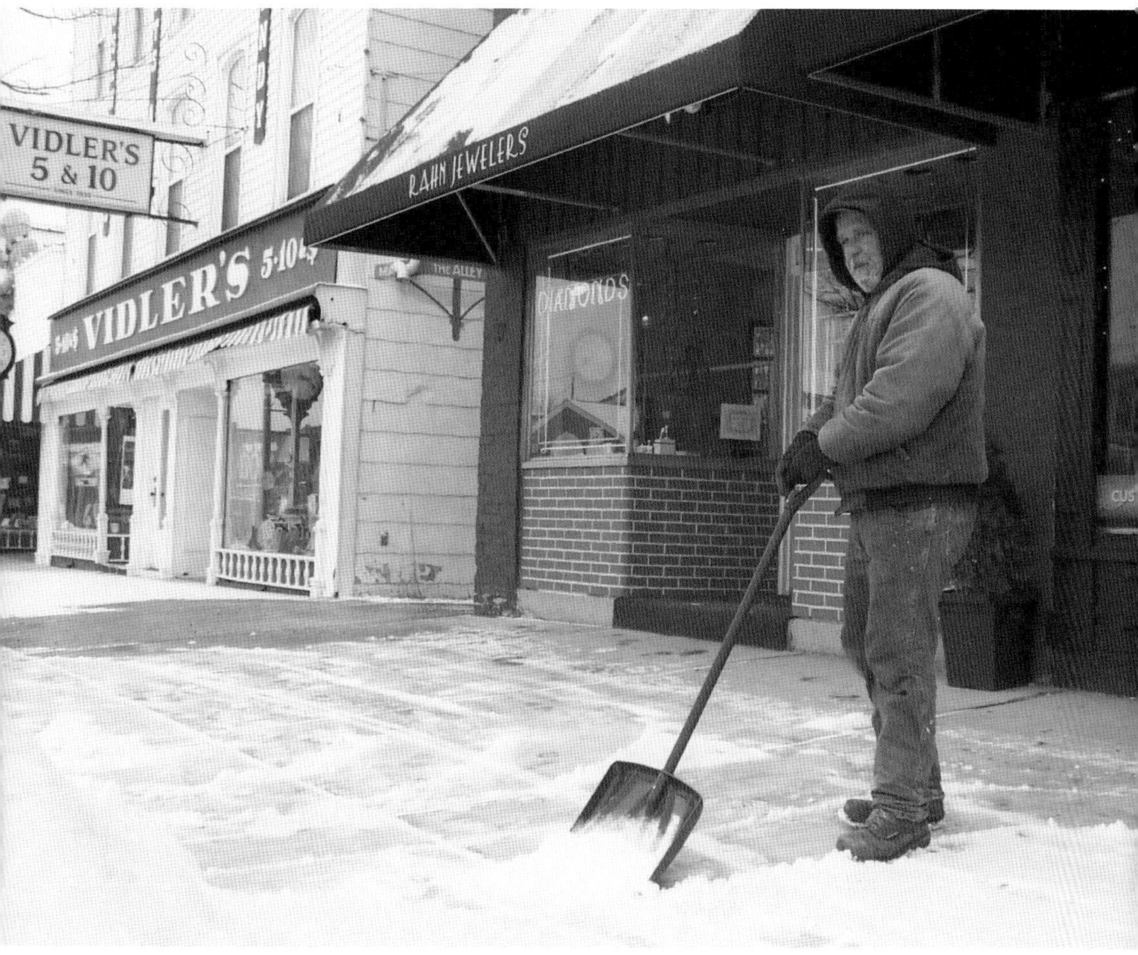

Old Man Winter's Nemesis

Old Man Winter has met his match in East Aurora. For more than a decade, Main Street business owners have put Nelson Welch in charge of keeping the sidewalks clear of snow. Welch, an East Aurora native, takes pride in the fact that the snow rarely has a chance to accumulate. He was even out during the two blizzards of 2014. During other seasons, Welch trades in the shovel for a rake. (Photograph by the author.)

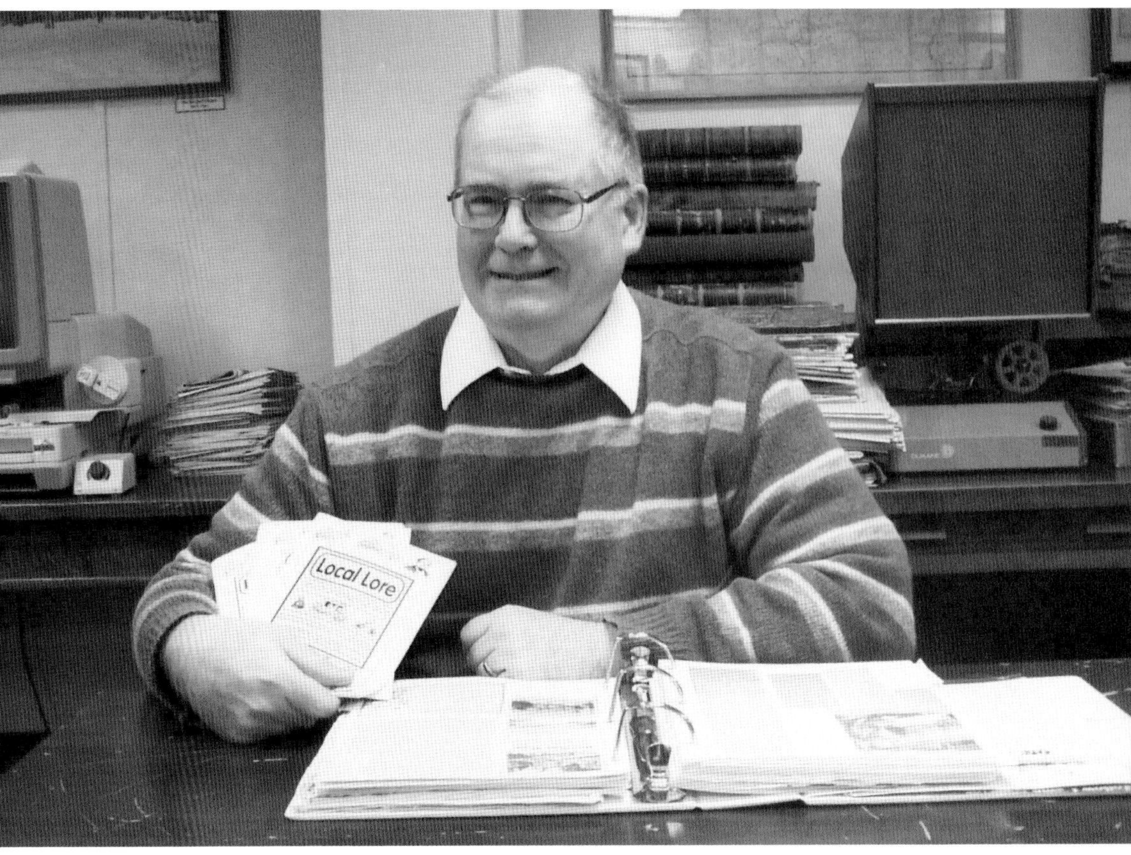

Drawing on History

When the editor of the *East Aurora Advertiser* solicited new ideas for the community newspaper, cartoonist Mike Kelly suggested a local version of the *Ripley's Believe It or Not!* cartoon series that appeared in newspapers in the 1920s. Since the mid-1990s, Kelly's "Local Lore" has highlighted unique and often-overlooked stories from the community's history. Topics have included the horse hitching posts still in existence around the village, famous visitors to the Roycroft, the history of the traffic circle, and the origin of the various manhole covers on village streets. Kelly spends countless hours in the Aurora Town Historian's Office and other area archives conducting research for his cartoons, which have also been featured in a series of books. (Photograph by the author.)

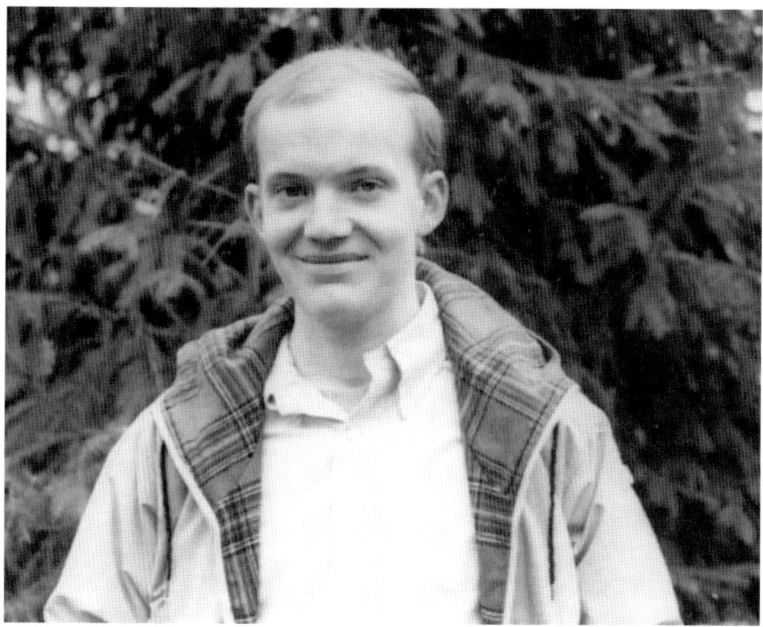

Artist of Architecture

Peter Andersen was the village's quiet artist. His long, contemplative—and often misunderstood—walks around the village and his careful examinations of the community's architecture led to well-researched renditions of important landmarks, including 898 East Main Street (below). For many years, his renditions were a regular feature in the *East Aurora Advertiser.* Andersen graduated from East Aurora High School in 1973 and earned a bachelor's degree in fine arts from the Rhode Island School of Design. Among the files in the archives of the Town Historian's Office are two large boxes labeled "Peter Andersen's Village." They contain a treasure trove of information, carefully gathered by Andersen, related to the architectural heritage of the village he loved. In the 1970s he spent countless hours on an architectural survey and helped garner National Register status for the Roycroft campus, which later led to National Historic Landmark status. Until shortly before his death at the age of 58 in February 2014, Andersen made weekly appointments with several people around town to share his latest drawings.

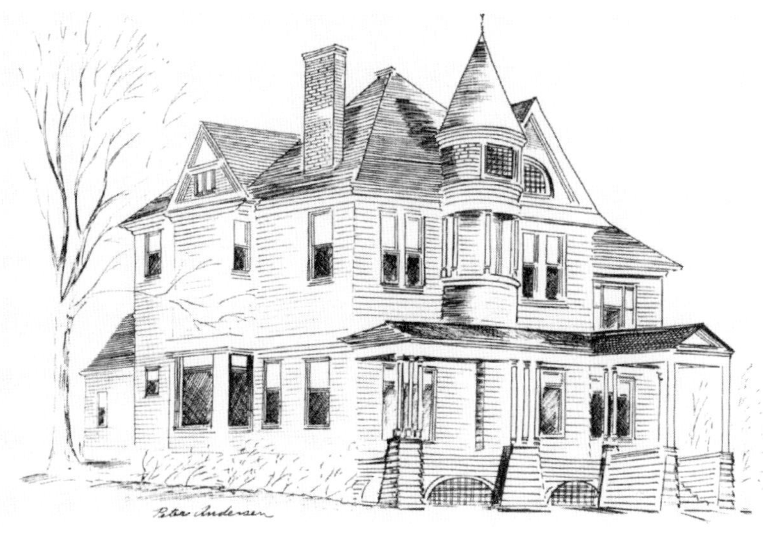

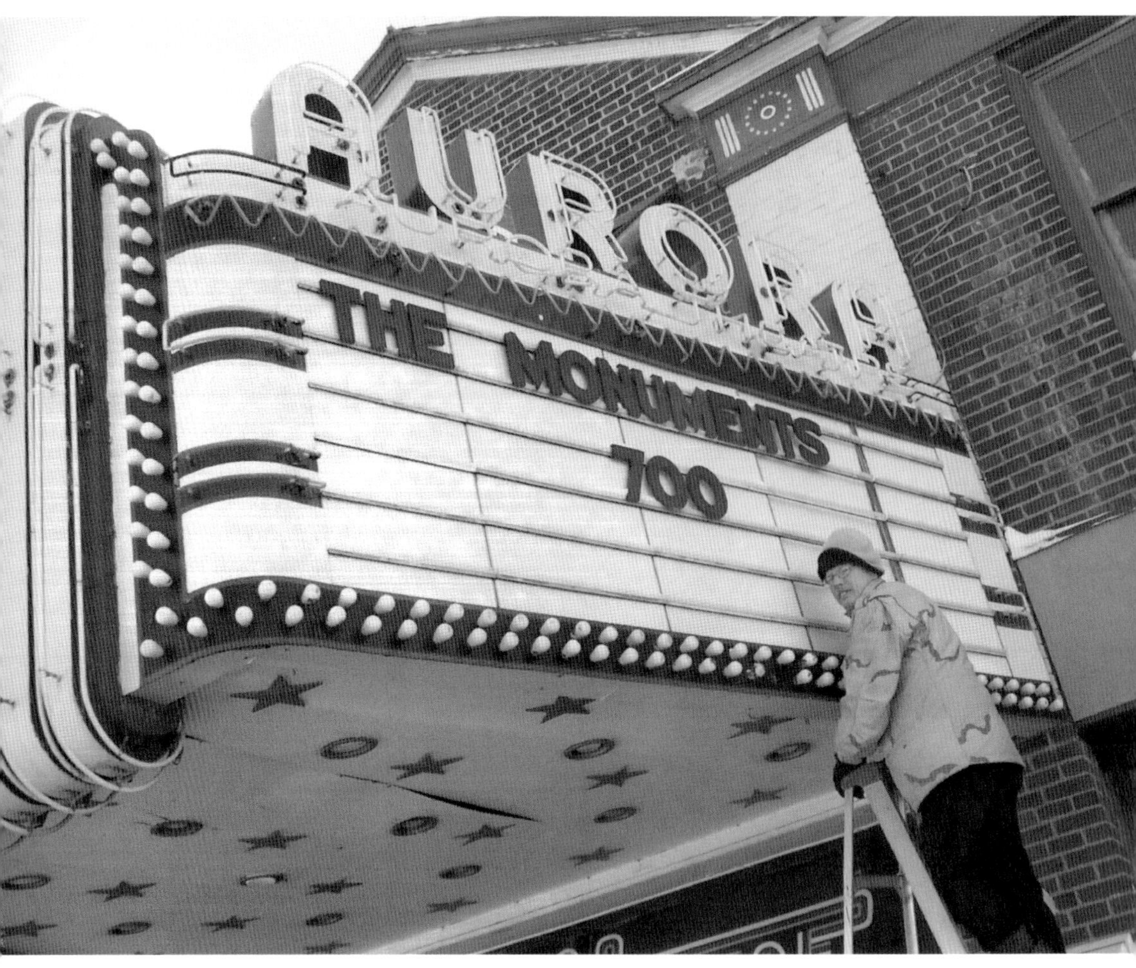

Man of the Marquee

Daniel Wurzer has climbed the ladder to change the letters on both sides of the Aurora Theatre's landmark marquee every week since 1985. No one has kept official track, but counting the times he has changed the sign for special events and birthday parties in addition to changing it for the new movies each week, he has made the climb nearly 2,000 times in his career. Wurzer started working at the theater in October 1981. When the employee in charge of the marquee left about four years later, the owners turned to Wurzer. "No one else wanted to do it," he says with a laugh. In addition to his numerous other jobs at the theater, Wurzer is in charge of removing snow from the marquee and making sure all the colorful lights are in working order. Owners have come and gone, but Wurzer remains a constant at the theater and on Main Street. "Lynn and Paul (Kinsella) are the fourth owners I have worked for," he says. (Photograph by the author.)

INDEX

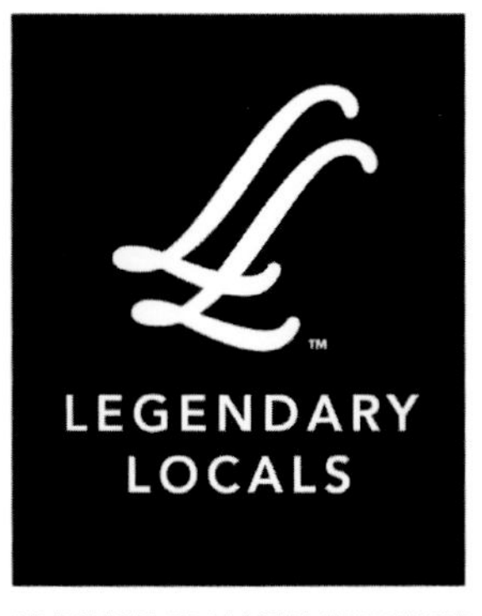

Consistent with our mission to preserve history on a local level, this book was printed in South Carolina on American-made paper and manufactured entirely in the United States. Products carrying the accredited Forest Stewardship Council (FSC) label are printed on 100 percent FSC-certified paper.

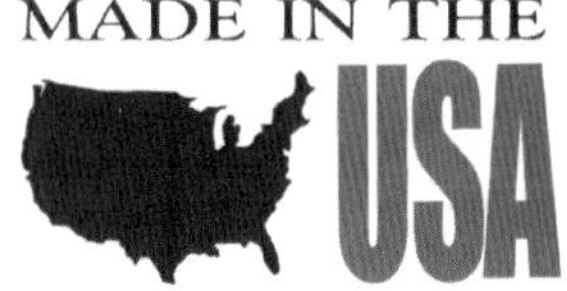